HEADS UP

My Life Story

ALAN SMITH

CONSTABLE

CONSTABLE

First published in Great Britain in 2018 by Constable
This paperback edition published in 2019 by Constable

1 3 5 7 9 10 8 6 4 2

A CIP catalogue record for this book is available from the British Library.

ISBN: 978-1-47212-785-3

Typeset in Bembo by Hewer Text UK Ltd, Edinburgh
Printed and bound in Great Britain by CPI (UK) Ltd, Croydon, CR0 4YY

Papers used by Constable are from well-managed forests and other responsible sources.

Constable
An imprint of
Little, Brown Book Group
Carmelite House
50 Victoria Embankment
London EC4Y 0DZ

An Hachette UK Company
www.hachette.co.uk

www.littlebrown.co.uk

To my incredible wife Penny, forever by my side
as a true friend. And to our wonderful daughters,
Jessie and Emily. Without you three, I would be lost.

Also, to Mom and Dad for your love and support.
You never pushed, only ever encouraged.

Contents

PREFACE

I've never liked revealing too much. As a naturally private person, I would always go down the road marked 'Keep Your Head Down'. Don't make a fuss. Just get on with it. Don't go telling the world about your inner thoughts. Well, now is the time to do exactly that. I'm quite a bit older, hopefully a little wiser and understand myself and the game better now than when still wearing boots. After so many years dismissing the notion, the timing seemed right to let it all out.

Time to explain the inner person – my ambitions and fears on a journey that began down the park, paused to sample the wholesomeness of non-league football before moving into a world that treated me better than I could have ever hoped. I have, after all, enjoyed some incredible moments that deserve a proper airing through my own words.

I will try to convey what it was like forging a career in the early 1980s when football was a very different entity to the shiny, cosmopolitan 'product' we see today; our relationship with supporters, much closer back then; the stain of hooliganism, almost taken for granted over two decades; our general outlook as footballers and how we were treated. What was it like, living that life?

That life changed when I joined Arsenal in 1987 and got to know Highbury, a uniquely atmospheric place reeking of history and tradition that could be deafeningly full one day and brutally empty the next, the only noise from the stands coming from a bloke bellowing profanities during a reserve game.

Soon, the team came together that went on to take part in what is, for me, the most dramatic match in English football history: Anfield 89. So much has been said about that incredible night. It's time to give my version, how it all felt back then.

After that impossible glory, the team evolved into one that could easily have gone on to become the first Invincibles, had Chelsea not spoiled everything one February afternoon. And we'll always have Copenhagen, my goal in that European Cup Winners' Cup victory marking a rare highlight in a dark period difficult to bear.

It was quite hard revisiting that period between 1992 and retirement. It rankles even now, how form and confidence nosedived so quickly before my career dribbled to a close.

Ah yes, saying goodbye to a game that has dominated your life. Having suffered the anguish, I can well understand how people cave in swiftly and spiral downhill. Adjusting to this huge change can't be easy for anyone.

Falling out with Arsenal wasn't easy either. I quickly turned from friendly former player, one of their own, to a critic, just like all the rest. Yet that shift in our relationship absolutely needed to happen if I was to ever be fully respected as an impartial observer.

As part of that, my media career has granted me the chance to look at the game in a more dispassionate way. How has it evolved over the years? How does a modern player's life differ from the one I experienced across the 1980s and 1990s? Do today's vast riches compensate for fewer laughs in quieter dressing rooms comprising multiple nationalities speaking different languages?

In essence, then, this book is about scratching the surface to see what's underneath in a profession generally considered to be the ultimate dream.

Above all else, I am in a position to describe absolutely everything, all the nooks and crannies, in my own words. By that, I mean writing it myself, not through a ghost writer, as is normally the case.

By sitting down at the computer to personally punch out the words, I hope to make my recollections a little more authentic. By cutting out the middleman, I can talk to you straight.

In any case, doing it any other way would feel like a cop-out. After twenty years of writing for the *Daily Telegraph*, covering four World Cups, four European Championships and countless club games at home and abroad, it would have been silly, not to mention lazy, asking for someone's help. I am more than capable of telling my story.

So this is all me. I was there throughout. I want to tell you my tale from the heart and head. Yes, a heads up. That's what it is. For someone known for his aerial ability and academic background, that title seemed to cover some apposite bases. Hope you enjoy.

CUT OFF AT THE KNEE

He didn't mess around. It was all pretty blunt. 'If you want to be able to play with your kids in a few years' time you've got to finish. There's no other choice.' John King was holding up scans to the light confirming that two operations on my right knee had failed to fix the problem. My surgeon had attempted to stimulate growth by pushing hot rods into the damaged bones. Microfracture, they call it, a technique pioneered by Richard Steadman in the US but fairly new to England at that particular time.

Sometimes this method works, other times sadly not. Mr King, it transpired, had done all he could.

Such a distressing outcome never crossed my mind when pulling up in pain one day at Millwall. It was 7 January 1995, a third-round FA Cup tie Arsenal were expected to win. On a cold, blustery afternoon, it was all a bit average as we huffed and puffed against determined opponents. As usual for that period, I found it hard going, the occasion once again failing to bring out the best in a disconsolate figure a long way removed from his old self. Would my form ever return to something approaching its best? It didn't seem likely on that dispiriting day as I reluctantly grappled with Keith 'Rhino' Stevens, who must go down as the coarsest, most belligerent defender I ever came across. Quite often, he'd completely ignore the ball in favour of manhandling his opponent, perhaps gripping them in a head-lock as play merrily continued elsewhere. It was quite surreal. I had never come across someone so blatantly crude.

But then came the moment that changed everything and it had nothing to do with my boorish mate. In fact, it all looked so innocuous – an awkward turn by the corner flag with no one around. The knee had locked stiff to end my involvement, which, if I'm being honest, came as a relief. Glad to be spared further wrestling bouts with Rhino, I limped into the dressing room thinking this was simply a case of torn cartilage – not insignificant, granted, but nothing to get too worked up about. Gary Lewin, our physiotherapist, certainly thought so after examining the joint at the end of a goalless scrap. For the record, I watched from Highbury's paddock – the traditional spot for non-playing members of the squad – as we lost the replay 2–0. In all honesty, that defeat wasn't a massive shock considering our plight at the time. The team had grown stale, lacking the quality, zest and hunger of previous years. George Graham's signings had gradually turned from inspirational choices into second-string triers. Though this failing didn't directly contribute to Graham's downfall, our struggles must have made the board's decision a little easier when it came to sacking their manager the following month.

But if the team's deterioration was a concern for everyone at the club, I would soon become preoccupied with my own situation, one that had taken a turn for the very worst.

This wasn't how careers were supposed to end, dribbling to a miserable close at the new Den, not the most glamorous of places to call it a day at the age of just thirty-two. And if the truth had been known on that January evening, I'd have felt a lot more depressed than I actually did while hobbling on crutches into our favourite restaurant. That was how Penny and I liked to spend our Saturday nights after matches – going out to dinner, either in London or somewhere more local. Sometimes it would be just the two of us, other times our close friends, Steve Bould and his wife Zoe, would make up a four. With babysitters sorted back in St Albans, we used to have a right laugh on those nights out, eating lovely food, drinking nice wine in some great restaurants.

Good food has always been a passion. In fact, a long-held ambition was to open a restaurant once I'd finished playing. I'd put that down in those questionnaires footballers were asked to answer in magazines like *Shoot*. What car do you drive? A Ford Capri 2.8i. Favourite pop star: Diana Ross. Ambition after playing: To open a restaurant. As time passed, though, that ambition faded as it dawned on me that I much preferred eating to the prospect of catering for others. And the King's Head in Ivinghoe on the edge of Dunstable Downs served the finest Aylesbury duck you would ever taste. Sitting there with Penny and my parents on that foggy evening, I began to cheer up, despite the discomfort.

Four or five weeks and then I'd be back. Cartilage operations using keyhole surgery were now standard practice, no longer the big deal of old. That said, I could never forget what happened to my great mate David Rocastle who had gone in for a similar operation a few years before. Like mine (though I didn't know it yet), Rocky's knee had suffered bone damage. Though they couldn't completely cure the problem, a combination of drugs, ice and rest allowed Rocky to continue for several more years without ever getting back to full mobility and fitness.

Chatting to Rocky before training, you could tell he was gutted about the situation.

'How's the knee feeling this morning, mate?'

'Oh, it's OK, Smudge,' he'd reply with a resigned shrug, rubbing the joint. 'It just feels a bit stiff. I thought the operation would have improved it a bit more. I don't know what they did but I've still got some fluid in there.'

'Yeah, I can see that. Looks a bit puffy. Can you feel it when you run?'

'A little bit, yeah. But I've just got to get on with it. Maybe it'll settle down in a few weeks.'

Unfortunately, it didn't. Much to everyone's regret, one of the most talented young players of his generation was never quite the same again.

That wasn't going to happen to me, though, was it? Rocky was just plain unlucky. This, on the other hand, all looked routine, only a matter of weeks surely before I'd be back. In any case, maybe the rest would do me good, take me off the front line for a while to allow me to view things from a different perspective. That had worked in the past when I was struggling. My manager at Leicester, Gordon Milne, pointed out the benefits one day. 'I'm going to get you to take a step back, Alan,' he said, gently breaking the news that I was dropped. 'Watch a match from the bench. It'll do you the power of good.' He was right, too, as he was about most things. Withdrawn from the fray, you see the bigger picture, how everyone reacts to certain situations, including the crowd. The exercise can declutter the mind in a very positive way, which would have been handy seeing as my own mind had tied itself in knots trying to figure out a route back to the good times. God knows, something needed to change, otherwise my Arsenal career was heading for the buffers.

Yet those two operations completely changed the narrative. After several hapless weeks pounding the Highbury track I started to suspect something was up. My knee just didn't feel right, the joint stiff and awkward, a million miles from how it should. I'd run down the stretch alongside the East Stand feeling horribly constricted, unable to sprint. This was hopeless. We were getting nowhere at all.

In an attempt to free the knee up, I went to hospital one day to have some fluid removed. Never a huge fan of needles, I looked the other way, eyes watering as the long needle went in. This wasn't nice. But the day got even worse when the syringe began to fill with a dirty brown substance featuring some nasty-looking debris. Gary Lewin and John King exchanged a look. They hadn't expected this. The consistency of the fluid made them concerned for what was going on inside that joint.

Fearing the worst, I went to see Ken Friar, Arsenal's managing director, to see what the club would do should I have to pack up. Financially, I mean. What kind of money would I get? For the first time in my entire career, one that had been thankfully short on serious injuries, I began to contemplate life after football and how we would manage without its safety net.

So off I went, climbing the famous staircase rising from the Marble Halls, the one that led to the boardroom, as well as the gaffer's office and that of our managing director. Walking through the heavy oak door I got straight to the point, nervously asking Mr Friar roughly where I stood. 'Oh, don't worry about all that,' he fired back straight away. 'You're going to be fine. Gary Lewin has assured me of that.'

Yes, I thought, *but have you spoken to Gary since he saw that horrible stuff coming out of my knee?* Maybe not.

As Arsenal's physio for all my time at the club, Gary had come to mean so much to the whole squad, not just as a physio but as so many other things – a go-to fixer, for instance, who, at late notice, could always sort out that extra ticket or car-park pass. Most importantly, his was the number you rang should one of your family get ill. But the fact that this bubbly, good-natured character was forever on hand meant he would also receive some strange phone calls at very odd times.

Paul Merson, for instance, once rang in the middle of the night because, while asleep, he'd poked himself in the eye. 'What shall I do, Gaz?' asked a worried Merse. 'Go back to sleep,' came the succinct reply. Some years later, Freddie Ljungberg rang at one o'clock in the morning to ask if, at this time of night, he was OK to park on double yellow lines. These were the days before player liaison officers, those poor souls who run around catering for every need of players who might be feeling totally lost in a strange country. Gary did it all back then. I don't know how he managed or indeed found the time. But he did, always with a smile.

So when he said I was going to be OK, it usually meant a fair bit. If he was confident, I should be as well. And he did remain confident, at least to my face, even after that worrying hospital trip. I certainly wasn't though. I knew my own body and one part didn't feel right. An ominous feeling had firmly set in.

Because of that, I asked Stewart Houston, our caretaker manager following George's dismissal, if I could join the squad on the upcoming end-of-season trip to China and Hong Kong. Injured, I wasn't originally on the list but that changed after Stewart heard my reasons. I explained this could very well be my last ever jaunt as a professional footballer. I badly wanted to go, just to be part of the group, enjoy the craic, even though I couldn't play in any of the friendlies.

As planned, I lapped up every second of that tour. Having never been to China before, it was fascinating just watching the locals go about their daily lives. If the swarms of people on bikes were expected, I couldn't believe the numbers having their hair cut on street corners, the hair covering whole pavements in parts of Beijing. In other parts, the ancient temples gave us a chance to take in some culture, which doesn't come naturally to every footballer. But we trod the tourist trail that year with a fair bit of enthusiasm, taken aback by the aura of this strange, spiritual place, a land unlike any other I had visited before.

Hong Kong offered something different with its high-rise intensity. The nightlife, for a start, was always going to get tested following the final friendly of that memorable trip. Unfortunately, that night in Wan Chai got famously out of hand when Ray Parlour was arrested for a drunken altercation. I had been drinking with Ray and several others that night but, come about four in the morning, I'd just about had enough so headed back to the hotel as Ray and a couple of others moved to another bar.

On surfacing the next morning, we were all shocked to hear Ray was in prison for punching a taxi driver after throwing prawn crackers into his car. If the second bit sounded like our mischievous teammate, the first part really didn't. You'd never call the Romford Pelé aggressive. Nothing like. Even so, he admitted the charges in court, sincerely apologised and stumped up the fines handed out by the judge and, later, the club. This harsh lesson, I reckon, proved a key turning point for someone who sorted himself out soon after that episode, going on to excel under Arsène Wenger.

For me, meanwhile, the chance to play for Wenger, or even Bruce Rioch, had gone up in smoke.

The Far East soon got swapped for the East End and a fateful date at the London Independent Hospital. Don't ask me what I thought on emerging from that building. The world suddenly felt like a much different place.

Gary had gone in with me to offer support, as he always did in these situations. Standing there on the pavement outside the hospital, he looked as shell-shocked as me, knocked for six by the verdict. 'I can't believe it, Smudge. I'm so sorry.' Forever conscientious, he took this kind of news personally, as if it marked a failure in his own work. It didn't, of course. There was nothing he could do or could have done differently.

Just over four months – that was all it took to turn me from top-flight footballer into unfortunate has-been. Gary maintains to this day he has never known such a short span between injury and retirement. And over twenty years after the episode, he shows great powers of recall to explain the precise medical problem. 'When you take cartilage out, the cushion has gone and it becomes bone on bone,' he says. 'Because of that, you always rehab slowly to let the bone harden. But your bones didn't harden. That's why we decided on a second op, the microfracture, when the drilled holes cause bleeding and that blood calcifies, turning into new bone.'

That's the theory anyway. For me, it proved sadly different in practice. Making matters worse at the time, I will never forget the excruciating pain in my right knee upon waking up from that second op. It was my own fault as well. The nurse had asked beforehand if I wanted a painkiller, one that would work when I came round. Having handled this kind of operation before, she obviously knew about the discomfort involved. For some inexplicable reason, though, I turned down her kind offer, saying I'd take one after if needed. And boy did I need it. As the anaesthetic wore off, I started thrashing about on the bed in absolute agony, yelping with pain. It felt like someone had taken a hammer and chisel to my right knee, which wasn't, I suppose, a million miles from the truth. Hearing my cries, the nurse appeared from nowhere, quickly flipped me over and dextrously shoved a pessary up my back passage – not the most dignified episode in my life but definitely one of the most welcome since the pain mercifully subsided within a matter of seconds.

Wincing at the memory, I come back to the present to hear Gary continue the sorry story. 'The way your bones degenerated so quickly was very unusual,' he says. 'It made John King's decision easy. Because your body reacted so badly to the microfracture, it was obvious it wouldn't cope without meniscus in the knee.'

Here comes the classic question. Why me? Why do I have bone type that can't function without cartilage? I only ask because two teammates, Lee Dixon and, as it happens, Ray Parlour, had cartilage removed when they were very young and had no problem playing on for about another fifteen years. I couldn't manage fifteen days.

More recently, players like Ledley King and Jamie Redknapp, with very similar conditions, managed to soldier on for quite some time by limiting training in between games. Arsenal's Danny Welbeck appears to have come through even better after undergoing the microfracture process.

Still, that's just how it goes, isn't it? Everyone is different.

So on that ruinous June day there was nothing more to be said. As Gaz headed off in one direction, bound for the training ground, I climbed in my car as one of the great unemployed, about to break the news to my best friend. Mind you, Penny didn't need telling. My face had already revealed most of the story.

I explained the diagnosis, what John King had said. The tears came quickly as I buried my face in her arms. At thirty-two, it was all over. The life that so many dream of but only a few achieve had come to an end after thirteen years. Barring my first year at Leicester, we'd been through all of it together, all the peaks and troughs of a memorable journey. And now this, the indelible full stop to signal the end.

It was weird. Suddenly, you feel like a different person. Something has been taken away that you can't remember ever being without. It definitely felt strange the day I went to say goodbye at the training ground. It was the first day of pre-season. Everyone was there, including Bruce Rioch and Arsenal's latest signing, a certain Dennis Bergkamp. I said hello to Dennis, wished him good luck, not knowing, of course, that he would go on to become one of the greatest players in Arsenal's history.

As for me, after twenty minutes or so, I couldn't wait to get away. The lads hadn't known quite what to say, it was all a bit awkward, while I felt like an outsider, out of the loop. The thing is, the bond had been broken. It sounds a bit brutal but, whatever way you look at it, I was no longer one of them. Their hopes and ambitions now differed from mine. They were heading one way; I was pointing another. In any case, they had training to be getting on with. A long pre-season lay ahead in which everyone would be trying to impress the new manager.

There was nothing else for it. I wished them all the best before driving away, feeling pretty numb about the whole situation. Twenty or so mates I saw every day had just been lost. That's what most ex-footballers will tell you they miss the most – rather than the actual football, it's the dressing-room camaraderie, the sense of togetherness between like-minded souls. It's that feeling of supreme fitness, elite athletes in their prime getting paid to play football. There's just no replacing that, as I found out in the coming months.

The hardest day, perhaps, came within weeks when I sat down to watch my old mates on telly. The first day of the season saw Middlesbrough visit Highbury, a match screened live on Sky on the opening Sunday. If my situation hadn't properly sunk in by then, it certainly did that afternoon as the teams ran out. There they all were – Bouldy, Dicko, Nige, Merse – looking lean and tanned, ready for another campaign as Arsenal teammates. For them, it was business as usual. Nothing much had changed. For me, nothing would ever be quite the same again.

On a positive note, I later found out that thirteen years in professional football is very good, seeing as the average career is much shorter, with younger players falling by the wayside or having career-ending injuries. I had been incredibly lucky to not only get where I wanted to go, to win every domestic trophy and a European one to boot, but to also hang around for quite so long.

Not that it felt that way as my situation sank in. Well, our situation to be more accurate, that of Penny and I, given that I was now out of work and in need of a job. With two girls under the age of six, the pressure was on. Yes, I had been sensible enough with money, investing in a pension that would now kick in. Though the Professional Footballers' Association (PFA) scheme normally paid out after you were thirty-five, being forced to retire through injury allowed an earlier start. That said, the salary in question was never going to keep us going on anything like the same standard of living. I'm not looking for sympathy here, far from it. Much more serious things happen to plenty of people. But it was a challenging time, to say the least – coping with the emotional aspect of saying goodbye to football alongside the practical issues on the financial side.

On the first part, it's easy to say I was devastated by the news, since everyone expects that kind of reaction. And I was devastated. It isn't often I crumple into a heap. The news marked a key moment in my life that shocked the system. But a big part of the reason for all the upset was the huge uncertainty now rearing up. Having my football career snatched away was obviously a blow, but I had long since stopped enjoying the daily routine in the way that I did as a younger man.

The state of my right ankle was partly to blame. Having twisted it so often and suffered countless kicks on the bone from persistent defenders, the joint was so inflamed that training had become a painful ordeal. To try and combat this, I was downing anti-inflammatory tablets on a regular basis to try and soothe the arthritic joint. Nobody wants to become over-reliant on these anti-inflamms. Taking too many can damage the lining of your stomach. But plenty of teammates did the same to mask stubborn niggles that could only be cured by prolonged rest. But who wants to go down that particular road? Drop out for two or three weeks and your replacement might impress enough to keep his place when you return. It's a longstanding predicament still around today. Players pop pills to get them through.

In my case, matchdays were different. With the adrenalin pumping, I didn't feel it so much. Only at the end, back in the dressing room, did the thing start to throb.

But on those London Colney mornings, especially the cold ones, I would be only too conscious of the way my ankle held me back. Jumping to head the ball, for instance, would mean shuffling my feet to make sure I took off from my left rather than the right. If I tried to launch off the weak one, I wouldn't get far at all. This adjustment wasn't just awkward, it was bloody frustrating. It took all the fun out of training, something I used to love so much.

To make matters worse, my general confidence had been low for quite some time. When the goals slowed down to a trickle around 1992, it deeply affected my life in a way only those close to me knew. The collapse in confidence had long since spread from matches into training, turning every day into something of a trial. To have that suddenly brought to an end can't help but feel good. You can only welcome the blessed relief. No more gritting of teeth to get through the discomfort. No more embarrassing moments in front of goal, stumbling over chances I would have previously snapped up.

Who knows? Things might have been different had I left Arsenal and started scoring again for another club. My enthusiasm for the game might have been rekindled. Not long after receiving the bad news, I got a call from a journalist friend of Harry Redknapp who wanted to know if I fancied joining West Ham. I had to tell the caller that the deed was already done, that my days of kicking a ball for anyone, never mind the Gunners, had come to an end. And as sad as that sounds, I felt that we'd reached a natural turning point. Time to move on and do something else.

But what would that 'something else' be? Football had been my life.

FIRST KICK

Poor Mom. I nearly killed her. Weighing in at a whopping 10 lb 10 oz, I must have caused quite a scene on 21 November 1962. Home births for the second child were common back then, so, with three-year-old David already running about, it was decided that our house in Arundel Road, Birmingham, would host the event. That said, I can't imagine the midwife would have recommended this method if she had known the size of the package.

Dad had been told some time before that home births required two things: loads of newspaper and untold amounts of hot water. So when it came to the big day he leapt into action, filling the kettle to the brim, putting several pans of water on the stove and preparing great piles of newspaper he'd been saving for months. Once Mom had somehow squeezed me out, Dad rushed to the midwife's side, eager to assist with all the necessary.

'What do you need?' he breathlessly asked, expecting only one answer.

'Could I have one sheet of newspaper to wrap the afterbirth, please? Oh, and would you put the kettle on for a nice cup of tea?' That was it. He had been wildly misinformed. It's a story Dad would tell for years to come.

On a more serious note, giving birth to me did knock Mom sideways. It took her a long time to recover from the traumatic ordeal. This was it for her. Like it or not, the family was complete.

With a rabbit in the garden and a cat in the house, those early years happily passed by, even though money was in short supply. With two children to feed and a mortgage to pay, Dad's modest wage from Lucas, the car and aerospace parts company, didn't stretch far. Mom used to recall the times, so tight was the family budget, that she and Dad shared a sausage after giving me and Dave one each.

I was brought up in Hollywood, a nice residential area sitting right on the edge of Birmingham's southern boundary, a divide between the suburbs and open countryside. During the summer holidays, if we weren't playing football, my friends and I would spend all day in nearby fields, walking for miles, messing about in streams, sometimes catching tadpoles with those little green nets attached to bamboo cane before taking them home in jam jars. I know that all sounds a bit twee, a bit Famous Five, but that's how it was for us in the mid-1970s.

As if to strengthen that image, building dens in the woods was also a favourite. One of the more solid efforts was formed of branches and ferns constructed in undergrowth on the edge of a golf course. Our hideaway just happened to be positioned right on the corner of a dogleg hole where, promisingly, the golfers couldn't see the fairway from their tee down the bottom of a hill. This was too good to resist. We'd wait under cover for a ball to roll up before sprinting out of the bushes to help ourselves. When the golfers appeared over the brow, there would be confused looks all round as they tried to figure out where their drives had ended up. The den quickly accrued a nice stash of golf balls, which we buried under leaves in a large tin. Yet on returning one day we were shocked to find the tin lying open and all the balls gone. This was a mystery. No one else knew about our little stockpile. Even if someone had accidentally come across our den, they'd struggle to find the well-hidden tin. Suspicious glances passed between our group. An inside job? We never found out.

By this time, Dad had gained promotion to earn more money, enabling us to move to a bigger house. The chosen one in Heath Rise, only half a mile up the road, was newly built and detached, a step up from the semi in Arundel Road. Unfortunately, it was a disaster from the start. Mom hated the place. It really affected her, to the extent her nerves became badly frayed. It didn't help that her dad's health was deteriorating before our eyes.

Mom was brought up in Snitterfield, a picturesque village just outside Stratford-upon-Avon, in a chocolate-box cottage complete with thatched roof. By the sound of it, young Elsie enjoyed a blissful upbringing, only disturbed by the Second World War. Though the German bombers didn't target Stratford specifically, Mom recalled the times they flew overhead on the way to Coventry and its many factories. On hearing the Luftwaffe approach, Elsie would run and cower under a sturdy oak table, just in case a stray bomb should head their way. Joining her under there was Audrey, a young evacuee from London, who, like thousands of others from the big cities, had been sent packing by her own family to take refuge in the countryside. As an only child, this was an odd experience for

Mom, to have this young girl move into her house. Mind you, imagine what it felt like for Audrey, wrenched from her family to live with complete strangers.

Following her mother's death, Mom's father came to live with us to see out his final years. A veteran of the trenches in the First World War, Granddad Bert was a diamond, a very kind man loved as much by Dad as by his own daughter. Unfortunately, Bert had developed an awful, chesty cough, caused, he said, by the Germans' deadly use of mustard gas. I can see him now, sat in his armchair, coughing away, trying not to make a fuss.

Granddad didn't last long in Heath Rise and neither did we. After his passing, Mom couldn't wait to get out so we packed our belongings and moved to a lovely place in Highters Heath Lane, which was bang in between our first house and the unhappy second. Sat on a generous plot, it stretched Dad's wage packet to the limit but he went through with it anyway for the sake of his wife. Whatever the cost, he had to get Mom into a new place. Thankfully, they got it right this time: that house remained a happy home for the next forty years.

A few years ago following Mom and Dad's deaths in quick succession, Penny and I were busy clearing out the family home when we came across an assortment of treasures stashed in a tin box at the back of a wardrobe. We found all sorts of mementoes from the Great War – Granddad's medals, his leather dog tag and a thick pile of postcards sent from the front. Addressed to his own parents in Birmingham, they are a poignant reminder of a soldier's forced optimism during those terrible times.

25 November 1916

Dear Dad,

Just a card to let you know I am in the 'Pink' and got a letter from Mother today. We had snow a few days ago. I am still on the same sort of job, not got the sack yet (some hopes).

With love to both,

Bert

5 December 1916

Dear Mother,

Just a card to let you know I am still in the 'Pink'. You have had some rough weather lately. How is my old shed looking? We are having nice weather now. I might get leave next month all being well. Hope this will find you and Dad quite well.

With love,

Bert

It wasn't so much what he did say in those cheery notes, more what he left out, the horrific details. A censor's stamp on the cards confirmed that, even if he'd wanted to, he couldn't reveal much.

I liked school. Always did from a very young age. Hollywood Primary was just up the road, only a minute's walk from Highters Heath Lane. With the lollipop lady yards from our door, shepherding children across a fairly quiet road, Mom would let me walk up to school on my own from the age of seven or eight.

For someone already obsessed with football, it was great that Hollywood had a decent pitch to host regular matches against local schools. It was a chance to measure myself against other kids, to see if I stood out, as my PE teacher suspected. On this theme, it all went off one day when a visiting dad took umbrage when the big lad up front in Hollywood colours started banging in goals all over the place. I'd got up to about seven in a sound thrashing when this irate bloke began shouting the odds. 'Get him off! It's not fair. He's too old!' I wasn't, by the way. Just looked it, standing head and shoulders above everyone else. But the chap wouldn't have it, despite our teacher's assurances. Eventually, my dad had to step in to put the man straight.

David also liked football when he was young. While I had a Birmingham City kit, his was West Bromwich Albion. But everything changed when a teacher started shouting at him during a match for something he was apparently doing wrong. Dave came home that day extremely upset. 'That's it! I'm never playing football again!' And he didn't. True to his word, my older brother headed in a completely different direction.

In the years that followed, model airplanes became one keen hobby. Naturally good with his hands and interested in anything to do with electrics, Dave once built a small plane from scratch. Complete with little motor, it was designed to buzz around attached to two long, steel wires for control. Once fully finished, he and his mate Peter couldn't wait to try it out over the same fields where we made that den. However, the one thing they hadn't noticed in this particular field was the presence of 11,000-volt power lines strung up above.

With the plane whirling round at quite some pace, Dave only noticed the power lines at the very last second. Realising it wouldn't be a good idea to have hold of the wires when the plane hit the lines, he managed to let go in the nick of time. If he hadn't, a few thousand volts could have done a lot of damage. There followed a huge flash and bang as the power lines collapsed, leaving Dave and Pete quivering on the ground amid a cloud of smoke. Coming to their senses, they sensibly decided to leg it, leave the scene of the crime before anyone came. All Dave remembers as he sprinted away was someone shouting from a nearby house, 'What the bloody hell's going on? All our power's gone off!'

Outside school hours, my friends and I, about ten in all, would spend a great deal of time down Daisy Farm Park. We're talking dawn till dusk, sometimes beyond. Mom would only start to worry if I hadn't come home for tea.

To get to the park, instead of turning right for school out of our front door, I'd turn left and walk the five hundred yards that took you past a newsagent's owned by Mr Cotterill, best known for wearing a boot with a huge platform to compensate for one leg being much shorter than the other. The effects of polio, back then, could be seen in many.

Mr Cotterill knew us all well, so often did we visit. I would regularly pop in to buy cigarettes for Dad. Ten Player's No. 6 tipped, that was his favourite at a time when most shops were happy selling fags to kids. And if I wasn't running errands, I'd be getting something for myself, wondering which sweets to buy from the big jars lined up on the shelves. A quarter of pear drops or pineapple rock? Cola cubes or liquorice allsorts? A tough choice that required plenty of umming and ahing. Alternatively, it could be some crisps, the ones made by Smith's containing the little blue bag of salt to tip in yourself.

That shop was an important stopping point on the way to Daisy Farm, a huge expanse of grass housing four or five full-size football pitches and a decent cricket square in the summer months.

When the sun was shining, especially around the time of Wimbledon, we'd take our tennis rackets to have a knock on one of the hard courts. To do that, you had to go and see the park-keeper in his little wooden hut and hand over a few pence to hire some time. Those parkies, it seems, don't exist any more but, back then, they held all the power in parks up and down the land. Because of that, you were always a bit scared of this figure of authority who seemed to delight in dishing out reprimands. That said, we'd gladly take any chance to wind him up, running off when he emerged from that little hut.

Next to the tennis courts, a playground area featuring slides, swings and roundabouts also kept us going. How far could you jump off one of the swings? We'd chalk a line on the concrete to measure each attempt. How fast could we spin the spider roundabout? I once got so dizzy I fell through the middle and badly cut my head.

It was mainly football, though. Yes, jumpers for goalposts, all the usual stuff, unless we played 'Wembley' in one of the big, netted goals. The games could get quite big, too, as kids of all ages gravitated over. Back then, everyone wanted to be George Best, Manchester United's wizard of a winger. You only had to beat one player and the commentary started. 'And here he is, Georgie Best, taking on the whole team. Beats one, beats two . . .!' I was no different. Those games in the park always came with a soundtrack. Thinking about it, Daisy Farm heard my first crack at commentary.

In terms of heroes, though Best was worshipped by all, I had some Manchester City posters pinned to my bedroom wall.

Mike Summerbee, Tony Book, Franny Lee – big stars at the time who'd won the league with City in 1968. My favourite player, though, was Colin Bell, a magnificent midfielder who took pride of place. A few years later, I would be taken for a tour behind the scenes at Maine Road, City's old ground. Walking into the physio's room, we must have caught them by surprise because there was Colin Bell, the great man himself, lying on the treatment table without a stitch on, completely starkers. It wasn't how I imagined meeting my hero.

Quite often, once a game in the park had got going, we'd be approached by a man loitering nearby. I know, that sounds dodgy right away. A grown man hanging around kids? Must be a pervert. Yet in those more innocent times we didn't really think that way. In any case, we knew why he was there. He wanted to join in. As for his age, well, when you're young, it's difficult to tell how old adults are. To us he seemed ancient with his slicked back hair. In reality, he was probably only about forty-five. And he always wore the same clothes – black baggy trousers held up with braces and a white granddad-collar shirt with one sleeve rolled up and the other flapping freely. He only had one arm you see, which should be a handicap when it comes to running around. But this man – we never found out his name – turned out to be beautifully balanced, especially with the ball at his feet. Very quick and nimble, he skated around the pitch like a spinning top, a real asset for whichever team had him on their side. He never said much during those games, just enjoyed taking part as if the company came as a welcome change. Where was he from? Did he have a wife and family or live alone? We never asked. After half an hour or so, having obviously got his fix, he'd wave his thanks and wander off, return to a life that remained a mystery.

As a well-behaved child, brushes with authority rarely came my way – a trait that fans of Leicester and Arsenal would later come to recognise. But a rare instance of rebellion occurred in the latter stages of primary school, much to the disgust of my angry Mom. David Geary was one of those friends your parents try to discourage as the type likely to lead you astray. No stranger to scrapes, David was known as a bit of a tearaway, always on the lookout for the next escapade. On this occasion, he thought it a good idea to bunk off school and somehow persuaded me to tag along. This was so out of character. Playing truant had never before even entered my head. But when David argued the case for a sneaky day off, I reluctantly agreed, anxious not to appear like a complete wuss. We might have got away with it, too, had we not stupidly decided to mess about in some builder's sand piled up on the path virtually opposite my house.

Not surprisingly, it wasn't long before Mom spotted us and marched across to drag me home, demanding to know what on earth I was playing at. Within seconds, she had put on some lipstick and thrown on her beige mac to haul me up to the headmaster's office. Shamefaced, I stood in front of the head as he delivered his rebuke, my cheeks turning crimson as the riot act was read. Usually, my mom was the gentlest soul you could possibly meet, never one to cause a fuss or lose her temper. But she went for it that day, outraged her boy had brazenly skipped school. Those hardline tactics shocked me. I'd never seen her like this before. Mind you, I'd never done anything quite so reckless. Mom's furious reaction ensured I would never again try this silly trick.

After passing the eleven-plus, I had a choice to make: King's Norton Grammar where they played football or King's Heath Tech where rugby ruled the roost. Knowing that, there was only one choice. I could never go to a school favouring the oval ball.

As a bonus, the grounds of King's Norton stood only a mile from Bournville, the Quaker village built by the Cadbury family in the 1800s for their employees. If the school's huge playing fields, a sizeable step up from Hollywood, were an instant attraction, the whiff of chocolate on the wind made them even better. It reminded me of the days when my friend's dad, a Cadbury worker, used to bring home the off-cuts in a brown paper bag. Living next door, I didn't go short.

Seven years at King's Norton passed happily by, with the accent on study and sport at this all-boys' school. Once in the sixth form, though, we'd have a bit more to do with the adjoining girls' school, only separated from our playing fields by a low hedge. House parties were the main way of meeting up, when the lads would turn up armed with kegs of Watney's Red Barrel or bottles of Strongbow cider. At the outset, I stood in the kitchen at these parties feeling a bit awkward, having had little to do with girls for a few years. Naturally shy anyway, I took time to settle before gradually making friends in this new environment.

As you'd expect, these get-togethers featured all the classic scenes – couples entwined in corners, clumsy dancing in the living room, drunken teenagers spewing up in the back garden. More often than not, though, we behaved fairly well as pupils from schools with good reputations.

Never top of the class, I wasn't stupid either. In football parlance you could say I was better than mid-table, usually good enough to qualify for Europe, thanks in part to a conscientious approach. Encouraged by Mom and Dad and driven by my own standards, I also put a lot of effort into homework and revising for exams.

Some of the worst memories involved cramming for A levels. To help, Dad had fixed up a desk in my bedroom, a piece of laminated chipboard screwed to the wall. For hours on end I would be sat there, often staring blankly ahead at the woodchip wallpaper to try and get my head around a certain subject.

To be honest, it was absolute agony, made worse by a method no one should try. For history, I decided to memorise whole essays word for word in the vain hope that, on exam day, the exact topic would come up. It was ridiculous. I spent weeks on end committing to memory endless paragraphs about the Reformation and Dissolution of the Monasteries when it would have been much more sensible to learn the salient points, all the facts and dates, then use them on the big day according to the slant of question. Instead, Mr Clueless over here simply regurgitated long, memorised passages, ignoring the examiner's specific request. No surprise I got a D in a subject that, heartbreakingly, took up more revision time than anything else.

French came more easily, the written part anyway. Languages seemed to suit my strengths – arts more than sciences – hence my wish to also study German at A level. There was one problem though – nobody else chose this subject so the school wasn't sure if I could go ahead. In the end, they relented, let me do German on my own, and I got one-to-one tutoring from Mr Flynn. With these choices, however, came a necessary evil.

A mile outside Birmingham city centre, a big white building sits back on the Bristol Road. To this day, every time I drive past my stomach turns over. That building, you see, witnessed my worst ever moment in education.

Talk about nerves. Forget about the hours leading up to Anfield 89 or the moments just before the 1994 European Cup Winners' Cup final. Those big-game butterflies do not compare with the sheer terror accompanying my French oral exam.

The days beforehand were nerve-wracking enough, what with trying to second-guess conversation topics before genning up on all the relevant vocabulary. While my French teacher had suggested a few likely subjects, he said nothing in the oral could be guaranteed. If that got me going, the actual day became a little too much.

Travelling up alone on the number 50 bus, walking as slowly as possible into the building, I had never felt this way in all my life. Given how petrified I felt, it was impossible to see how I would ever get through the ordeal. Sat in the waiting room, I felt like heading for the door, scarpering altogether, forgetting all about this diabolical test.

At this point, people often say the nerves die down a touch. Once things get going, they don't feel too bad and are able to give a good account of themselves. Well, that certainly wasn't the case here. A bone-dry mouth produced incoherent nonsense during twenty minutes that felt like two hundred.

They must have sounded horrendous, my stuttering replies. They must have grated like chalk on a squeaky blackboard. From her expression, I could tell the examiner had heard much better French that morning from other students. She treated my answers with kindly tolerance, a hint of pity briefly crossing her furrowed brow.

I staggered out at the end grateful to be liberated. Though all my darkest fears had been horribly realised, the surge of relief felt truly wonderful. Running for the bus, I couldn't wait to get away.

'How did it go?' Mom and Dad eagerly asked later. 'Oh, OK,' I lied, not wanting to admit the hideous truth.

If that proved a nightmare, I didn't experience many setbacks on the football side, either at school or for my Sunday team. Mind you, I'll never forget the day very early on at King's Norton when I rushed up to the noticeboard to check on the team for our very first game. Quickly scanning the line-up from one to eleven, fully expecting to be named as one of the forwards, my heart sank on realising I had been left out. What? This had never happened before. In primary school, I was always the best, an automatic pick. Turning away from the board, I felt a bit sick. Once home, the tears wouldn't stop. Luckily, things improved from that point and, after doing well for the school, I'd get picked for the district and then West Midlands County.

With Dad busy at work during the day, Mom would ferry me around Birmingham for those representative matches, with us often having to catch two or three buses. She'd stand on the touchline in all sorts of weather, not really understanding all that was going on, but sticking it out anyway to show support before taking me home to cook our tea. Afterwards, I'd sit by the front window waiting for Dad's headlights to swing into the drive, anxious to tell him how I'd got on. This was the game I loved, the one I never wanted to go away.

A CHURCH EDUCATION

It was only a year. One solitary season. But that 1981/82 campaign, the year after leaving school, completely changed my life. I went from being an anonymous student at Coventry Polytechnic and part-time hopeful earning £18 a week (plus £5 for a win), to a professional footballer, soon to be known nationwide as a promising prospect.

Alvechurch, the likeable village where I played part-time football, lay seven miles from home, in the Worcestershire countryside just over the county border. The pitch at Lye Meadow was well known for its slope, falling away from the touchline nearest the main road to the opposite flank down by the clubhouse. It took a bit of getting used to, that sizeable gradient, but once you had come to terms with it, this could be used as an advantage.

If the state of the pitch was questionable, the clubhouse could best be described as homely, the dressing rooms basic. On matchdays, the lounge bar was full to overflowing. In a room packed with people who quite liked a drink, fighting your way to the bar took some persistence. As for those dressing rooms down a short corridor, they were pretty rough and ready, with a slatted wooden bench running around three walls and a battered treatment table wedged in the middle. After every match the lads would bang their muddy boots on the tiled floor, the aluminium studs making a right racket as steam drifted through from the showers. Loud voices, dirty jokes, the thirst for a pint – this was Alvechurch in the early 1980s, a friendly, raucous, good-natured place.

That season at Lye Meadow taught me so much. For a start, how to cross the divide between junior and senior football, a less forgiving world where, for some, a win bonus meant they could pay the mortgage that month. For others, with good full-time jobs, this was more about enjoyment. Yes, they took it very seriously, everyone wanted to win, but it was also about having a laugh with mates at the weekend.

I had to grow up quickly in this new environment. The old hands may have heard all about this bright young kid coming through but that wasn't going to grant much legroom at all. You had to quickly prove that, as a raw teenager new to this level, you wouldn't start doing stupid things to cost precious points. Going further, you had to earn their respect by holding your own, not hide away because it got a bit rough. This might be the tricky part. As a fairly placid character, not one for putting myself about, could I survive in this hard-nosed world?

It wasn't that I was weak. Standing over six feet tall, I was bigger than most, with very strong legs that could hold off opponents and protect the ball. Physically, there was no problem at all. It was more my laidback nature and being slow to understand the occasional need for muscle and bloody-minded resolve.

As a schoolboy, I'll never forget being substituted in a county match after a particularly quiet performance. Standing there dejected in my tracksuit, Dad pointed to the face of one of my teammates furiously scrapping for the ball. 'Look at his face, Alan! Look at that determination. You need to be a bit more like that, otherwise games will pass you by.'

As it happens, Dad was talking about Victor Hollier, a busy little midfielder courted by lots of clubs, who fought like a terrier in that middle ground. Victor had ability, no doubt about that, but a never-say-die attitude was probably his biggest strength.

Unfortunately, the poor lad never got a rest from his father's advice. Unlike my dad, normally a passive observer who only occasionally piped up, Hollier senior would be at it right through the match, showering his son with a relentless stream of directives and bollockings. Not only that, Victor's dad would always like to tell us who'd been on the phone the night before. Aston Villa, Birmingham, West Brom, Wolves, you name it. By his reckoning, the boy was going to have them queuing up, begging for his signature.

'Your son will do all right,' he once said to my dad, totally oblivious to the condescending tone. 'He'll make a decent living in non-league. But my Victor's going all the way. He's going to be a top professional.' Dad bit his lip, nodding politely, but never forgot that patronising prediction.

I felt sorry for Victor, having to put up with a domineering parent constantly giving it out. It can't have been easy, coping with that. The burden of expectation must have weighed heavy. I think Victor did eventually sign for Villa, as his dad proudly forecast, but nothing much happened in the following years. I wonder if his upbringing had anything to do with it.

As for me, the situation was totally different. Gently encouraged more than forcefully pushed, my easy-going nature could potentially be a problem when gritted teeth were needed more than languid skills. Don't get me wrong, a dogged determination lay deep inside. Without that, I wouldn't have got very far. But some must have wondered in those early years if I was made of the right stuff to progress in this game.

That sort of reservation stuck right through my career. Too nice. Needs to be nastier. To a degree, I would accept those criticisms. I used to look at Mark Hughes, a fine centre-forward with a combustible streak, and wish I could adopt some of those qualities. A bit more fire in the belly would have helped no end, possibly propelling me to the next level.

Still, you can't change who you are. I have always kept that thought close. I might lose out in one direction but gain in another through keeping a cool head when the heat is turned up. For instance, in the two biggest games of my career – Anfield 89 and the Cup Winners' Cup final – I retained my composure and kept my concentration. The results, even if I say so myself, were two fine performances. Hugely satisfying to do that when it mattered most.

Going back to Alvechurch, we had some great characters in that pokey dressing room. Chrissy Birch, the captain, a tough centre-half, loved belting out songs in his best baritone voice. 'I am a linesman for Notts County!' he used to bellow in a slight variation of the Glen Campbell classic. Then there was Randy Reg from Rugeley, our moustachioed goalkeeper from coal-mining country. Dougy Devlin, a funny, intelligent Scot, was never short of a word. Neither was Phil Harper, a skilful striker and born comedian from Wolverhampton. I will forever be indebted to these colourful characters. They took me under their wing, looked after the youngster who showed considerably more talent than practical know-how.

The manager was Rhys Davies, a Welsh schoolteacher with a mischievous sense of humour and background in athletics. To balance that off, John Mason, his assistant, was a football man through and through who'd played for Alvechurch a decade before. Together, they made a useful double act, Rhys skilfully man-managing this assorted crew, while Mase's enthusiasm and knowledge proved a constant winner.

As luck would have it, Mase lived in Coventry where I had ended up after my A levels. Coventry Polytechnic certainly wasn't first choice. I'd gone for interviews at Manchester and Kent universities, neither of which went especially well. The conversations, admittedly, didn't go quite as badly as my French oral but I came out of both meetings feeling flat and disappointed.

In any case, I failed to get the grades demanded of those establishments, my B, C and D leaving little choice. It would have to be Coventry, a decaying city fifteen miles up the road. Just to give you an idea of the state of Coventry at the time, the Specials partly based 'Ghost Town' – released that very year, 1981 – on a hometown tarnished by shuttered-up shops and high unemployment.

On the bright side, at least this short move meant I could still play for Alvechurch, and even pop back to train during the week. I'd catch a bus to the Novotel hotel where Mase would pick me up and drive us over to Birmingham, an hour filled by friendly chat and advice from this infectious character.

Training took place on a Tuesday and Thursday, either in Rhys's school gym in Great Barr, north Birmingham, or under lights. Afterwards, we'd retire to the Three Crowns, a pub run by the club's vice-chairman, Allan 'Schoey' Schofield, who also happened to be my future father-in-law. Linda, Penny's mom, would sneak me a hot beef sandwich carved from the joint in the kitchen. Linda says she felt sorry for this lad her daughter clearly liked, knowing I was going back that night to my Coventry digs.

Oh yes, my digs. I'd had a bit of a nightmare in that direction. Because I was late sorting out my uni, I was also late applying for a room in the halls of residence. By then, all the halls were full, forcing me to go private in search of accommodation.

Mr and Mrs Windmill, a couple in their thirties, lived in a respectable semi on the outskirts of the city. My heart sank, though, when they showed me my room, the smallest in the house, which didn't hold much beyond a single bed and wardrobe. For a six-foot-three teenager, it felt really claustrophobic, not somewhere I'd want to spend lots of time.

To be honest, that applied to the house in general. No fault of the Windmills – they could not have been more welcoming – but it didn't feel like the kind of place a young student should be hanging out. For them, a normal working-class couple with a young baby, the extra twenty quid a week must have come in handy. For me, the whole situation didn't seem right. Sat there in the lounge watching *Coronation Street*, I felt out of place. People like me were supposed to be down the Students' Union bar knocking back pints and talking about everything from football to girls to the meaning of life, not discussing why Deirdre had left Ken yet again.

The thing was, though, I had decided to study Modern Languages, namely French, German and Spanish. It made sense. With decent grades at A level in the first two, this route seemed like my best chance of moving forward and getting a job at the end. This kind of degree traditionally attracts girls and my year was no different, with only one other boy on the course. Yes, I know it sounds brilliant. Spoiled for choice. Even so, I also wanted to make friends with like-minded lads who'd be there for some social during the week.

But that never happened in those early months. After lectures, I found myself catching the bus back to Binley Road to get on with some work or sit with the family. The food wasn't great either. Obviously on a tight budget, Mrs Windmill's signature dish was sausage stew, cooked in a huge pot, the remains of which would sit in the kitchen overnight. It didn't make for a pretty sight at breakfast, this congealed mass of grey with globules of fat sitting on the top. And if that wasn't enough, more solidified fat lay in the grill pan at the top of the cooker. The residue from cooking bacon, that fat would melt when I toasted some bread, leaving my breakfast tasting a bit strange.

Inevitably, I couldn't wait for Friday mornings to come around when, with no lectures scheduled, I could clear off home for the weekend. Quite often, to give me more time, my dad would even drive over on a Thursday night. No reflection on the Windmills at all, but I felt so relieved to walk out of that door and jump in the car.

Dad knew I was unhappy and I think it upset him, but there wasn't a lot he could do. We both knew I had to get on with it. With a career in professional football looking increasingly unlikely, I had to make the most of a degree course that could lead to a good job. In any case, things would surely get better as time went on, especially the following year when I could enjoy more independence by sharing a house with other students.

As it happened, I did make some friends during the second term and a house had been earmarked for that following year. My spirits lifted as I looked forward to the classic student experience of sharing a scruffy bedsit with a bunch of mates. This was more like it. My student life could now begin for real. Then just as we were about to sign the rental contract, another sort of contract came within reach. Leicester City's keen interest changed everything.

By that time I'd played twenty games or more for the mighty 'Church, getting to grips in the process with all the eccentricities and habits of non-league football. Looming large in those customs were the away matches. Well, not really the matches, more the coach journeys back that usually involved stopping at a few pubs. Now, I was only eighteen and not much of a drinker. I used to head into Birmingham with my mates, go to nightclubs like Boogies where we'd naturally have a drink. Never one much for pints, I drank Pernod and lemonade for a time. Then dark rum and Coke took over for a bit. But gulping down gallons of lager has never been my thing.

Most of the Alvechurch lads, in contrast, absolutely loved a pint. Not only that, the chairman and board members were not averse either. It meant a two-hour journey home could take all night after stopping at a couple of boozers along the way. Then there were the food stops, usually at a chippy. One time, we felt like a change so popped into a Kentucky Fried Chicken joint where a merry Randy Reg instantly took a shine to a life-size cardboard cut-out of Colonel Sanders. Our bargain buckets bought, the Colonel joined us on the coach where he stood stiffly up front for the rest of the journey back to Worcestershire.

Allan Schofield would always play a central part in these escapades. As a publican himself, he was the one to have a quiet word with the landlord if closing time threatened to get in our way. What a character. With his shiny patent leather shoes and trademark silk hanky poking from a blazer pocket, there was no mistaking Schoey. With a million one-liners and a nickname for everyone, our vice-chairman's Brummie tones could always be heard. And on these away trips he would come into his own. Never without a fat wad of cash, Schoey was in familiar territory when looking after bar staff, always on hand to slip a handsome tip so that we could enjoy a rowdy lock-in.

Mind you, I didn't mind these stop-offs one bit if Allan's daughter had come along. I'd sit chatting to Penny, playing footsie under the table, rather than get hammered up at the bar. Young love in full bloom. It amused the older lads no end. They thought I was treading on dangerous ground, flirting with Schoey's daughter, seeing as he had a reputation for knowing all the right people. If something needed doing, they said, he could find a way as the landlord of a pub frequented by some of Birmingham's handiest villains. At the time, I didn't have a clue if all this was true. I could never rely on this kind of rumour, especially from teammates trying to wind me up. And seeing as Penny was only fifteen at the time, the lads would make all sorts of jokes about me getting sorted. Kneecaps, I seem to remember, got regularly mentioned. I did wonder, while laughing nervously along, if Schoey really did have the hump. How dare this gangly teenager flirt with his little girl?

Fortunately, my kneecaps stayed intact as the goals started going in. It seemed that the Southern League Midland Division wasn't too good for me after all. As confirmation, I got picked for the England semi-professional squad that took part in a four-team tournament up in Aberdeen. That was another eye-opener, especially the game against Italy involving a style of combat I'd never encountered before. The little tugs and shoves, the tight man-to-man marking came as a shock to this innocent teenager. Back in Worcestershire, though, more and more scouts started visiting Lye Meadow to have a glance at Alvechurch's young centre-forward.

This was great news. The prospect of making it as a pro had, in my mind, virtually disappeared. I knew several lads, Victor Hollier included, who had been snapped up by professional clubs. They were obviously better than me. Had more about them. That's what I thought, anyway, when nothing materialised.

Being a philosophical sort, not one to really get the hump, I simply got on with things, telling myself that it wasn't meant to be. Alvechurch therefore looked like a logical step, a good level of football to keep me involved. I gave it my all without any misgivings or indeed any aspirations to stand out from the crowd to try and fulfil my childhood ambition. Who knows? Maybe that attitude helped, allowing me to relax and play well without constantly fretting about missed opportunities or tightening up because someone was watching.

But what do you know? Those opportunities, it seemed, weren't totally lost after all as my performances drew an increasing amount of admiration. Among those interested, Leicester, who were in the second tier – the old Second Division – figured prominently, with Ian McFarlane, Jock Wallace's number two, coming several times. Mind you, Ian wasn't alone. Villa, Blues, Coventry, West Brom – all the Midlands clubs – had a good look during that season.

Ron Atkinson, however, definitely topped the bill. Arriving in a Rolls-Royce for our cup tie against Billericay, Manchester United's flamboyant new manager, expensive sheepskin and all, caused quite a stir on that cold winter night. I heard afterwards that he hadn't hung around for the full ninety minutes. To me, that didn't feel like a good sign, though Ron has always insisted since that he intended coming back for a second look. Unfortunately, the game he had in mind got postponed due to heavy snow and he never made it back. That was his story anyhow.

Leicester, in contrast, quickly made up their mind and an offer of £15,000, plus another £7000 depending on appearances, got laid on the table. Too good to turn down. Despite its status and reputation (Alvechurch hold the record with Oxford City for the longest FA Cup tie – five replays in 1971/72), they were basically a village team dependent on a few hundred fans coming through the rusty turnstile. Not only were they never going to deny me this crack at the big time, the club simply could not afford to be spurning such sums.

And so it was that Dad and I travelled over to Leicester to 'negotiate' terms. I use inverted commas because Jock Wallace, who had never seen me play, laid down the offer bluntly as if any kind of haggling had never entered his head. Mind you, Jock had such a strong Glaswegian accent you could never really tell. We sat there quietly as he grunted out the figures, explaining that I would have to learn my trade in the reserves for a good two or three years before hopefully progressing to the first team. Walking out afterwards, my dad turned to me: 'So, what did he say they'd pay you? I couldn't understand a word!' Thanks, Dad. A fine agent you turned out to be.

Luckily, I had just about understood the important bits, namely that I would be paid £180 a week, augmented by an appearance fee of £220 should I play for the first team. That's fair, I thought, seeing as most of the first team, according to Jock, were on £400 a week. As it turned out, I played in the first team on the opening day of the 1982/83 season and didn't look back. The big Scot had inadvertently sorted me out.

As for my studies, I tried to find a way of continuing them alongside the football. Just because Leicester had offered a path to my dreams, I didn't really want to abandon an education I might need in a few years if things didn't work out. The trouble with Modern Languages, though, is you have to divide the third year between living in French- and German-speaking countries. That was going to be impossible now unless, of course, Leicester loaned me to Lyon and Bayern Munich. As a compromise, I suggested switching to Modern Studies, which didn't require such a commitment, but Jock wasn't having it, arguing with some reason that I should solely concentrate on the job that paid.

To be honest, I didn't take much persuading. Neither did my Mom and Dad. For parents who had always encouraged me to study hard, to give it everything, they could see my Coventry adventure was not working out. In any case, they, like me, were excited by the prospect of me becoming a professional. They knew only too well this was what I had wanted from the beginning. All those years playing schools football, climbing up the ladder from district to county. All those school holidays over at Daisy Farm, persisting till it was too dark to see the ball. Finally, it had come good. A little later than for many but that didn't matter. In fact, I would find out thirteen years later that my prolonged education, and my interest in language, would lay the ground for a second career.

I signed on the dotted line and waved goodbye to Alvechurch, a wonderful club full of glorious characters.

TAKING MY CHANCES

My Leicester career hadn't got off to a great start. That's what I thought anyway. What are you supposed to think when the manager sods off only a matter of weeks after signing you? That's what happened with Jock Wallace, whose departure for Motherwell left me feeling uneasy. It was Jock, after all, who had shown faith, who had addressed me that day in his office, talking through a career path leading to the first team in a couple of years. He was the one taking the punt. Nobody else.

Now all of a sudden, we had Gordon Milne, a very different personality from his predecessor, with different ideas about the game. What was he going to think? How would I figure in his plans? If at all. As an aside, Milne's appointment had proved a little controversial, having spent seven years with local rivals Coventry. He'd become a big favourite at Highfield Road. From the outside, he seemed to be Coventry through and through, which didn't sit well with many Leicester fans.

For different reasons, I was also sceptical. You see it all the time: a new man comes in and overhauls the playing staff. Those previously in favour quickly get ditched. One man's meat is another man's poison. These were the thoughts running through my head in the days leading up to my first day at work.

Oh God. My first day. The butterflies flapped wildly as I left home at the start of a commute that would become second nature over the next five years. M42, M6, M69 – the journey took an hour, give or take ten minutes. Adding to the tension was the fact I had only passed my driving test a few weeks before. The pressure was certainly on that day. With my Leicester contract signed and the first day of pre-season looming, life was going to be very awkward if I couldn't drive. Happy in Birmingham with Mom and Dad, I never even contemplated moving to Leicester. So how would I have made that hundred-mile round trip every day? Catch the train? What a longwinded pain. No, I simply had to pass. There was no other choice.

Luckily I did. And though my mom was nervous about me driving up the motorway, insisting that I phone to let her know I'd arrived, I wasn't bothered at all about the driving bit. It was what waited at the end that twisted my stomach.

Walking into a dressing room full of strangers, that's what did it for me, the prospect of entering a room full of professionals looking me up and down, sizing up this kid from non-league. Though you could never describe me as an extrovert, at eighteen I was verging on shy, making this kind of situation all the more terrifying. Once on the Narborough Road, the main thoroughfare leading into Leicester, I pulled my bronze Ford Escort into a lay-by next to a phone box. Scrambling for change, I dialled home. 'Hi Mom, yes, got here OK, no trouble. No, don't know what time I'll be back. Depends on how long training lasts. Got to go now, Mom, or else I'll be late.'

Turning into the Filbert Street car park, I took a moment to compose myself before heading in. Just take a deep breath, son, and open that door.

Once in among it, of course, it is never as bad as feared. The lads were loud and chatty, as friendly as you like, a tangle of voices in a crowded room. There was Nicky Walker, aspiring goalie and part of the Walker's Shortbread family, a welcoming presence on that first day. Ian Wilson, Andy Peake, Paul Ramsey, Larry May: they would all become good mates over the next few years. Changed into training kit, the next task was to find a lift for the short journey to Belvoir Drive. That's what happened back then. With precious few facilities at our training ground, we got changed at Filbert Street before jumping into cars, taking it in turns to act as taxi. In winter, we'd often return caked in mud, laying towels on seats to protect the upholstery.

No such problems this day, the first of pre-season, the pitches pristine after a summer of care. And funnily enough, with those nerves about meeting new faces now easing, I didn't feel so apprehensive about the football side. This was what I knew, what I was pretty good at, even if the standard had noticeably cranked up. It didn't take long for me to feel comfortable.

The hardest aspect, in reality, was coming to terms with full-time training, having only been used to a couple of sessions a week. I did feel a bit jaded in those early days as the body reacted to an extra workload that tested my brain as well as my legs. But I also felt exhilarated, excited by the challenge. And before long, it got even better.

Halfway through pre-season, Northampton Town brought a big squad along to Belvoir Drive for a couple of friendlies between first teams and reserves. Unsurprisingly, I was in the reserves – the stiffs – just trying to get to grips with my new life.

At half-time, I hear a shrill whistle coming from the adjoining pitch. It was the boss, calling me over. Walking across, I didn't know what to think. Maybe he had some advice, having seen snatches of my unremarkable first-half display. But no. 'You're going on for the second half,' he says, nodding at the first-team pitch. Oh right. Here we go. He wants to have a look.

I suppose we all recognise moments like this, the ones that can affect your entire life. Take the chance, seize the day and you may never look back. But if it doesn't go so well, you could end up back at square one lamenting missed opportunities, forever wondering what might have been. In this case, we're talking back to the boondocks of the reserves while the manager goes out and buys an alternative. If that had happened, I'd have faced an even steeper climb than the one presently staring me in the face. In fact, it could have been more of a downhill spiral as the manager moved forward without me in his thoughts. Looking back, then, this moment was definitely a big deal. Mess it up and my career could have headed in a much different direction.

That said, you don't tend to think like that at the time. Well, I didn't anyway. I didn't feel particularly nervous walking on to that pitch, fretting about the consequences should I fall flat. In fairness, that has always been a strength – taking things in my stride, never getting too worked up about big moments. My sixth-form PE teacher once remarked on that, telling Dad how I seemed to navigate every step up in football with little fuss.

Perhaps that laidback attitude came to my aid here, because I somehow stayed calm to grab a hat-trick. A hat-trick! Bloody hell, this was good news. Over forty-five minutes, my standing at Leicester had markedly improved. Sharp and bright, clinical in front of goal and linking well with Gary Lineker, Leicester's emerging golden boy, I hadn't just taken my chance, I'd hollered my claim from a metaphorical rooftop, a claim Gordon Milne couldn't ignore.

Talk about a watershed moment. Alan Young, a Scot signed from Oldham three years before, was brought off that day to give me a run-out. Youngy would soon leave the club, along with several other Jock Wallace signings, and I would start up front in the first game of the season.

Charlton Athletic came to Filbert Street that day, 28 August 1982. On paper it looked a decent start for genuine promotion contenders. After finishing eighth the previous season under Big Jock, it was thought that Lineker's goals would go a long way to making the crucial difference.

For me, of course, this day was huge. To be included in the starting line-up so soon after signing was something I certainly hadn't expected when Jock memorably laid down the law a mere two months before. It might not have been a big crowd by today's standards, but the 11,038 attendance was nearly 11,000 more than I had been used to.

What a buzz. I enjoyed every minute, even though we ended up losing 2–1. And I did OK. Nothing spectacular but held my own. Bill Anderson, the *Leicester Mercury*'s longstanding football writer, was even kind enough in his report to name me man of the match. I wasn't sure about that, a rare bit of sentiment from Bill possibly being involved. Even so, I'd definitely take it, seeing as, in the next three years, you would do very well, with Lineker about, to get a look-in as 'Man of the Match'.

On the following Tuesday we travelled up to Rotherham where the great Emlyn Hughes was player-manager. I had watched Emlyn on the telly so many times, seen him lift trophies for Liverpool on a regular basis, that beaming smile never far away. Not only that, he'd become a household name on *A Question of Sport* where, as a team captain opposite Gareth Edwards, the Welsh rugby legend, he would make the audience laugh with his high-pitched antics.

Now here he was on the same pitch trying to stop me from finding the net. It was an early indication of my change in circumstance. While earthy Millmoor might not have provided the most glamorous of backdrops, the presence of England's former captain was more than enough to spur me on. The night got even better when I anticipated a back pass and nipped in to flick the ball beyond Rotherham's goalie. What a moment. If I wasn't pleased enough about my first goal in league football, a 'well done, son' from Hughes at the end left me floating on air. If he thought I played well, I might just have a future. The rest of that season confirmed as much.

Helping enormously was a partnership with Gary that clicked straight away. I didn't have to worry too much about forging a bond when that side of things was taking care of itself.

Gary had already been around the first team for a couple of years, starting on the wing before moving inside. As a local boy, he quickly became a fans' favourite with those darting runs and natural eye for goal.

Looking from the outside, it was the kind of playing style that should have suited us no end; me, holding up the ball with my back to goal, flicking on headers; him, lurking on shoulders, running in behind. It seemed a perfect blend. Yet what looks good on paper doesn't always pan out on grass, so it was lucky that Gary and I hit it off pretty quickly.

'You know what it's like, Smudge,' my old teammate says now. 'You have a little look when a new striker turns up. Is he any good? Is he a threat to my place? But I could see straight away you were much different to me. Tall, good in the air with a good touch, I thought you'd make a decent partner, even in those early days. Without blowing smoke up our own arses, we weren't dopey footballers, we could work things out, so it didn't take much for us to get going.'

Off the pitch, too, we got on very well. Penny became friendly with Michelle, Gary's girlfriend, which led to us going out for meals or spending time at Michelle's house where her lovely parents, Roger and Julia, always made us feel welcome. With a grand piano in the lounge, Roger would sometimes entertain everyone by tickling the ivories with no little panache. Gary's party piece, meanwhile, was a lively impression of an excitable chimp. He'd hop around the room, scratching armpits and screeching.

One time, after a home match, we had arranged for Gary and Michelle to see us in Birmingham. Well, Walsall to be more accurate, where Penny and her mom, after Linda's divorce, were renting a charming, if chilly, Victorian terrace. With room at a premium there, our visitors checked into the Post House Hotel just off the M6 and we duly picked them up to go back for some dinner. All good so far. At the end of the night, though, we got a real shock when I dropped them off in the hotel car park. Gary, at the time, had a sponsored car, a modest little Fiat. The trouble was, with his name plastered in large letters down the sides, it tended to stand out. More than that, in an area short on Leicester fans, it obviously wound somebody up. Some smartarse had decided to nick a fire extinguisher from somewhere and completely cover Gary's car with the foamy stuff. It was a right old mess. We cleaned it up as best we could before our friends drove back to Leicester.

On another occasion, the four of us met in Stratford-upon-Avon for a day out. The weather was lovely, the sun shining down warmly on Shakespeare's hometown. And what do you do on a day like this? Well, you rent out a boat, of course, and enjoy a gentle row along the river. For half an hour or so, we splashed about in classic fashion while managing to avoid any collisions. Even the final bit proved entertaining as we tried to ease our vessel into port. Gary found himself straddled between dry land and water, his feet in the boat, his arms on the jetty and the gap getting wider. Helped by his shipmates and a bloke on the side, he just about managed to avoid total embarrassment and pull the boat in. Walking back into town, our little trip felt like a roaring success. Only later, when it was time to go home, did the smiles start to fade. Trying to find his car keys, Gary went through that familiar ritual of patting himself down, checking every pocket several times over with increasing panic. They were nowhere to be found. We had to face facts. The keys must have slipped into the river during that comical attempt to grasp terra firma. No use going back. The water was dark and deep. And none of us fancied going for a dip.

There was only one thing for it. No other choice. We drove the couple back to Leicester where Gary picked up his spare keys before we turned the car round and returned to Stratford. Now where did he park again? Ah, there it was. His Toyota Celica, a clear step or two up from that little Fiat.

I didn't often fall out with Gary. As two fairly laidback characters, we rubbed along nicely. On the pitch, he was doing his job and I was doing mine. As the goals flew in, the situation was not only proving beneficial to Leicester, it was doing no harm at all to our own reputations. Gary, in particular, was creating plenty of headlines as well as plenty of interest from bigger clubs.

One time, though, he did get the hump. Our coach, Gerry Summers, started banging on one day about how much I passed to Gary and how little he passed to me. Though he said it half jokingly, you knew Gerry was trying to make a point and was implying that Gary was greedy. Then he turned to me and said, 'Go on, Al, tell him he should pass to you more.' Stupidly, I went along with the charade, repeating with a smile the same sentiment, more to shut Gerry up than have a go at my strike partner. It was only later when he got me alone that Gary's face darkened. 'If you've got something to say, fire your own bullets, not someone else's.' He was angry that I had even entertained Gerry's point. I tried to defend myself, explaining I just said it as a joke, not meaning anything by it. But Gary wasn't having it. The perceived criticism had stung.

I don't suppose it helped that Gary and Gerry did not really get on. For a start, our star centre-forward was not a big fan of training, which tended to wind up Gerry no end. Gerry's attitude was that if he had taken the trouble to devise a session, the least the players could do was buy into that work by giving it their best. Gary, however, did not see it like that.

'It wasn't that I didn't like training,' he explains now. 'I didn't mind it as long as it was finishing, or something I was getting some benefit from. Even fitness training, I liked. But all that other stuff, five-a-sides and everything, I didn't see the point. The goals were too small for a start. They'd ruin your confidence!'

Three o'clock on a Saturday, that's when it counted for him. That was often his comeback, delivered with a wry smile, if we gave him playful stick for ducking out of training with a stiff groin.

Mind you, it was difficult to argue with his logic when, come the big day, our man looked razor sharp, banging in a couple to win the game. Some players need to train well all week – I would say the majority – in order to feel right for the serious stuff. Gary was the exception, a rare one indeed. He could do the bare minimum from Monday to Friday and then roar out of the blocks with great success. Even on a matchday he did very little beforehand, eschewing the traditional warm-up out on the pitch for a stint in the bath. His routine was always the same – standing in just a couple of inches of hot water, he would go through some gentle stretches. After that, it was all systems go.

It was as if Gary didn't need the help of any coach. Even at that early stage, the striker had a firm grasp of what was required. And as the years passed, as the England caps piled up along with the goals, as the Barcelona spell lent sophistication, that understanding reached an enviable depth. I will never forget his words on returning from Spain to join Tottenham. 'Come on, Smudge,' he said one day. 'It's quite easy to get twenty goals at this level if you know when and where to run, don't you think?' What? No, I didn't think, to be honest. I might have just won the Golden Boot in Arsenal's 1988/89 title-winning season but the business of scoring still didn't feel that simple.

The thought of success with another club barely entered my head in those early Leicester years when football was a very different proposition to the multibillion-pound 'brand' on worldwide show now. Back then, no one had thought of calling the supporter a customer. The game was less glitzy, more aggressive on and off the pitch, and overall perhaps just a little more real, with much less distance between player and fan.

At Leicester, we knew many supporters by name, so often did they wait outside the ground. Strolling to your car after training, you'd have a quick chat as a photo from *Shoot* magazine was held out for signing.

Don't get me wrong, this obviously still happens, but in a more controlled way. It's much harder these days to get within touching distance, such are the tight security measures in place. Gated training grounds, for one, make it more difficult, especially when there's a sign outside warning fans that players won't stop for autographs.

Essentially, I don't think the make-up of an autograph hunter has ever really changed. The most serious are fanatics, devoted to their team, deriving tremendous pleasure from a quick word and scribble. That sort should be valued, not kept at arm's length.

To give an idea of the close bond with fans, we players would go along every year to the Coalville branch of the official supporters' club for their Player of the Year do. It was a homely affair, held in a social club of what was back then still very much a mining town. A long trestle table would be laden with food, cheese cobs and pickled onions always a favourite. During the course of the night, a Goal of the Season trophy would also be awarded. Thinking about it, I've still got one buried up in the loft. Then there was the annual Miss Coalville competition, involving a string of local girls parading up and down in front of a panel of players. The single lads were always keen to volunteer for that. But whatever the function, we'd hang about all night chatting with fans, never really thinking this was a bind. It was just what you did, a part of the job.

In fairness to today's lot, we were under less pressure, not just in these public situations but more generally, including on matchdays. It led to a more relaxed approach, especially by some.

Mark Wallington was a wonderful character, who, when he turned pro, was in the process of qualifying as a PE teacher. Clearly a bright bloke, there was always a really calm aura about our goalie, not to mention a mischievous glint in the eye. On the one hand, he worked extremely hard to become number one when Peter Shilton left. On the other, he never took life too seriously, even on a Saturday.

Goal kicks gave an opportunity for one favourite party piece. Backing away from the ball to take the kick, Wally would go right into the goal, reaching back with his hand to grab the net. Then, in moving to step forward, he'd pretend his hand was caught, causing him to stumble back, a huge grin betraying the practical joke. It was the same when a fan threw back the ball from the stand. Reaching out to catch it, Wally would quickly straighten his arm to bounce the ball back with the inside of his elbow. The fans loved all this clowning as much as our goalie. It created a connection, brought the two halves together in a way that doesn't happen so much these days.

Something that definitely wouldn't happen now involved Wally again, this time away from public view in the dressing room at half-time. Like most footballers, our keeper was a creature of habit, superstition even, and his ritual involved heading for the toilet cubicle tucked in the corner as soon as he walked in. As the boss delivered his team talk, Wally would be sat there, toilet door ajar, listening in. Even better, he'd do it with a fag in his mouth, idly puffing away. I think he sat on that loo to get out of the way, to stop his smoke bothering anyone. And it all seemed so natural. Gordon Milne didn't bat an eyelid and we just took it as read, an everyday thing, just as normal as the kit man keeping whisky and brandy miniatures in the skip, just in case someone fancied a swig to calm the nerves.

I was lapping up life in my first year of a career that had always been the dream. Every day was a good one, laughs never far away. That included the business of actually getting to training, a journey that eventually turned into a car share of giant proportions. For now, it was just me and Stevie Lynex, him travelling from Dudley, me from Hollywood. We'd meet every morning at nine at Corley Services on the M6 where we'd take turns to drive the rest of the way.

Steve was a proper Black Country lad, born in West Bromwich with an accent to match. Sporting a droopy moustache with a tendency to narrow his eyes, we all called him Charlie, after Charlie Chan, the fictional detective. He'd come through the Baggies' youth ranks but never made the first team, so followed Johnny Giles to Shamrock Rovers in Ireland before coming back to spend three seasons at Birmingham City, followed by Leicester. It was funny with Charlie. Despite shining for Leicester as a Filbert Street favourite scoring plenty of goals, the pacey winger always hankered for a return to his beloved West Brom.

We got on really well as travelling companions and fellow West Midlanders, soon becoming roommates for overnight trips. A lover of big cars, Charlie drove a gold Ford Granada, the plush 2.8 Ghia model with all the bits. Like me, he also loved his music (Motown being a joint favourite) and kept a pile of cassettes crammed in the glove box. Inevitably, the daily debate was which album to play. For a month or so, Charlie was hooked on Five Star, Romford's own version of the Jackson 5, who became quite big in the mid-1980s. By the time we moved on to something else, I think we knew every word of all their hits.

The song choice wasn't so straightforward when more players joined the group. Bob Hazell was the first, signing from QPR in 1983. But Bob still had a house in Walsall, having started his career up the road at Wolves. Reluctant to move to Leicester, he started coming with us, which happily meant less petrol money for me and Charlie. Born in Jamaica, Big Bad Bob was a hulk of a man, boasting the kind of generous frame you don't see in football much now. He had particular problems with Leicester's shirt, the one with Ind Coope plastered on the front. Made from cheap polyester, it tended to create an awful lot of static, especially if snug fitting, as it was on Bob, who was less than happy that Admiral, the kit manufacturers, couldn't make one big enough. As it was, the mixture of sweat and polyester proved uncomfortable for Bob who ended up sticking plasters to his nipples to stop the rubbing.

Fearsome on the outside as a tough centre-half, Bob was friendly and funny in the dressing room, with a chuckling laugh that got us all going. Mind you, I wasn't always smiling sat in his car, a powerful Saab turbo he loved to push hard. 'Look at the needle!' he'd enthusiastically shout, pointing at the turbo dial as it shot up to maximum. Still, we always got to work safely, and never late.

Next to join the party was Peter Eastoe, a striker of some talent on loan from West Brom. Gordon Milne brought him in to add a bit of know-how, which certainly worked for me because I learned quite a lot watching Pete go about his work. I also laughed a lot listening to him talk. Pete was something of a comic genius, full of funny stories from his varied time in the game. And his car was a classic. Well, maybe not a classic in the true sense of the word but certainly a sight to behold, especially when full. We're talking about a huge grey Citroën CX estate, complete with air suspension that could make you feel seasick as it bobbed up and down. This thing was like a hearse, cavernous inside, which was just as well when goalkeeper Mark Grew and young Mark Hutchinson from Aston Villa also joined the crew. That made it six in all, meaning we had to travel in Pete's Citroën when everyone turned up.

Though Pete didn't play a lot for Leicester, mainly backing up me and Gary, on one of the few occasions he did it ended in horrible pain. Manchester United were the visitors, a talented team featuring Kevin Moran, Remi Moses, Norman Whiteside and Bryan Robson. Those familiar with these names won't be surprised to hear this lot knew how to handle themselves, taking few prisoners in the tackle. Ron Atkinson's side also included Gordon McQueen, the big Scotland international unfamiliar with niceties. Few of us saw the incident in question, but we did see Peter lying on the floor clutching his face. It turned out McQueen had elbowed our man off the ball, shattering his jaw in several places. For many weeks afterwards, with the jaw wired up, Pete could only take in food by sucking through a straw.

Another time, I was jogging back for a corner alongside the notoriously robust Joe Jordan when Southampton's centre-forward, right out of the blue, threw an elbow at my throat, catching me bang on the Adam's apple. For a few seconds, I could hardly breathe, but remember accepting the blow as part of the game. Big Joe simply took the chance to lay one on an opponent when nobody was looking.

I'm not trying to single anyone out here, more to give an indication of the climate back then, when multiple cameras and retrospective action weren't around to deter such dirty tricks.

I was learning all the time. Though non-league was far from gentle, it lacked the cynicism and cunning of the professional game where livelihoods and standing were very much at stake. That soon became clear at Leicester where our own status remained in the balance going into the last game of my first season. The day witnessed a quite tumultuous climax, featuring one of the most infamous games of recent times.

Fulham had been strong favourites to win successive promotions but when they started to stumble we managed to peg back their sizeable lead for the third promotion spot, helped by a gritty 1–0 win at Craven Cottage. The momentum, we felt, had swung our way. Level on points going into the final fixtures, Fulham appeared to face the tougher task, away at Derby County who needed a result to avoid relegation. We, on the other hand, were at home to Burnley, who, it should be noted, were also fighting the drop. For us, though, a win would be enough to remove any doubt.

In the event, we found it tough going on a hot and tense day. Chances proved hard to create against a Burnley side featuring Trevor Steven and a young Lee Dixon, a future friend and teammate a few years down the line. Mind you, I really should have scored when put through on goal but messed up my attempt to lob the keeper. When the final whistle blew at 0–0, our fans swarmed on to the pitch, having heard that Fulham had lost at Derby. As they celebrated outside, we did the same in the dressing room, grabbing the champagne to start the party. Yet the corks had barely popped when Gordon Milne appeared to break the news. 'Hold on, lads. There's been an appeal at Derby. Fulham want the match replayed.'

Seeing the TV pictures later, it wasn't hard to understand why Malcolm Macdonald, the Fulham manager, felt so incensed. With Derby 1–0 up thanks to Bobby Davison's volley, the fans had spilled out of the stands onto the sidelines. So close were they to the touchline, there was barely enough room to take a throw-in. Even worse, some idiot kicked out at Fulham's Robert Wilson. Seconds later, when the referee blew for a free-kick, the hordes thought it all over and swamped the field. Deciding enough was enough, the ref called it a day with two minutes still to play, hence the appeal from an aggrieved Fulham.

It wasn't until the following week, when we were in Torremolinos on an end-of-season jolly, that the Football League denied their requests for a replay, perhaps working on the proviso that Fulham would have needed to score twice in those two remaining minutes to change the situation. Whatever the reason, our San Miguels tasted much sweeter after the verdict. See those lads on the beach? They're now First Division footballers.

It was another of those moments that change careers. Ten months before, I'd taken my chance to score that hat-trick against Northampton. Now the fates had conspired to put me in the big time. With Leicester promoted, my journey gathered pace.

FLYING WITH THE FOXES

The opening game gave us a clue. Notts County were no great shakes, having mooched around the lower half of the First Division the season before. Yet they waltzed into Filbert Street and gave us a right pasting, as well as an early indication of the difference in class between the top flight and those below.

Martin O'Neill scored the first for a team also featuring Justin Fashanu, Nigel Worthington and Brian 'Killer' Kilcline, who just happened to be the sweatiest centre-half I ever faced. You would try and hold off the bearded beast only to find your hand slipping on his sopping-wet shirt. No other defender seemed to perspire quite as much. But he was no mug, Killer, and I didn't get much change out of him that day as County went about putting us in our place.

How to explain the 4–0 pounding? First-night nerves? Just a slow start after the buzz of promotion? No, the step up in standard hit us like a brick. As confirmation, the first ten games passed without a win. Ten bloody games. And it wasn't as if we were coming particularly close. Of those ten tussles, we managed to lose eight, most by generous amounts. It looked like the 1983/84 season was going to prove an uphill slog ending in a swift return to the Second Division.

Our first point on the board arrived in late September when we scraped a 2–2 draw with Stoke City. Mind you, I wasn't around at the final whistle, having been carted off to hospital for some dental repair after having my front three teeth kicked out. Steve Bould was the culprit, a future Arsenal teammate and very good friend. He certainly wasn't in my good books that day, though. Receiving the ball on my chest in the middle of the pitch, Bouldy swung round a leg from behind to try and kick it away. As I would later discover, that was typical of the bloke. Persistent and aggressive, the big centre-half rarely gave an inch. On this occasion, sadly, his size thirteen boot missed the ball completely, smashing instead into my face.

Falling to one knee, I reached for my mouth, thinking the blood pouring out was due to a cut. But then Stoke's Mark Chamberlain, future father of Alex Oxlade-Chamberlain and an England winger at the time, started picking things up off the turf and handing them to the ref. It suddenly dawned. These were my teeth, kicked cleanly out, roots still intact. As I walked slowly to the touchline, our coach, Gerry Summers, came across for a look.

'You OK, big Al? You'll be all right to carry on, yes?'

'No I bloody won't, Gerry! I've just had my front three teeth kicked out!'

By this point, serious pain was taking over from the initial numbness, perhaps caused by shock. Back in the dressing room, our physio, John McVey, thought it wise to put the molars in a cup of milk. I think he'd read somewhere this would keep them fresh. In the event, John may have been right, because at Leicester Royal Infirmary a very nice lady gently pushed back my teeth into their gum holes.

'They won't stay there forever,' she kindly explained. 'At some point you'll have to have a bridge. But they should be OK for a year or two.'

Standing alongside, Penny looked concerned, having rushed to the hospital after seeing the incident from her seat in the stand. Listening in, her concern was matched by a certain fascination. Not surprising really. She was a dental nurse at the time.

Furthermore, the doctor's forecast was right. Not until my Arsenal days, after Big Bad Bouldy pitched up, did I require the services of the club dentist who made that aforementioned bridge and also, for protection, a gumshield.

Sadly, that draw against Stoke proved more port-in-a-storm than notable turnaround. With me recovering on the sidelines, we lost at Birmingham and Norwich before drawing with Ipswich. The First Division was proving a merciless bedfellow, offering little encouragement, no matter what we tried. Consequently, you can imagine the spirit within the camp. Rock bottom, desperately in need of a boost.

But then came the volte-face in the most unlikely of places, both for the team and their number nine. Never mind that we ended up losing a two-legged League Cup tie with Chelsea on penalties, a win at Stamford Bridge with me grabbing a goal seemed to infuse some self-belief.

Finding my feet once more, the nagging doubts began to subside.

I had, after all, come a long way in a short space of time. From non-league to top flight in little more than a year: making the leap without setbacks would be asking a lot. Was I even good enough? It looked up in the air for a good while.

Off the pitch, the routine remained – car sharing with Stevie Lynex and co, travelling across every day from the West Midlands. For the most part, it worked perfectly. Never a hitch. Never late. The only snag came when we trained in the morning ahead of a night game. I couldn't go home. What to do in the afternoon when I should be resting?

The answer came in the shape of two very good friends – Ian Wilson, our hardworking midfielder, and his lovely wife Tracey. From the word go, this down-to-earth couple, both from Aberdeen, took Penny and I under their wing. With a lovely house in Oadby, a small town just outside Leicester, they'd often invite us over for something to eat.

And on the day of those night games, I'd go back with 'Wils' for a bit of lunch, after which he'd usually retire to bed. Back then, in my very early twenties, I didn't feel the need for an afternoon kip. To be honest, that suited Wils no end. I could look after Greg, their adorable one-year old son, who had taken a liking to this lanky Brummie. Tracey, meanwhile, might grab this chance to do some shopping, leaving me to babysit for an hour or two. I'd sit there with Greg, idly playing along, only half-thinking about the match. Once Tracey got back, she'd make chilli con carne before Wils and I left for Filbert Street.

Leicester's first season in the top flight miraculously turned into a decent campaign. For me, grabbing a hat-trick in a 5–1 demolition of Wolves screened live on the telly was probably the highlight, although beating Arsenal 3–0 was also right up there, having managed to score past the great Pat Jennings. The day after, I cut out the photo capturing the moment from a Sunday newspaper, sticking it straight in my scrapbook. For many years afterwards, I faithfully kept such cuttings to chronicle a career that was always going to be fun reviewing.

After that horrendous start, losing our first six games, we ended up securing safety with two games to spare. That took some doing. The recovery in form and morale had been quite remarkable. On a personal front, I had enhanced my reputation with sixteen goals. More generally, we were forging a name as an exciting side whose games were rarely short on incident.

At the end of that 1983/84 season, Wils, Tracey, Penny and I travelled to Cyprus for a fundraising game organised by the army. We were looked after royally on that week-long trip. Apart from the match at Happy Valley between the armed forces (our team) and a local side, there was an official function in the officers' mess at Episkopi Garrison, all ceremonial uniform and shiny medals. Then there was the drinks reception at the Governor's magnificent residence where brandy sours, the island's signature cocktail, came reverentially served on silver trays. That evening, we met the Governor's wife, Lady Langley, who, during the course of conversation, offered to teach me and Wils to windsurf.

'It's easy!' she exclaimed. 'You boys will pick it up in no time!'

Buoyed by her faith, off we went the next day to a quiet bay where Lady Langley gracefully demonstrated the art of standing on a board holding on to a sail. Just as she said, it did look fairly easy. Nothing to it. But when it came to having a go ourselves, neither I nor Wils could get the hang of it, continually falling into the warm sea. After four or five tries, a giggling Lady Langley decided to call it a day, her students not quite so adept as she had imagined. Afterwards, we said our goodbyes, never thinking our paths would cross again.

Four years later, Arsenal travelled to Bermuda for a bit of R & R. Another great jaunt. A bit of golf, a bit of sun and some evening entertainment: what could be better? For some reason, George Graham's son also came on that trip. Only about eighteen at the time, an innocent Daniel wanted to be part of the crew, which meant coming along on a night out. Oh no, this was asking for trouble. The opportunity for skulduggery couldn't be ignored. True to form, someone decided it would be quite fun to spike Daniel's drink, just to see how the youngster coped. The answer, predictably, was not very well. After a few extra-strong cocktails, Graham junior expelled his innards outside a bar before staggering back to the hotel. I'm not sure the boss ever found out.

Thankfully, it was a bit more civilised the evening we attended a function at the Governor of Bermuda's mansion. This felt familiar. I'd been in this situation before. Even so, I wasn't prepared for what happened next.

'Alan! Alan!' came a sudden cry from across the room. 'Oh, how delightful to see you! How are you? How is Penny? How are Tracey and Ian?'

It was, of course, Lady Langley, my old mate from Cyprus who had followed her husband to this latest posting. We chatted for a while, me explaining that my windsurfing abilities hadn't much improved, her laughing at the memory. At the end, once she'd moved away, the other lads couldn't wait to ask about my pal.

'How the bloody hell do you know her, Smudge? Got friends in high places, haven't you?'

'Ah, yes,' I said casually. 'We go way back, me and Lady Langley. Known her for years.'

* * *

Leicester's status as a side whose games were full of incident certainly gained traction in the 1984/85 season when we played Burton Albion in the third round of the FA Cup. Although the Northern Premier League side was drawn first out of the hat, the game got moved to Derby County's Baseball Ground for safety reasons. Their manager, Neil Warnock, was in the first flush of management, yet to make his name in the football world. He was, in fact, a qualified chiropodist and on the eve of the match did a piece for *Football Focus*, the BBC's Saturday lunchtime favourite, attending to someone's bunions while talking up his side's chances.

Derby's pitch was always one of the worst, a total mud heap in the middle of winter. It wasn't much different during that campaign – hardly a blade of grass to be seen, particularly down the middle. Even worse, the mud had frozen solid overnight to leave treacherous ruts in various parts of the pitch. Inspecting the icy surface beforehand, we couldn't quite believe the match was still on. It certainly wouldn't take a stud. Most of us wore pimpled trainers to try and cope.

To start off with, the precarious conditions acted as a leveller, Burton equalising to make it 1–1. But then the trouble started behind one goal and their keeper, Paul Evans, got hit on the head by a block of wood, believed to be part of a seat. Down he went, feeling groggy and nauseous. Though he continued after some treatment, Paul claimed not to remember the next two goals going in. I got the first of those and, in fairness, my close-range header came from a cross the keeper may well have come for had he been OK.

Because Evans was still suffering at half-time, the referee charitably extended the break by five minutes to give him more time. A doctor had a look and advised him to come off. But Evans wasn't having it and, in those days of being allowed only one substitute, Burton had already made theirs, so were naturally reluctant to go down to ten men.

It didn't matter. We scored another three to run out 6–1 winners, Lineker bagging a hat-trick and me getting two. Job done. A prominent banana skin had thankfully been sidestepped to leave us thinking about the fourth round. Hold on a minute, though. Not so fast. Talk turned at the end to a possible replay as Warnock argued with some reason that hooligans should never be allowed to change the course of a match. In our dark, wood-panelled dressing room, confusion reigned. Gary and I walked over to Gordon Milne. Did we enquire after the keeper's wellbeing? Did we ask about the crowd trouble? No, our concerns lay a little closer to home.

'Boss, if the game has to be replayed, will our goals still count?'

It was a legitimate question, even if slightly self-centred at that particular moment. But that's strikers for you. Goals are their lifeblood. To have these efforts struck off would definitely have rankled.

As for the tie, a replay was indeed ordered, this time behind closed doors. We ended up playing at an eerie Highfield Road, home of Coventry City, where Paul Ramsey's early strike decided a lifeless contest. And for the record, our goals in the first game thankfully counted.

But if that represented good news for me and Gary, the reason for the replay certainly didn't. Hooliganism: a stain on the game dating back to the 1960s that had almost become part of everyday life, something you accepted with a resigned shrug. Coming from Alvechurch, I'd never experienced any real aggro, unless you count the time our keeper, Reggie Edwards, swapped punches with a fan at Cheltenham. When the bloke started yelling insults at the end of the game, an incensed Reggie chased the culprit to have a go back. That aside, there were rarely enough people to create a crowd scene, never mind cause trouble.

In the professional game, however, violence was getting progressively worse, as Penny found out one day at Filbert Street. Just as she and her brother, Greg, were getting out of the car before a game with Chelsea, an angry mob of away fans stampeded past, some pouring with blood as bottles flew through the air. Diving back into the car, quickly locking the doors, they sat there for a minute to let the herd pass. When venturing back out, they had to tiptoe over a carpet of broken glass.

Unfortunately, that wouldn't be the last time she encountered such havoc. A few years later, she was walking down to Highbury with friends before an Arsenal–Millwall game when evasive action became necessary: a fan came crashing through a window of the Gunners pub on the corner of Blackstock Road. As a nice comedic touch, the startled bloke was still sitting in his chair as he landed on the pavement amid a pile of glass.

Such violence simply formed part and parcel of the matchday experience. It was almost taken for granted, something to avoid if you possibly could, and often prompted by fashion-conscious kids calling themselves Casuals, smartly kitted out in Fila, Ellesse and Sergio Tacchini. These gangs were well organised, plotting away days and scraps weeks in advance.

Unlike today, football lacked any kind of cachet among respectable people with decent jobs. Down the local accountancy firm, for instance, they probably didn't chat over coffee about last night's game, debating a manager's decision to switch to 3–5–2. Your doctor was unlikely to launch into some friendly banter about his or her team beating yours the other day. Football played a much smaller part in everyday life, the casual observer rare in a world made for die-hards.

Nineteen eighty-five was the year of Heysel, the Bradford disaster, the Luton–Millwall riot, of English teams banned from European competition. The country's national sport had never sunk so low, prompting *The Times* to describe the game as 'a slum sport played in slum stadiums and increasingly watched by slum people'. Incredible. Newspapers can't get enough of the game nowadays. It's a prime concern of editors to beat the competition by producing special pull-outs and signing famous columnists.

Back then, however, football had become a dirty word, especially among politicians. Prime Minister Margaret Thatcher demanded to know what the FA was going to do about hooliganism. FA Secretary Ted Croker argued this was society's problem more than just football's, pointing to the 1981 riots in Brixton, Toxteth and Tottenham. Even so, compulsory ID cards for fans were seen as one answer for quite some time, only shelved after the outcry following the Hillsborough disaster in 1989.

Attendances were inevitably affected during those dark days. For Leicester's opening game of the 1984/85 campaign against Newcastle United, we attracted only 18,000 people to Filbert Street, a crowd that would have been boosted by a healthy number of Geordies. A few weeks later, 12,000 turned up for the visit of Watford. In a ground capable of holding 22,000, empty seats were everywhere. It was different for the terraces where the cheapest tickets lay, and where, among others, your average hooligan hung out. Compare and contrast the situation now. It's usually a sell-out at Leicester's King Power Stadium, with more than 30,000 souls keen to see the action.

That 1984/85 season, just like the last, quickly became clouded by the threat of relegation. But despite our best efforts to mess things up (we lost eight of our final eleven matches), we once again finished fifteenth with fifty-one points, exactly the same as the previous year. In fairness, we weren't getting any worse but neither were we improving. Only hapless Stoke, who finished bottom that season by an embarrassing margin, had conceded more goals. That would teach Bouldy to kick out my teeth. But if it hadn't been for our firepower, we'd have been doomed. And everyone at the club knew that such a perilous status quo would inevitably lead to the loss of the player mainly responsible for those life-saving goals.

And so it was that Gary Lineker joined Everton in a £800,000 move. Leicester's favourite son, the local golden boy, unavoidably left home in search of success. It marked the start of something new, not just for him but also for me, his erstwhile partner. Greater responsibility had suddenly shifted my way. As Leicester's main striker, I'd be expected to make up some of the shortfall Gary's departure obviously created. How was that going to work out? Nobody knew, especially me.

For Penny, too, the transfer had an effect. Not only was her close friend Michelle no longer around, her matchday routine had to be changed. As a rule, she'd go into Leicester town centre to meet Paul Ramsey's girlfriend, Sally, who worked for

Christian Dior on the beauty counter at Boots. After a coffee with Sally, Penny would then walk across to the market where Gary's brother, Wayne, would be selling fruit and vegetables on the family stall. Off they'd drive to Filbert Street in the fruit and veg van, Wayne taking in a bag of cherries or grapes to share around. None of that now. Wayne wouldn't be going. Gary's departure had messed everything up!

Or had it? You did have to wonder when Gary's new club pitched up at Filbert Street on the opening day of the 1985/86 season. Everton were champions, a powerful and classy outfit, featuring the bite of Peter Reid, the elegance of Kevin Sheedy and goals of Graeme Sharp. What a team. They'd just run away with the league, coasting home thirteen points ahead of bitter rivals Liverpool. With Lineker in their ranks, Howard Kendall's side would surely only get stronger. Yes, our chances looked slim on that sunny day. But football being the gloriously unpredictable game that it is, we ended up winning 3–1, with me scoring one and Mark Bright grabbing two to suggest that life after Lineker wouldn't be so bad after all. The supporters were ecstatic, having feared the worst. We all headed home with hope in our hearts.

False hope, as it turned out. The next nine games slipped by without a win. Brighty couldn't kick on from his opening salvo as we continued leaking goals at an alarming rate. As autumn turned to winter, highlights became dreadfully scarce. The best moment by far came two days after my twenty-third birthday when we handsomely beat Manchester United, yours truly scoring two. A furious Ron Atkinson kept his stars – Paul McGrath, Gordon Strachan, Mark Hughes and all – locked in the away dressing for a good hour afterwards. A corner seemed to have been turned, particularly when, a couple of weeks later, we completed the double over Lineker's Everton, triumphing 2–1 at Goodison Park.

'I just knew you would score,' Gary told me afterwards. 'When you went through on Neville Southall, I just knew you'd tuck it away.'

To be honest, so did I. Despite the team's problems, I was feeling very confident as the main man up front. Rather than struggling without my old partner, I found that his absence gave me new life by freeing up key areas inside the penalty area. Forwards soon learn, if they've got anything about them, the best place to go when a ball is about to arrive. Coaches used to call it the POMO (position of maximum opportunity), having studied the statistics to work out that spot. Strikers, on the other hand, tend to sniff it out in a more instinctive way.

So instead of Gary making that dash into the six-yard box, it would be available for me if I so fancied. When Stevie Lynex was looking to cross the ball from the right, I could offer him the best option, find the best position. In other words, no longer did I have to work off Gary in terms of movement, drifting to the back post, for instance, if he went near. Used as a lone striker a lot of the time now, I had my pick of runs.

The upshot was that I ended up scoring more goals. Not loads more, not quite as many as Gary had bagged, but enough to enhance my reputation as a young player heading in the right direction.

Helping me along was Gary McAllister, an elegant midfielder who, together with Ali Mauchlen, more of a tenacious bulldog, had arrived from Motherwell the summer Lineker left. Not only did Gary bring a classy intelligence to the team, I benefitted straight away from his acute football brain as we quickly built up a good understanding. For example, when the ball was played into him, I knew there was every chance he'd help it round the corner first time before quickly spinning to offer a return pass. In putting us on the front foot, the move also forced the opposition to take a step back. In addition, Gary's early ball, because I was expecting it, gave me an advantage over my marker. I could take it in my stride or lay it off before the defender had time to get close. It was all about speed of thought and movement – more than welcome in this post-Lineker age.

Watching from the sideline, Gordon Milne was enjoying this brand of neat, slick football, even though it didn't lead to many victories. As one of Bill Shankly's first signings at the start of the 1960s, Gordon had been reared on a fast passing game responsible for Liverpool's emergence as a top club. This industrious right-half played a big part in promotion from the Second Division before picking up two title medals under a manager in Shankly whose beguiling charisma vied with Beatlemania for Merseyside's attention.

Experiences like that are bound to leave a deep mark, your whole football philosophy shaped by those salad days. The boss would always convey a deep regard for the game, enthusiastically rubbing his hands while addressing the squad, the compact figure in shorts imploring us to move the ball with speed and imagination. To encourage this, he'd have us playing small-sided games (the staple of Liverpool's training regime), sometimes joining in to give a glimpse of a talent that won fourteen England caps under Alf Ramsey.

In hindsight, I was very lucky to have 'Milney' as my first manager in the professional game. For a start, he recognised my potential by promoting me to the first team at a time when the reserves appeared to be my level. After that, he spent time nurturing that potential with lots of advice during one-to-one chats on the training ground. Man-management was a strength, no doubt about that. Gordon had a talent for getting to the heart of the matter and using his vast experience to lend valuable perspective in this over-hyped sport: 'Remember, you're never as good as they say you are and you're never as bad.' It was a useful morsel to retain in the years to come. He'd also have a word when the England manager, Bobby Robson, came to town, reassuring those in the spotlight they need not try too hard. 'Don't feel you've got to do anything special,' Gordon would say. 'He isn't looking for that. Just play your normal game. You'd be surprised by how little he expects.' Nuggets like that helped you to relax.

More generally, Milne fostered a really good team spirit within our group, even if that squad lacked enough quality to prosper in the top flight. That fact got hammered home once more in the 1985/86 campaign, at the end of which Gordon's people skills came again to the fore. As usual, we were right up against it at the bottom of the table, every point vital in our fight for survival. In April, we travelled down to Southampton to face a useful team featuring Jimmy Case, Liverpool's former hard man, the fearsome Joe Jordan, previously mentioned for a swipe at my throat, and Peter Shilton, long-time England goalie of prodigious reputation.

And seeing as the match ended up goalless, it was actually Shilts who did all the damage. Racing on to a through ball, I toe-poked it past the onrushing keeper, only to get caught by his forceful dive. Crashing to the turf, I knew this wasn't good.

In clattering into Shilts, I'd twisted my knee in a way bound to tweak the ligament. Every footballer recognises that particular threat when the joint is opened up by an awkward challenge. The pain tells you straight away something has happened. And it had, even though I somehow managed to finish the game.

But it always feels worse afterwards once the adrenalin has subsided, and John McVey quickly diagnosed the problem. No MRI scans back then to inspect the joint in detail. It was down to the experience of medical men who took a considered view after talking to the patient while gently manipulating the injured area. In my case, the conclusion was a badly strained medial ligament, meaning I'd be out for a few weeks, just when the team desperately needed points. Still, there was nothing else for it. I simply had to hope I could still play some part in a battle set to last until the very end.

And so it proved. With me *hors de combat*, we lost our next three games, which may have happened anyway given the opposition included Manchester United and Liverpool. Here we go then, all on the last match – a home fixture with Newcastle United, safe in mid-table. The situation was clear. If Ipswich Town lost at Sheffield Wednesday and we won, it would be them going down, not us.

Lying on the treatment table at the start of that week, I could see him coming a mile off, our concerned manager.

'Alan, we need you on Saturday,' Gordon earnestly began. 'I know your knee's not right yet but John tells me it would be possible to play with a pain-killing injection. I wouldn't normally ask but it's the end of the season. You'll have all summer to recover. And as you know, this is a massive game.'

I couldn't argue there. None of us wanted to be playing in the Second Division. For someone like me, an emerging target for bigger clubs, the backwards step could have proved costly, stunting development and discouraging suitors.

On the other hand, I was well aware how many players had practically crippled themselves by leaning too heavily on cortisone steroid jabs. Used too often, I knew it could do all sorts of harm to joints, tendons and cartilage. The stories you heard sent a cold shiver. Not only that, any attempt to kill pain is, by its very nature, preventing the body from emitting warning signals. The ligament in question might get badly damaged.

Weighing everything up, though, Gordon's persuasive powers were just about enough. I reluctantly agreed to the jab, eager to help my teammates get the job done. And we did, beating Peter Beardsley's Newcastle 2–0, a potentially fraught afternoon running quite smoothly. What's more, my knee passed with flying colours, never once hurting that day or any time afterwards. Then came welcome news of Ipswich's defeat at Hillsborough. Another season in the sun had been secured.

As pleasing as that was, I couldn't help feeling disappointed when Gordon announced that summer he was moving upstairs to take up a role as director of football. After four years, he felt he couldn't take the team any further, so stepped aside to let Bryan Hamilton take over.

That was some call by the Leicester board – to appoint a fledgling manager who had only operated in the Fourth and Third Divisions, latterly with Wigan Athletic, a club Milney knew well having played and managed there. Yet our old boss seemed convinced Hamilton was the right choice, explaining his reasons some years later.

'He had a totally different personality to me, which I thought was the right way to go.'

Maybe so, but that bubbly personality brought with it a very different way of managing, a way that grated with some who had got used to a more grown-up approach. I, for one, just couldn't take to some of his methods, especially 'fun-filled' warm-ups that had him standing in front of the group shouting 'Do this!' or 'Do that!' It was a well-worn drill when you only copied what the leader was doing (hands on head, hands behind back, etc.) after the order 'Do this!' If you so much as twitched a muscle after 'Do that!' it was always ten press-ups or some other punishment. I know these games are designed to keep the brain sharp and all that but they felt a bit tiresome and childish compared to what had come before.

That said, the first few months of the season offered some promise. After beating the mighty Liverpool and drawing with Manchester United, we won five on the trot, including two in the League Cup. This was more like it, some kind of consistency. Maybe this time we wouldn't be constantly haunted by the threat of relegation.

Some chance. As winter set in, so did the blues. Over twenty-two games we managed a paltry three wins, which left us flailing badly down in the mire.

Towards the end of that bleak run, we travelled up to Anfield for a fixture bearing all the hallmarks of a comprehensive home win. But as that early season success at Filbert Street suggested, Leicester had represented something of a bogey team for Liverpool dating right back to the early 1960s when the Foxes won three in succession at the home of Shankly's all-powerful side.

Much more recently, Ian Banks had added to my early opener the day after Boxing Day in 1983, the second match for both sides in twenty-four hours. That put us 2–0 up, only for Liverpool to storm back to grab a draw, with Graeme Souness spurning an opportunity to steal the show by generously missing a late penalty. To put that result in perspective, four months later that Liverpool side would complete the treble by winning their fourth European Cup.

Talking of Souness, this 2–2 draw represented my first brush with this fearsome competitor, and it wasn't long before a firm introduction was made. I can picture it now, the ball rolling into my feet and Souness blatantly going over the top to plant six studs into my shinpad. Such was the force of impact, I felt the shin bend inwards as the moustachioed midfielder pulled the kind of snarling face that left no doubt as to his intentions. Luckily, I walked away unscathed, thinking that all the stuff I'd heard about the formidable Scot was no exaggeration.

A year later on the same ground, not only did I manage to avoid any leg-breakers, my team went one better, Lineker and I scoring to claim a Boxing Day win.

So travelling to Merseyside didn't fill us with fear in the way that it did for many others. And on the day of this latest match, Valentine's Day 1987, all the papers were referring to Leicester's love affair with this particular fixture. Not only that, the tabloids billed the game as a straight shoot-out between me and Ian Rush. Who would come out on top, they wondered – Liverpool's prolific kingpin or the lad making waves for land-locked Leicester?

In the event, we ended up losing 4–3, with Rush grabbing a hat-trick and me claiming two. Not bad, I thought. Disappointing to lose but we could hold our heads high, as could I personally with a well-taken brace. In a way, that had to go down, I reasoned, as a moral victory – scoring two at Anfield for a struggling side. The papers, however, didn't agree, claiming Rush the clear victor in this striking sideshow.

Nevertheless, we were coming to the end of my time at Leicester. Those same papers declaring Rush the champ that day had been full of stories linking me to several top clubs. With Lineker long gone, I was next in line to be sold by a club not in any position to turn down large sums. Within six weeks of that plucky Liverpool defeat, I'd be signing a contract with 'Arsenal Football Club' printed on the top.

LONDON CALLING

The phone rang. It was around half past seven one winter's evening in early 1987. I was sat in the living room with Mom and Dad, just about to watch *Coronation Street*, a habit in our family since the series began. Mom went to answer the phone, which sat on a small table out in the hall. After a few seconds she returned to the lounge.

'Alan, it's Alex Ferguson,' she said, a little hesitantly. 'He says he wants to speak to you.'

'What, *the* Alex Ferguson, Mom?' I was shocked to say the least. 'Do you mean the Manchester United manager?'

'Well, yes, I think so, dear.'

Ferguson had only been at United for a couple of months after inheriting an ill-disciplined team floundering at the foot of the First Division. He was in the very early stages of trying to rebuild the club from top to bottom and that principally meant overturning the playing staff to construct a side in his image.

'Hello?' I said, nervously picking up the phone.

'Yes, hello, Alan. Alex Ferguson here.'

I could tell right away from those broad Glaswegian tones that this wasn't a prank call from one of my Leicester team-mates. It was indeed Ferguson. And he had a proposition.

'Alan,' he continued, 'I know Arsenal are interested but I'd like you to wait till the end of the season. I want you to sign for Manchester United.'

The whole football world knew of Arsenal's involvement. The Gunners wanted to sign me sooner rather than later, before the transfer market closed in March. And now it turned out United preferred the summer when, with me out of contract at Leicester, they might not have to pay quite so much money. In fairness, Ferguson's revelation should have made me think. You don't turn down a club of that stature lightly, even if they are suffering at that particular time. Sure to recover eventually, they may never come knocking again.

But I was unequivocal that night talking to their manager.

'I'm sorry, Mr Ferguson, but I've already made up my mind. I'm going to sign for Arsenal. I want to sign for Arsenal.'

The conversation after that didn't last long.

'OK, son, if you've made up your mind. No problem. I wish you good luck.'

And that was that. I walked back into the living room, and briefly relayed the conversation to Mom and Dad before sitting back down to watch the rest of *Coronation Street*. Mind you, I'd be a liar if I said I fully concentrated on what Hilda Ogden was saying that night. Ferguson's phone call kept going round in my head. *Have I done the right thing? Wouldn't it be better to wait? This could be the biggest mistake I will ever make.* Yet I never felt that way about my other option. During that same winter, I received a call from Gordon Milne to tell me Chelsea were keen. Ken Bates, the chairman, and John Hollins, their manager, wanted to travel up and talk in person.

'I don't fancy Chelsea, boss,' I said. 'Doesn't really appeal.'

'But Alan,' Gordon countered, a hint of anxiety in his voice, 'you should go and speak to them, hear what they've got to say. It's good manners and you just never know.'

Now, I don't know if Leicester knew the kind of fee Chelsea were prepared to pay. Maybe they did, and it was very generous, hence Gordon's eagerness for talks to take place. In any event, I reluctantly agreed, and so it was arranged we'd meet the following evening at the Post House Hotel in Walsall, the very place Gary Lineker had had his sponsored car defaced a few years before.

In a private room, Ken Bates spelled out Chelsea's ambitions for the future, while John Hollins explained how I'd fit into an attack already boasting Kerry Dixon, David Speedie and the mercurial Pat Nevin.

I nodded along in all the right places, without properly listening to their argument. The thing was, I just wasn't interested, no matter how persuasive and impressive the sales pitch. When it came to asking questions, all I could manage was a lame query about the dodgy state of the Stamford Bridge pitch, notorious back then for cutting up. I didn't even think to ask about money. Stupid, that. If I had, their offer would have served as a useful yardstick for negotiations with Arsenal. Anyway, we eventually parted, with me having made it clear the move didn't appeal.

A few years later with two league titles in the bag, I was waiting for the lift at the Grosvenor House Hotel, venue that year for the PFA awards dinner. As the doors opened, there stood Ken Bates, staring straight back.

'Evening, Mr Bates,' I ventured tentatively, not quite sure how this outspoken character would react. I was just stepping out at my floor when the answer came. 'Alan,' he hissed, a grin spreading across those bearded features. 'You made the right choice.' The lift doors were closing as I smiled back.

I didn't agree with everything Ken said during that turbulent era for Chelsea, when financial problems and hooliganism marred their reputation, but I certainly couldn't argue with his quip that night. It would be a long time indeed – after my retirement, in fact – that Chelsea would emerge as a serious heavyweight. They actually got relegated the following season after our meeting.

As for United, it would be another six and a half years before they won the title. Would I have lasted the course in those intervening years? Ferguson, what's more, was a long way from becoming the revered figure we now take for granted. While his achievements for Aberdeen were impressive, nobody knew if he could hack it in England. And he may not have, had United not won the FA Cup in 1990. That said, you could level similar doubts about George Graham. Who was to say the former Millwall manager could bridge the huge divide and become a success? Personally, I didn't have a clue. One thing I did know, though: the young players being promoted to the first team had plenty of promise.

Tony Sealy first made me aware of Arsenal's interest. He knew George Graham from their time together at QPR where Tony was a striker and George a young coach. Due to this connection, furtive messages started passing down the line. 'George wants to know if you fancy it,' my Leicester teammate would ask out the corner of his mouth. I don't know if you'd call this tapping up, but it was something that happened, and definitely still does, right across the board. Managers want to

I seem quite impressed by Mom's creation for tea. *(author's collection)*

Dave's homemade trolley was clearly better than mine. *(author's collection)*

On holiday with my best friend, a ball. *(author's collection)*

Hollywood Primary School's all-conquering outfit. Not sure about the pumps though. *(author's collection)*

Ten years on: my first taste of international football with England's semi-pro team. *(author's collection)*

Learning the ropes at Alvechurch. *(author's collection)*

eicester City secretary Alan Bennett making ure I sign in the right place. *(author's collection)*

On the ball at Leicester. *(David Cannon/Allsport/Getty images)*

Gordon Milne: he taught me so much in those early Leicester years. *(Trinity Mirror/ Mirrorpix/Alamy Stock Photo)*

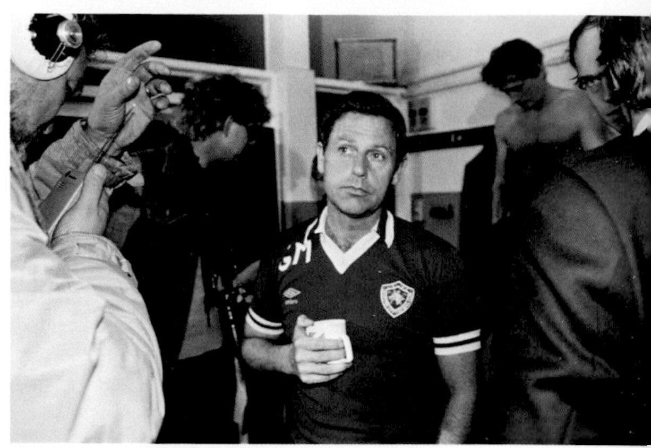

Prematurely celebrating promotion with Leiceste in 1983. *(Neville Chadwic Photography)*

Not a bad strike force: Gary, 'Charlie' and me. *(Neville Chadwick Photography)*

See you next season.’ How the hell did David O’Leary know that? *(Professional Sport/Popperfoto/Getty images)*

George Graham: ‘Tell Alan to f****** get hold of the ball!’ *(Professional Sport/Popperfoto/Getty images)*

Just about made it! With my best man, Mick. *(author's collection)*

Family and friends on our big day. *(author's collection)*

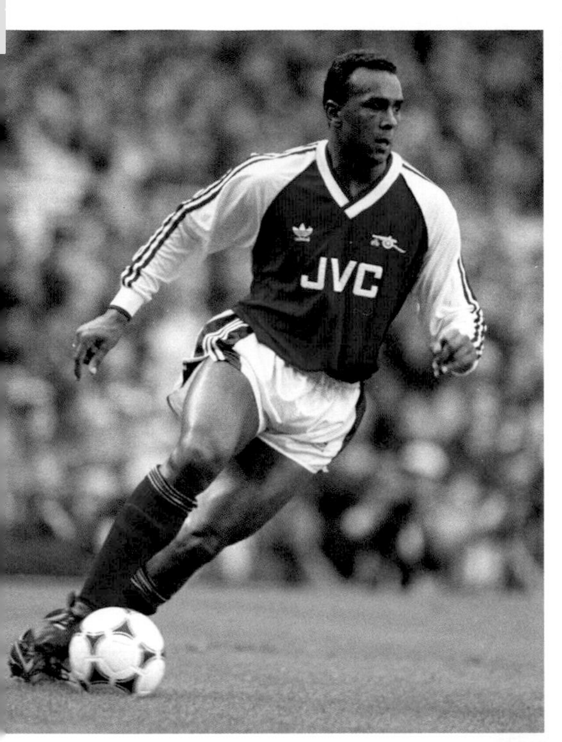

Rocky: the skill of a Brazilian; the heart of a lion.
(Bob Thomas / Getty Images)

Sharing the good times with Rocky. I still miss him now. *(Colorsport)*

One down, one to go: Anfield, 26th May 1989. *(author's collection)*

The most famous goal in Football League history. *(Colorsport)*

know how a player feels before taking the trouble to make an offer. These days, agents do most of the talking when it comes to sounding out players. Back then, a third party like Sealy might do the bidding.

'Yeah, of course I fancy it, Tone,' I'd reply. 'Tell him to make his move.' This went on for a while during the 1986/87 campaign when Leicester were once again struggling towards the bottom of the old First Division. With Lineker gone two seasons before, I had succeeded in stepping forward as Leicester's chief goal-getter. Now it was my turn to attract some attention.

The connection with Arsenal continued for several months, as did my quiet chats with Tony Sealy. But what really hit home were some other words shared at the end of our game on Boxing Day 1986. In our fight to stay up, Leicester had just earned a creditable point in a 1–1 draw with Arsenal. I hadn't scored but had acquitted myself OK against David O'Leary and an emerging Tony Adams. Walking up at the end, David shook hands and uttered something that knocked me for six. 'See you next season,' he casually said, as if the move was all sorted and he knew the details. I would come to learn later that as a longstanding servant, David knew the club inside out, everything from the manager's next target to the chairman's wife's birthday. He always seemed to know what was going on, much to the amusement of teammates speculating on his source. Not that I knew all this at the time of our memorable exchange. 'You'll never guess what,' I said to Penny and my parents in the players' lounge afterwards. 'David O'Leary just said, "See you next season." How come he knows something I don't?'

In fact, it was a good couple of months into the new year that Arsenal's interest began to firm up. Eventually, Gordon Milne, by now the director of football, approached me on the training ground to say a bid had been made that Leicester were accepting. For bargaining reasons presumably, my suitors had left it late in an era when the third Thursday in March traditionally marked transfer deadline day. Up until that point, clubs could do business with each other throughout the season. After that point, they had to wait until the end of the season – all a bit different to the frenzied activity across two transfer windows now.

That said, this particular deal turned into a bit of a rush. It was arranged that Ken Friar, Arsenal's managing director, and chief scout Steve Burtenshaw would attend our home game with QPR on the Wednesday night, 25 March. Straight after, they'd whisk me down to London where we'd conduct negotiations the following day. As it happened, George Graham was in Portugal with the team on a mid-season break. He wouldn't be around for negotiations. So if I did sign, I'd have to wait a while to meet my new manager. Not to worry. After a 4–1 win over Rangers played in front of a small crowd, I nervously jumped into Mr Friar's car bound for his house in north London.

This was it. This was my big move so many in the media had long been predicting. To be fair, I was ready for it too. Five years at Leicester were just about right. Having learned so much under Gordon Milne after pitching up as a non-league rookie, it was time to make the step up to a bigger stage where the prospect of silverware replaced the scrap for survival. And Arsenal were on the up, a club going places with a history and tradition very few could match.

The plan, then, was to get up in the morning and have a general chat about money and such like before driving down to Highbury to tie up the details and sign the contract. A big, big day. Full of anticipation, I went to the bathroom to make myself presentable. Once showered and shaved, I was ready to go downstairs where the lovely Mrs Friar was cooking a full English. Only one problem – I couldn't open the bloody bathroom door. The lock on the knob was playing up, and no matter how many times I twisted and pulled, it wouldn't play ball. This was embarrassing – locked in the bathroom of Arsenal's managing director. Not exactly how I wanted to kick off the day, never mind my relationship with my prospective new club. Faced with few alternatives, I simply had to bite the bullet by knocking on the door and shouting out for help in my politest voice. 'Hello? Hello? Anybody there? I can't seem to get out.' In the end, Mr Friar came to the rescue, unable to suppress a giggle as he opened the door.

After a good laugh over the bacon and eggs, I went through to the lounge to talk serious business. This was the bit I was dreading – just me and Ken, no adviser or anything, talking brass tacks. Back then, agents were nowhere near as widespread as they are today. Some players had them, but an awful lot didn't and, to a certain extent, I was in the second category. I say that because a financial chap from the Professional Footballers' Association was going to meet us later at Highbury to try and make sure I got the best deal. We had known each other for a while through the PFA's commercial arm, which offered this service virtually for free.

For the time being, though, I was on my own, forced to talk figures in Ken's living room. I thought back to the evening at

Sutton Coldfield Golf Club when Vic Crowe, a former player and manager at Aston Villa, came into the back kitchen to have a word. As a member of the club where Penny's mom was steward, Vic had taken an interest in my career. And knowing I was set to hold talks with Arsenal, he wanted to give me a steer on the figures I should be talking as a young striker very much in demand. He wrote down a number on a scrap of paper and handed it over: £100,000. I should settle for nothing less. That was 100k a year, by the way, rather than a week as is the going rate today for many Premier League players. Mind you, that was an awful lot of money in 1987. To be fair, it still is now to most people. But I wasn't 'most people' at that particular time. I was the latest proven goalscorer to come on the market and, as such, in a great negotiating position. Not that I fully appreciated that fact sitting on Ken's settee as he set about explaining Arsenal's position. After a bit of flannel to justify the club's stance, he quoted £60,000 as their best offer. To be honest, this didn't fill me with joy, seeing as I'd been getting £40,000 at Leicester for some time. What I should have done at this point was lay down a marker, say that I was thinking more along the lines of double that, and be prepared to settle for 100k, just as Vic had recommended. But I didn't. I bottled it, mumbling something about hoping for a bit more.

With nothing properly agreed, we soon left for Highbury, a twenty-minute journey from the Friars' home, where the bloke from the PFA and Gordon Milne had gathered to try and see the job through. Left in one of those historic wood-panelled rooms for private talks, I told my adviser I wasn't happy with the offer, that I thought Arsenal should be paying more. He duly went off to relay my feelings before returning with their reply. This to-ing and fro-ing went on for a while, until Gordon poked his head round the door to say that time was ticking on. This was deadline day after all. We had to get a move on, he said, otherwise my registration wouldn't go through on time. Mind you, it wasn't as if Arsenal were going to use me straight away. The plan was to immediately loan me back to Leicester where I could hopefully help them avoid relegation. Only in the summer would I come south to join my parent club. It was a cosy arrangement that suited both clubs. Arsenal would secure my services before the end of my contract when it would have become a free-for-all, while Leicester got their money (£800,000) but still kept me on the firm for the vital run-in. What a stitch up – the pawn in the middle properly played.

Looking back, I was incredibly naive. I held the power, after all. It was them that wanted me, so I really should have issued an ultimatum – 100k, take it or leave it, otherwise I will wait until the end of the season to become a free agent when I'll be in an even better position to call the tune. But I didn't say that. As is usually the case when it comes to money, I settled for less when I could have got more. In the end, as a compromise, Arsenal agreed to increase my signing on fee. It wasn't ideal and it wasn't a lot, but there you go.

The good news was that I was officially an Arsenal player now, which made me feel incredibly proud. Even more so when Steve Burtenshaw gave me a tour of the ground, emphasising the great history and tradition as we strolled past Herbert Chapman's bust towards the dressing rooms. Finally, he led me on to the pitch and into the centre circle.

'Alan, a lot of players have worn the number nine shirt here,' he said, grandly sweeping his arm around all four corners of the pitch. Then came the punch line. 'But not many have been able to make a success of it.'

Bloody hell, I thought. *That's all I need to hear.* But it didn't take long the following season to know what Steve meant. If you weren't strong enough, the expectation and pressure could turn promise into paralysis, a much different situation from the one at Leicester.

I don't know what especially appealed about Arsenal. When I was younger I really disliked them, the way some of their players always seemed to be moaning. Funny how things like that leave a mark. Maybe a particular game on *Match of the Day* had stuck in my head, when the Arsenal players were having a right go at the ref. My opinion didn't even change after turning professional, though that was more down to traffic-delayed coach journeys ending with a slow crawl down the Holloway Road, which, it has to be said, was a much scruffier thoroughfare than it is now. Looking out the coach window, I was less than impressed. 'I couldn't play for a London club,' I whined, as if a footballer would live right next to the ground. 'Look at the state of it round here!' Funny how life turns out. Only a couple of years later my Arsenal medical took place on this same road, in the Royal Northern Hospital, now sadly demolished.

Within months of joining Arsenal, though, I came to regard the Holloway Road with a lot more affection. As a regular route to Highbury, it became a part of my life, as it did for my wife who, on matchday, knew to turn left at the Baker's Oven. Not only that, certain pubs on that stretch were always fondly mentioned by the likes of Paddy Galligan, a much-loved do-it-all man at Highbury, who regaled us with stories of long drunken nights awash with Guinness and Irish folk music, some of them even including a young Niall Quinn.

As for the change of heart, perhaps it had something to do with the youngsters coming through. Tony Adams led an impressive charge from the youth set-up featuring David Rocastle, Paul Merson, Michael Thomas, Niall Quinn, Martin Hayes and Gus Caesar. Looking from afar, something seemed to be happening under George Graham, a fairly inexperienced manager but clearly an ambitious one charged with turning around the fortunes of his old club. After winning the double as a player in 1971, Graham joined from Millwall intent on bringing back the good times, which meant, in his opinion, overhauling an ageing playing staff past its sell-by date to introduce more youth, hunger and energy, either recruited from within or the lower leagues. The added benefit, some said, was the wage bill being slashed, which must have gone down very well in the boardroom.

If my experience was anything to go by, a cost-cutting policy seemed to be in force. Arsenal were not in the mood for handing out big contracts, as I found out during negotiations.

For now, though, it was back to Filbert Street and a relegation scrap. When we followed up that comfortable win over QPR with another handsome victory – 4–0 at home to a struggling Manchester City – we began to believe survival was possible. For my part, I managed to get my head around this unusual situation to settle down and score a few goals. Despite this, one football reporter constantly had a go. He kept saying in print my heart wasn't in it, that my mind was on Arsenal rather than Leicester's plight. God knows what made him think that, seeing as my form and goal output had hardly changed. He clearly had an agenda that wasn't going to be affected by anything happening out on the pitch. To him, it clearly seemed impossible that I could still give it everything in Leicester colours. Oh well, you can't convince everyone. I ignored the criticism, determined to keep going.

But now came the tricky one, a trip to Highbury. You may have noticed that players hardly ever turn out against their parent clubs these days, thanks to an agreement when the loan deal is done. Personally, I'm not a big fan of the arrangement, since it means one team not having to face a particular player (who might be key) when everyone else must. That kind of manipulation cannot be right. Not that this crossed my mind at the time. In my innocence, I assumed I wouldn't be forced to play against Arsenal, that the two clubs had come to an agreement. Feeling uptight, I walked up to Gordon Milne one morning to politely ask if I could sit this one out. Keeping focus, I explained, would be very hard. But Gordon was having none of it. 'We need you, Alan. It's a vital game for us. This is why you came back on loan – to help avoid relegation.' I couldn't believe it. This was going to be awkward.

And that's how it turned out. Never mind the result – a thumping 4–1 home win – this embarrassing day couldn't end quickly enough. At one point, it grew even more surreal when the Leicester fans gathered up in the Clock End started singing my name, in an effort, perhaps, to let me know they hadn't yet abandoned their departing centre-forward. As always, I turned to acknowledge the chant, giving them a quick wave and clap. Nothing too untoward there. On hearing this, however, the North Bank defiantly launched into a song of their own, keen to point out I was their player now. Oh blimey. What to do? There was nothing else for it. I swivelled round to salute that dense mass of people, a loyal congregation I would soon need to impress. At that point, I got a real bollocking from Gary McAllister. 'Hey Smudge, concentrate on the fucking game, will yer?' Fair comment, I suppose. Fighting for their lives, Leicester badly needed a result. Unlike me, Gary and the rest wouldn't be swanning off to London at the end of the campaign, looking forward to a new and exciting career. If things carried on like this, they'd be heading for the Second Division where Shrewsbury and Scunthorpe helped provide the glamour.

But the club wasn't doomed yet, and my teammates were entitled to 100 per cent commitment. Mind you, it's not as though I didn't perform that day. I did OK in a one-sided contest. Might even have scored but for Rhys Wilmot pulling off a fine save from a point-blank header. At the final whistle it was handshakes all round. And this time it wasn't just David O'Leary saying, 'See you next season.'

Before this new adventure could begin, though, my saddest experience at Leicester had to be endured. Following that drubbing at Arsenal, we lost at home to Watford, and lost away at Chelsea before a damaging 1–1 home draw with Coventry City in the penultimate match left us dependent on others on the last day. Winning at Oxford United would be useless if Charlton Athletic beat QPR. Predictably, they did just that, as we thought they might, while we ground out a lifeless goalless draw at the old Manor Ground.

Off came the shirt and into the crowd it flew as I waved my thanks to fans who had been so supportive over five happy years. Back in the dressing room, the lads were pig sick. A season of occasional highs – beating Liverpool and thrashing Sheffield Wednesday 6–1 – had been ruined by a whopping twenty-two defeats. Over the course of a long season, you get what you deserve. We could have no complaints.

As for the lads at Oxford that day, their dark mood wasn't helped by my behaviour. After a shower, I reached into my suit carrier for a tuxedo. As chance would have it, Arsenal were holding an end-of-season dinner that evening at the Hilton hotel on London's Park Lane. There wasn't much time to spare. I had to quickly get dressed and jump in my car, parked right outside for a sharp getaway. Unsurprisingly, the sight of me getting spruced up, fastening my dicky bow and slipping on shiny shoes, didn't go down well. 'Don't worry about us, Smudge. You fuck off to Arsenal. We'll be OK.' I must admit, I felt a bit guilty, leaving them like this. But what could I do? A return to the Second Division wasn't in the plan. In the cold light of day, my run was perfectly timed after four instructive years in the top flight. This was the right time to go. I knew that well enough. Even so, I felt a bit flustered leaving the Manor Ground that night, scraping my car trying to squeeze out of the tight car park.

Once out, however, the guilt quickly faded. Driving down the M40, I grew more concerned about the evening ahead, meeting new teammates and all that entailed. On the outskirts of London the stomach started churning. The butterflies didn't improve when I pulled into the Hilton's underground car park. Across the way I could see Viv Anderson, right-back for club and country, getting out of his car. *Great, I'll have someone to walk in with. That'll make it easier*. I tentatively waved. He quickly gestured back before heading towards the exit. *Oh, he's going to wait for me at the lift*, I thought. *Introduce himself there*. But when

I got to the lift he had jumped in and gone. Charming. Not very friendly at all. That made me even more nervous. *Is that how they behave in these parts?* I knew London was going to be different, the pace of life so much quicker, but this was a bit worrying – shunned by a new teammate on my first day.

Up in our room, Penny was getting ready, having driven down earlier. 'You'll never guess what, Pen. Viv Anderson just blanked me in the car park. Left me standing there like a lemon!' In fairness to Viv, I'm sure it wasn't like that. Maybe in his mind he was just having a laugh by winding up the new signing with a classic bit of dressing-room humour. I bet he rushed to tell the lads that he'd just left me stranded. That was something else I would have to get used to – a more cutting wit, shaped by the big city.

Funnily enough, I don't think I even spoke to Viv that night. Never got the chance afterwards either. He was soon on his way to Manchester United as part of George Graham's plans to refresh the squad. Tony Woodcock had already gone, so had Paul Mariner, Tommy Caton and Stewart Robson. A new dawn was breaking, one which would heavily involve the club's latest signing.

Sat at our table, Penny and I were getting to know some familiar faces. Graham Rix, for instance, had been a longstanding fixture for Arsenal and England. I'd watched him on the box many times, weaving clever patterns with that imaginative left foot. A Yorkshireman by birth, Rixy was friendly and funny, as was his wife, Gill, who talked to a nervous Penny, only twenty at the time, about the best places to live.

Talking of twenty-year-olds, a cool, elegant figure soon walked across. 'Hi, I'm David,' he said, in a well-spoken voice.

'If there's anything you need or want to know just ask.' He stood there chatting for a while, those handsome features drawing us in, making us feel welcome. Once he'd gone, I looked at Penny. We were thinking the same thing. What an impressive young man, to come over like that. So mature and polite. It made our night, to be honest, meeting David Rocastle, a very special person who would quickly become a much-loved family friend.

Later that evening, I bumped into Ken Friar. 'Got all your bags packed for tomorrow then, Alan?' That completely threw me. I knew the team was flying out to Cyprus the next day for a charity match and break, but I was sure we had arranged I join them a day later, once I was properly organised following a chaotic week. 'Er, no, I haven't, I'm afraid.' After a few puzzled looks from Mr Friar, wondering, perhaps, what kind of idiot Arsenal had just signed, he said not to worry, the club would book a later flight. And so it was that I flew to Cyprus on my own, again full of nerves, this time at the prospect of properly mixing with the lads.

Standing at the baggage carousel in Larnaca airport, waiting for my suitcase, I wondered if I'd see anyone at the hotel. It was pretty late. They might all be in bed. Alternatively, they might be just going out! Whatever, it was going to be past midnight at this rate. My bag was taking forever. And then, to my horror, the carousel stopped, having delivered everything from the plane's hold. The only one left in the arrivals hall, I slouched across to the lost luggage desk to wearily break the news. That's all I needed, to arrive with no gear. Still, I didn't have much choice but to climb in the car that had come to pick me up. Hopefully my bag would arrive the next day.

In the meantime, I checked into the hotel and went to meet my roommate who had kindly hung around to greet the new signing. As suspected, the rest of the team had strolled into town. David O'Leary, as mentioned, knew the ropes inside out, making him a good choice as my guiding light. In the morning, he kindly took me around every room to introduce me to a bleary-eyed set of lads who, following their night out, had only been in bed a few hours. At the same time, he asked if I could possibly borrow a piece of clothing, whether a T-shirt, shorts or pair of flip-flops. A bit embarrassing, but it helped break the ice. Those of the same size gladly made a donation. I was badly in need of the stuff, too, seeing as my suitcase had somehow ended up in Switzerland and wouldn't get to Cyprus for another few days.

As for the rest of the trip, we enjoyed a few nights out, with Charlie Nicholas leading the way on the dance floor. We also played a friendly against a select eleven on a hard, dusty surface best remembered for the great George Best, at that point long retired, swaying about in midfield. Despite the vast reduction in powers, it was a genuine thrill to share the same pitch.

Talking of thrills, I had always fancied having a go at parasailing, that watersport when you get pulled along by a speedboat hanging from a parachute. From a distance, it looked like a good laugh, something to tick off the bucket list of adventure pursuits. And there it was, on offer at the beach we visited one day. Reasoning this was as good a time as any, I excitedly handed over my cash before getting strapped up as the bloke in charge went through the instructions. I was told that, on his shout, I should just start running towards the sea and let the billowing parachute lift me into the sky. 'Go!' Off I shot, legging it down the sand as the boat in the shallows gently pulled away. Thankfully, this all went swimmingly and I soon found myself sailing high above the blue Mediterranean. Down below, I could see the lads on the beach, shielding their eyes as they looked up. Ah, this is the life. Messing about in the Med as an Arsenal player. At that moment, Alvechurch and the Southern League felt a lifetime away. Drifting back to the present, I began to get a grip of this whole experience. Once up there, floating harmlessly along, it was pleasant enough, but nowhere near as thrilling as I had imagined. It felt a bit tame to be honest, far from the expected adrenalin rush.

That said, I found out later that the scene didn't look so serene through the eyes of Ken Friar. Lounging on a sunbed, he glanced up to see this gangly figure, legs dangling, being towed along – in his mind, precariously. Turning to a colleague, he casually asked who it was, no doubt expecting a shrug of the shoulders. Instead, the answer jolted him back.

'Oh, that's our new signing, Ken.'

Our managing director nearly choked on his pina colada. 'What? We've just paid £800,000 for him! Who let him up there?'

The boy in the bathroom had gained his wings.

ROLLING OUT THE NEW GUNS

It was a burning hot day, the kind I never used to like when it came to playing football. Growing up, I always got a bit overheated in these sweaty conditions. In the end, I think I convinced myself I couldn't perform when the temperature rose. Still, no room for any such excuses now. This was my Arsenal debut, when the visit of Liverpool, no less, marked the beginning of the 1987/88 campaign. And Highbury was absolutely packed. On top of the 55,000 crammed in that day, every wall and ledge was lined with expectant fans, many of the blokes topless, lapping up the sun.

A few enterprising souls had even managed to clamber on to the roof of the North Bank. Despite tannoy announcements pleading for them to come down, they just wouldn't budge. Like everyone else, those Arsenal supporters were anxious to see if we could lay down a marker as title contenders by beating the team that had been gloriously overcome only four months before in the Littlewoods Cup final. This Liverpool side, however, looked a little different. With Ian Rush leaving a huge hole by joining Juventus, Kenny Dalglish had signed John Barnes and Peter Beardsley to give the team a slightly different feel.

And Barnesy soon did what he would do many times hence – hurt us with a bit of magic from those mercurial feet. A clever cross from the left found a lurking John Aldridge who glanced home the opener off the inside of the far post. Without question, the visitors were good value for their lead, playing all the football as we struggled for rhythm.

For me personally, it was turning into a difficult day. Feeling nervous after all the attention, I couldn't get hold of the ball. It kept bouncing off. And on the few occasions I did manage to retain possession, Alan Hansen would quickly nip in to make me look leaden-footed. Knowing it wasn't going well, I could feel myself tensing up whenever the ball came my way, which only made things worse.

The only bright spot, to be honest, was when I held off my man to set up Paul Davis's equaliser with a nicely cushioned header. As Davo wheeled away, I grabbed hold to celebrate, both delighted and relieved to make some kind of a mark. Unfortunately, another headed touch would not end so well. With two minutes left, Liverpool won a free-kick on the left edge of the box. When Barnes curled one in, I thought I had done enough by heading it firmly away. Unluckily, the clearance flew straight to Steve Nicol whose instinctive dip of the head saw the ball rebound and miraculously float into the far corner. It was a freak goal. How many times would you see a goalkeeper beaten by a header from all of sixteen yards out? Well, it happened that day to spoil the party. We returned to the dressing room with nothing to show for our sub-standard efforts. I wouldn't look back on my debut with much fondness at all.

Games at Manchester United and QPR didn't go much better. Having managed a goalless draw at Old Trafford, Loftus Road's bone-hard plastic pitch witnessed a comfortable home win. That made three matches I hadn't exactly graced with a stellar performance. Adjusting to new teammates in a different environment felt like hard work.

As for the hike in expectations, that hit me like a brick one day at Arsenal's training ground in London Colney, near St Albans. Sat on the treatment table before training, I picked up the *Sun* to kill a bit of time, totally unprepared for the main football splash.

ARSENAL GO FOR DIXON, ran the bold headline, under which it was 'revealed' that George Graham wanted Chelsea's Kerry Dixon because 'Alan Smith has failed to impress'.

Bloody hell, I thought. *I've only played three games! Is that how little time you get at a big club?* Well, not quite. But this back page was a sobering symptom of my new world where pressure trumped patience by some distance. The conjecture even delved into my private life, with one reporter continually claiming that Penny, my fiancée, couldn't settle in the south. God knows where he got that one. Penny had found a good job in St Albans as a beauty therapist and had made new friends in an area she loved. She never once thought about returning home. Still, that didn't stop some chancer from writing it, even after Penny had strongly denied the story when the reporter rang our home when I was away. That seems incredible now – firstly, a journalist having the home number of a top-flight player and, secondly, that he should question my partner in my absence. It wasn't as if we'd given him our number. He'd clearly done a bit of delving to obtain the information. All in all, these goings-on felt like quite a contrast from life at homely Leicester.

Later that week, the gaffer sat us down after training to talk about the next game, Portsmouth at home. He was leaving out

Charlie Nicholas, my strike partner so far, in favour of Perry Groves, a modest £50,000 signing from Colchester the season before. At that point, Charlie thought he could smell a rat, suspecting George wanted him gone, so playing him against newly promoted Pompey when there might be a few goals about could make matters awkward.

And Charlie was right in one respect. There were indeed a few goals about, three of them for me in a 6–0 romp. The first was a tentative poke of the left boot when Graham Rix dispossessed a sleepy Alan Knight in goal. The second was more emphatic, pouncing on a loose ball, while the third, a close-range header, had me jumping for joy in front of the Clock End. What a great way to get off the mark. Maybe that *Sun* reporter would have to change tack. As for Charlie, he didn't play again, consigned to the stands and reserves before leaving for Aberdeen.

To be honest, that didn't come as a major shock. We could see that our teammate, labelled 'Champagne Charlie' by the press, would struggle to fit into George's new regime where everyone followed orders within a strict framework. Chas was more of an individual, a skilful crowd-pleaser heavily associated with the previous era under Don Howe.

Soon after that thrashing of Portsmouth we launched into a fourteen-game winning run that saw us beat Tottenham away in my first north London derby as well as progress in the Littlewoods Cup. As it turned out, that cup competition would prove the season highlight, at least until we reached the final.

The FA Cup, for a time, looked just as promising, particularly after beating Manchester United in a rip-roaring battle. That was the day Nigel Winterburn gave Brian McClair all sorts of grief before and after the Scot missed his penalty. It marked the beginning of a feud between the two sides that erupted at Old Trafford in 1990.

Ill feeling apart, that fifth-round tie meant a lot personally following a difficult spell worryingly short on goals. Those newspaper doubts about my ability resurfaced again over several weeks. A far-post header, however, in front of the North Bank released a lot of tension, allowing me to go on and have a really good game.

Four days later I added another in the semi-final second leg of the Littlewoods Cup. What a night that was. The visit of Everton generated an incredible atmosphere, the best at Highbury I have ever experienced. People came early, swarming through the turnstiles to see us warm up, with seven thousand unfortunates roaming outside, unable to get in. Once underway, the action felt frenetic, powered by this throbbing congregation urging us on.

The portents didn't look good when Rocky somehow managed to miss an open goal, but we eventually eased away from Colin Harvey's side, the thunderous noise rarely receding. At the end of the 3–1 win, the pitch quickly filled with fans, overjoyed to have reached a second League Cup final on the trot.

Up in the dressing room, the fizzy stuff flowed, soaking a TV reporter trying to have a word. We hung out of the windows above Avenell Road, waving at the crowds amassing below. This felt really special, not just to me, new to this business, but to everyone involved on that tumultuous night. Don't ask me why. Some people might wonder what was so extraordinary about reaching a League Cup final, a lukewarm achievement for many these days. But it was different back then, at least through Arsenal eyes. This was a young, exciting team full of hope and desire, led by a manager bristling with ambition. I think our supporters, in turn, sensed the beginnings of something exceptional. Another trip to Wembley only confirmed the notion.

During these opening months of my Arsenal career, David Rocastle had quickly become a good friend. Only just turned twenty, fairly new to the first team, still a young pup among senior pros – his maturity didn't square with someone of his age and standing.

That aspect of his character largely transferred to the pitch where an outstanding attitude and outrageous skill had begun to attract plenty of attention. I watched a piece on the BBC's *Football Focus* in which they showed a map of London to explain the convoluted route Rocky took every morning via bus and underground to get to Highbury from his home in Brockley, south London. He was being touted as an emerging star in George Graham's project. To back up that billing, Rocky spoke eloquently in front of the camera about his hopes and ambitions for the next few years. He clearly had something about him, this strikingly good-looking lad with flawless manners. There was an inner resolve, a real determination to make something of himself, no matter the obstacles lodged in his way.

Strangely enough, his feet, the makings of his career, were the only part that didn't match the smooth persona. Disfigured by corns and bunions, those size tens looked a right state, totally out of kilter with the rest of his body. Rocky put the affliction down, always with a laugh, to a deprived childhood when his mother couldn't afford to buy new shoes, forcing him to squeeze into pairs he had outgrown. If this was a drawback, you would never know. Those feet rarely struggled to do as they were told.

And forget about trying to intimidate him in matches. Rocky would never back down if someone started getting rough to test his mettle. On the contrary, he relished all that, giving as good as he got, that powerful frame well capable of absorbing heavy blows before striking back with a meaty thump. In those early years before knee surgery affected his mobility, Rocky was the complete package, blessed with the silky skills of a Brazilian, the tackle of a rhino and heart of a lion.

One day at Nottingham Forest, he marched in at half-time buzzing with excitement, laughing about a running battle with Stuart Pearce that included some verbals. Forest's no-nonsense left-back had piled in with plenty to try and overpower his young opponent. Yet that kind of tactic was never going to work, only serving to energise our spirited number seven who saw it all as an enjoyable challenge. This feisty attitude endeared him to everyone, not least George Graham, who loved a fighter.

I loved him for other reasons too. Off the pitch, Rocky had a more gentle side to his character, especially when with Janet, his girlfriend at the time, later to become his wife. The boy from Brockley, who grew up without a father, revelled in family life. When Melissa, the first of his three children, was born in February 1989, he became the biggest doting dad you could ever meet, a hands-on modern parent entranced by his little girl.

Alongside, he loved to look good, spending fortunes on clothes, regularly turning up in a new bit of gear, something stylishly expensive by Armani or Prada.

The great thing about Rocky, though, was that he never took himself seriously or got carried away by the growing adulation. He had a great sense of humour, always at the forefront when something needed picking apart, his booming voice making everyone laugh. That irreverence even extended to colour, to his fellow black players in our dressing room, the likes of Paul Davis, Gus Caesar and his old mate Michael Thomas. He used to call them 'the brothers', which was his way of bringing everyone together by taking the piss out of any perceived divisions.

As it happened, all these lads were picked for the League Cup final, a contest with Luton Town we were expected to win, on 24 April 1988.

Gus made the cut due to David O'Leary's injury, an enforced change that would play a crucial part in the result. Mickey, on the other hand, had already eased ahead of Steve Williams in the midfield pecking order, partly because he represented the future.

Steve had quite a distinctive character. For a start, he travelled from Southampton every morning, chauffeured by a mate. A keen student of the stock market, he'd spend that couple of hours in the back seat studying the *Financial Times*, an interest he shared with our goalkeeper, John Lukic.

More to the point, he was a lovely footballer, so smooth and cultured in everything he did. In fact, Steve's partnership with Davo in the middle of the park must go down as one of the most elegant pairings ever fielded by Arsenal. It really caught my eye on arriving at the club.

But 'Willo' had a failing – he couldn't keep schtum. If he felt something needed saying, he wouldn't hesitate, whether or not that riled the boss. A prime example cropped up during that 1987/88 season when Willo had a run-in with George during training. A belligerent sort, our midfielder simply wouldn't back down following a bad-tempered session involving some needle.

'Just drop me then,' Steve snapped defiantly, staring George in the face. 'Go on, drop me. Just drop me!'

Our manager held his temper, letting the argument fizzle out, to leave us all wondering if he was going to accept such blatant insubordination. We should have known better. You just didn't speak to him like that. And if you did, he'd get his revenge. That particular dish, so the saying goes, is best served cold, and the boss waited until the day of the final to strike back in earnest. Left out of the starting eleven, Willo stormed out in a huff, never to play for the Gunners again.

That week, we had enjoyed a few days in Marbella on the south coast of Spain, just like we had before the first leg of the semi-final against Everton. It worked then, so why not now? With the sun on our backs in a different environment, it felt like a good way to get ready. The mood, you might say, was fairly relaxed. Training consisted of a bit of light jogging in the morning before we were left to our own devices, which meant frequenting the bars of Puerto Banús.

Incredible to think that now – that a team on the eve of a major final would be allowed to drink. But that's just how it was back then, not only for us but for most teams. On one occasion, Kenny Sansom slept all night in a random boat moored in the port. We could have lost our left-back had the boat set sail without noticing its extra passenger.

Back in England, our focus sharpened up, especially when the youth team beat us 3–0 in a practice match. For me, the trip to

Wembley was the kind of occasion I had joined Arsenal to experience, a major cup final in front of a huge audience. Because of that, I was desperate to do well and disprove the doubters who had pointed to some lean spells during my debut season.

The jury, in fairness, had still to reconvene to pass judgement on my suitability for this new job. In my mind, there was never much doubt. I knew I could thrive at the sharp end of this talented young team. It was just a question of convincing everyone else by producing the goods on a more regular basis.

The final itself was a lively affair, particularly in the second half when we stormed back from going an early goal down. Three minutes after Martin Hayes's equaliser, Mickey Thomas's pass found me free in the box and, on the stretch, I managed to beat Andy Dibble in goal with a right-foot drive.

'One goal in his last nine games. All that's forgotten now!'

This wouldn't be the last time Brian Moore's ITV commentary would provide the soundtrack to one of my goals.

And what a great moment – to deliver on the big stage at a vital time. With fifteen minutes left, I wasn't far away from becoming Arsenal's match-winning hero.

Unfortunately, Luton had other plans that came into force once Dibble saved Nigel Winterburn's penalty. That would have put us 3–1 up. Game over. End of story. But a famous moment of indecision by our own Gus Caesar saw the tide turn towards Bedfordshire. Danny Wilson's stooping header breathed new life into Luton before a sharp finish by Brian Stein, his second of a swelteringly hot day, meant there was no coming back for the strong favourites.

It had been a thrilling to-and-fro, perhaps deservedly won by one of the best teams Luton have ever built, managed by a clever coach in the modest Ray Harford. Time to lick our wounds, to finish the season as best we could and hope the following campaign would deliver more.

In our final game we beat Everton 2–1 to leave us twenty-four points behind champions Liverpool. We left Merseyside that day happy with the win but also disappointed by our sixth-place finish. At the same time, I think we all believed much more was to come. This squad had huge potential. That much was clear. The core of home-grown players was improving all the time. Rocky and Mickey – two south London lads full of ability and fight. Merse – a cheeky kid from Harlesden with outrageous skill. And then there was Tone, Tony Adams – not only a formidable defender but a born leader to boot.

Alongside, those brought into the fold were beginning to settle down. I had scored sixteen goals, some in big games, which amounted in my eyes to an OK return. Nothing special, mind, but something to build on. Nigel Winterburn had been given plenty of run-outs, many at right-back, while Lee Dixon and Brian Marwood, arriving in the January and March respectively, got a useful touch of the ball. Very soon, Steve Bould would pitch up to complete the jigsaw.

And twelve months on from this win at Everton, when Martin Hayes and Mickey Thomas provided the goals, we'd be returning to Merseyside for another joust. As history records, young Michael would once again feature, this time a little more famously across Stanley Park.

MIRACLE ON MERSEYSIDE

'Cheer up lads! This is the week we're going to win the league!' Bob Wilson, Arsenal's goalkeeping coach, was only trying his best, having turned the corner to see us all sitting there, looking quite down. We smiled back in the way that you do to a kindly uncle who clearly means well.

It was the morning after Liverpool played West Ham, the morning after I went to the 1989 Football Writers' Dinner and helplessly sat there as news filtered through of the mounting score up at Anfield. 1–0 (expected), 1–1 (hold on!), 2–1 (expected), 3–1 (oh well), 4–1 (oh dear), 5–1 (bloody hell!).

In a room full of journalists it wasn't long before someone worked out the result meant that, in Friday's shoot-out, we would have to beat Liverpool by two clear goals to win the league. Oh, is that all? That's the champions of England we're talking about, the dominant force for a good sixteen years, four-time European Cup winners that had long since turned Anfield into a forbidding fortress thanks to a succession of top-class players. It was no different this year. Hansen, Barnes, Rush, Aldridge, Beardsley: quality all the way, suffused with a winning mentality. To face them was to know how quickly they moved the ball about. It could be quite dizzying, chasing those famous red shirts, never quite getting near enough to put in a tackle.

And when you did win the ball, there was always the feeling you had to make the most of it, or else risk another few minutes huffing and puffing trying to regain possession.

We all knew how they trained. The method had been set in stone since Bill Shankly's time. Small-sided games – that was the key – with an emphasis on passing and movement, zipping the ball about at breakneck speed. Because of this, the technique of Liverpool players always seemed to be on a different level, more on a par with European teams than anything in England. That would partly explain why they kept winning the European Cup. Few could outplay this well-oiled machine that kept up its revs no matter the personnel. And the latest model was no less impressive, John Barnes a prime example of their enduring class.

And we had to go there in a couple of days' time and give them a bit of a spanking? No wonder we looked glum when Bob delivered his prophetic line.

I mean, we couldn't even beat Derby County or Wimbledon in front of our own fans in the days leading up to the final denouement. The wheels seemed to have fallen well and truly off as Liverpool edged in front thanks to a storming run lasting five months. Twenty-one wins and three draws saw them lift the FA Cup in an emotional affair against Everton and move ahead of us by three precious points. But a chance still remained, however slim. Victory by two would bring us level and match their goal difference. Under those circumstances, the only thing separating us would be the number of goals scored. Our superior tally would bring home the bacon.

That's how tight it was at the end of a season tragically scarred by the horrors of Hillsborough. When Arsenal hosted Newcastle on that fateful day, 15 April 1989, I watched from the paddock, unavailable after fracturing my cheekbone in training. I'll never forget the impact when Al-James Hannigan's forehead butted my face instead of the ball. What a nightmare. This practice match against the youth team was only supposed to be a gentle run-out to go through some moves. But you can never be sure in these kinds of contest. The youngsters are always pumped up, eager to impress in front of the boss, while the first-teamers try their best to do the least possible. And young Al, a no-nonsense Londoner, definitely fell into the committed category, although I don't think he knew how else to play. In fairness to him, it was only an accident. I just got there first, much to my cost.

Collapsing to the turf, I gingerly reached for my cheek, which didn't feel right at all. George's assistant Theo Foley came jogging across to offer encouragement eerily similar to that of Gerry Summers at Leicester when my teeth were knocked out. 'Come on, Smudge, you'll be OK. Let's get on with it.' 'I don't think so, Theo. My cheek has caved in!' Luckily, when Gary Lewin saw the damage, he got on the phone straight away. As the right side of my face swelled up to the size of a small football, I was whisked away to St Mary's Hospital where they operated that night. Sat up in bed the next day, I was pleased to see Penny, given a real fright by Gary Lewin's phone call. Trying to lighten the mood, she told me this was the very place – the Lindo Wing – where Princess Diana had given birth to William and Harry.

Well, not much consolation for me, set to miss several weeks of a season that had been going so well, with nineteen league goals helping us into a promising position. I was absolutely flying, feeling like I would score in every game. And now this, an unwanted interruption that could disturb the flow. Still, it was done now so, with Niall Quinn taking my place, I sat down for the Newcastle game hoping the lads could keep things going.

At half-time, I walked into the players' lounge, the old Halfway House just off the tunnel, to get a cup of tea and check out the scores on the little telly perched behind the bar. But rather than showing the usual half-time scores, the screen was filled by pictures from Hillsborough where, it seemed, there had been crushing in the crowd before Liverpool's FA Cup semi-final with Nottingham Forest. At this stage, reports were a little sketchy but I went up to the dressing room to relay the news.

'There's been trouble at Hillsborough,' I told the lads once the gaffer had said his bit. 'They reckon people might be hurt.' Only at the end of our 1–0 win did the full horror in Sheffield start to become clear.

From that point on, everything changed. All-seater stadia would later come into force while techniques in crowd management markedly improved. No doubt about it, this was a watershed moment that eventually heralded a different attitude to football. Soon it would become more fashionable to follow, thanks, in part, to Italia '90, that wonderful World Cup England really should have won.

For now, though, we knew Hillsborough's dark cloud had cast a forbidding shadow that would take the gloss off any sporting achievement. Paul Merson can vouch for that, having found out shortly after the disaster that he'd won the PFA's Young Player of the Year award.

'It's probably the best thing you could ever win as a youngster,' Merse emotionally recalls now. 'But I didn't want it. I didn't want it. Football had gone out of the window for me then.'

To a certain extent, we all felt the same. It seemed so meaningless, this business of kicking a ball about for ninety minutes. What was the point, when people in the crowd could get the life squeezed out of them?

I thought back to the night my dad came to watch us play at Coventry. When he arrived at Highfield Road, it looked like the seats had been double booked because the aisles soon filled up with people without a seat. At the end, when it came to filing out, Dad got crushed in the crowd as it condensed through an exit. His feet lifted from the ground as panic set in, air leaving his lungs at an alarming rate. Fortunately, the crush subsided before any real damage was done. Nevertheless, Dad never forgot that night. It was a sobering reminder of the dangers involved when something goes wrong inside a ground.

And now something had gone badly wrong. Tragically so. In total shock, Liverpool suspended their fixtures, which included our game at Anfield. It was soon decided everyone else should stop too. In those first few days, as Liverpool's distraught players began attending funerals, nobody quite knew what would happen. To us, it seemed entirely possible the season could get abandoned as a mark of respect. Who could argue with that after ninety-four people, eventually to become ninety-six, had lost their lives?

We came into training each day in a state of limbo, just trying to tick over, waiting for a resumption of duties, or perhaps the opposite. As you might expect, the mood was subdued, lacking the playfulness of normal get-togethers. Sat in the canteen, we spent more time discussing the possible consequences of this dreadful episode than anything connected to actual football. Perhaps sensing our state of mind, George Graham sat us down to urge concentration. 'We must remain professional, lads,' he said. 'These are awful circumstances but after working so hard over the months to get to this point, it would be senseless to let it all slip away now.' He was right, of course. No point in giving up. That would help no one.

Acting on his words, we sprinted out of the traps when football recommenced. May Day marked the visit of Norwich City, league leaders up to Christmas but now falling away. Available again after missing only two games due to the break, I grabbed a couple in a sound 5–0 thrashing televised live on ITV, a black eye the only sign of Al Hannigan's head. That was it. We were back on track, and a 1–0 win at Middlesbrough, though an ugly affair, reinforced the notion this could be our year.

Then came the damaging double-header at Highbury, first a nervous performance against Derby when Peter Shilton decided to have a stormer. Though I managed to beat England's keeper with a consolation header, the overriding memory from that hugely disappointing day was two-goal Dean Saunders talking afterwards about how much he valued his brace as a Liverpool fan, how much he hoped it would help them win the title.

If that wasn't bad enough, a 2–2 draw with Wimbledon four days later really did feel like the end. Despite Nigel Winterburn opening the scoring with, of all things, a right-foot belter from twenty-five yards, the Crazy Gang took revenge for our 5–1 opening-day win with a defiant display in trademark party-pooper style.

Shoulders slumped, we trooped around at the end thanking the fans for their support in a season that looked like falling just short. An air of resignation hung over Highbury. You could hear it in the half-hearted applause. You could see it in the fans' faces. Next year perhaps. Yes, next year, that would be it, armed with more experience, better equipped. The vibe in the home dressing room didn't much differ. Though the boss wasn't prepared to concede anything just yet, he congratulated us on a fine effort that season, as if the game was nearly up. Peter Hill-Wood, the chairman, came down from the boardroom to offer similar sentiments. I drove home that night feeling totally deflated. When Liverpool thumped West Ham a few days later, it really did feel like the game was up.

Friday morning: the lads wander in one by one, not knowing this day would go down in history. We mill idly about the area at the top of the corridor where Gary Lewin's small treatment room forms a natural hub. One or two newspapers lie around the place.

'Look at this, lads!' Rocky shouts out. 'Look what Graeme Souness is saying about our chances tonight.'

MEN AGAINST BOYS ran the provocative headline, under which Souness explained why his former club would win the day with their superior brand of football, their cultured passing style over our more direct approach. Rocky wasn't having that. He pinned it to the noticeboard, full of defiance, before bringing it on the bus for our journey to Liverpool on that sunny spring morning.

It turned out that everyone imaginable had come along for the ride. People we didn't recognise were already on that bus, some sat, no less, in our regular seats, not realising the superstition that comes with this kind of thing. After some polite requests to move, we all settled into our usual habits. Card school at the back – Bouldy, Merse, Tony and Nigel – while the rest of us chatted or read the papers.

Inevitably, though, a slightly different atmosphere ran through the coach that day. An air of excitement at what was to come made that trip up the motorway a bit livelier than usual. What did we have to lose? Nobody fancied us (least of all Souness!), so our underdog tag seemed to relieve some tension. That certainly felt the case in the afternoon when it was time to try and get some sleep at our Liverpool hotel, Atlantic Tower.

That was always tricky, sleeping in the afternoon. As much as you desperately wanted to get some kip, the mind would be racing, thinking of the match. Normally, I'd lie restlessly in bed, unable to ignore the peeping daylight at the edge of the curtains.

This time, however, the script took a turn for the better. David O'Leary and I, roommates since I'd joined, somehow slept like babies for a good couple of hours. And when we went downstairs for tea and toast, most of the lads said they'd also slept well. Don't ask me why. Perhaps everyone felt the pressure was off.

Mind you, when it came to the team meeting after tea and toast, George Graham didn't treat the match like a free hit. On the contrary, he made us believe the seemingly impossible was actually doable, as long as we managed to keep a clean sheet.

'Concede one and it's virtually all over,' George said as he stood next to the flipchart illustrating our tactics. Oh yes, our tactics. Three at the back. When the boss first announced he was going to use this system, we thought he'd gone mad. Yes, we could all remember the experiment at Manchester United, when Tony Adams scored at both ends to start the donkey chant. Bouldy came in to form a back three with Tony and Dave O'Leary. I suppose it worked OK. Nothing spectacular. Certainly nothing to suggest it would get another airing in the club's most important game for eighteen years, when Arsenal last won the league.

A back four had got us into this position. We knew the shape inside out. Why change that now in this, the biggest game of our lives? But George had a plan for negating Liverpool's two wide men, John Barnes and Ray Houghton. Push Nige and Dicko on to the danger men by using them as wing-backs. And the three centre-halves would offer more cover.

'We don't want to go chasing the game just because we've got to score two goals,' George continued. 'I want us to be nice and patient, stay solid and frustrate Liverpool. Let's see how they react to the situation. It might not be easy for them knowing they can lose 1–0 and still win the league. So let's keep our shape, stay nice and tight and see how things go. Once we get the first goal, and we will get it, it only takes a second to get the second. But lads, we've got to stay in this game. Remember that. That's why keeping a clean sheet is so, so important.'

That team talk, for me, was the finest George ever delivered. It not only inspired us, made us believe, but those words cleared our minds for the challenge ahead. That was absolutely vital in a situation like this when the momentous occasion could have easily overwhelmed. George's genius that night was to simplify our task by breaking it down into separate parts.

So off we went to Anfield, a ten-minute drive from our waterfront hotel, knowing the next ninety minutes of football could define our careers, never mind our season. On a personal level, I was vying for the Golden Boot with John Aldridge,

Liverpool's deadly marksman. And as sponsors of the award, Adidas wanted to get me and John on the pitch beforehand to publicise the shoot-out.

Did I mind doing it? asked the Adidas representative poking his head round the door. 'Yeah, that's fine,' I shrugged. Looking back, I don't know why on earth I said that. Agreeing to something like this minutes before such a huge game? What was I thinking? But then word came back that Aldridge wasn't keen. 'OK, no problem,' I said. Then he agreed, before once again deciding it wasn't for him. God, make your mind up! I wondered if this was a sign of his nerves. And if so, had these nerves spread right through the home dressing room?

No matter. We had our own job to do, though preparation took a knock when we heard that, due to traffic problems on the M6, the start would be delayed by fifteen minutes. Straight away, we had to readjust, turn back the clock in our warm-up routines. I sat back down for a bit, read some more of the programme, before repeating my stretches. Then, with minutes to kick-off, George went through his team talk again, this time with one or two extra lines.

'Don't have any regrets, lads. You will probably never be in this situation again so do yourselves proud out there. Above all else, you're doing it for yourselves and your families. Let's go!'

He stood by the doorway to shake everyone's hand, something he never did. If we hadn't realised before, we knew at that moment this was something special.

One iconic image that night was the sight of us running out armed with bouquets of flowers to hand to Liverpool fans in a mark of respect for the Hillsborough tragedy. Ken Friar, our managing director, was responsible for that, a gesture well received by all in the ground. I handed mine over to a lady on the far side before jogging back to the middle where, by kicking off, I would get the first touch of a match famously defined by virtually the last.

A frenzied pace characterised the start. Well, not just the start to be honest, but the whole match. The ball didn't stand a chance as tackles flew in at breakneck speed. Rocky on Ronnie Whelan, Mickey on Steve McMahon. It's funny looking back. No one made a fuss about getting walloped. They simply picked themselves up, brushed themselves down and resumed a scrap bordering on violent. The referee, in turn, didn't react by flashing yellow cards all over the place. That's just how it was during that era. Much more was allowed. The laws hadn't been tweaked to try and minimise injuries. 'Excessive force' was more of a compliment than the barometer used now to determine red or yellow. In addition, you tried not to show weakness by letting an opponent know he'd hurt you. Turning away, you'd wince a little before jogging back into position, careful not to betray any pain by limping. Oh no, that was frowned upon. Hobble about and your opponent gets a lift, happy to have left a mark on his adversary.

While I've never been one to blithely claim things were better in our day, I do find it sad that this kind of attitude has been lost to the game. In a match of this magnitude now, players would be rolling over and screaming, making the most of every challenge to gain an advantage, get opponents sent off. It's an ugly facet of modern football that does our sport no favours. Watching re-runs from 1989 only hammered home the point. And because of this fury, the game couldn't settle to find any rhythm. The ball rarely stayed with one team for long, such was the urgency to win it back.

We were a vocal team back then, with no thought given to hurt feelings if you weren't pulling your weight. Kev Richardson was often at the forefront, comfortable firing off bollockings as a no-nonsense Geordie. 'Hey, fuckin' liven up!' he'd yell at someone, no matter who they were. 'Put yer fuckin foot in!'

On this occasion, though, such shouts were rare given that our attitude, our stomach for the fight, was never going to be lacking. Whether it was Kev, Tony Adams or Rocky, it was more about encouragement, geeing each other up, making sure we didn't let our intensity slip.

As for chances in that first half, the closest Liverpool came was an Ian Rush drive from outside the box that damaged a muscle, forcing him off. Small mercies. Peter Beardsley, surprisingly left out of the starting eleven, trotted on to offer a different threat. Up the other end, we came a bit closer when Mickey sprinted to the byeline to clip over a cross that Bouldy headed firmly at the far post. But for Steve Nicol getting in the way, we would have taken the lead at a stage that might have seen the contest head in a different direction.

Up in the stand, my wife still hadn't arrived due to the traffic. A beauty therapist at the time, she and her close friend and workmate, Clare, had skipped half a day off work by writing fake appointments in the salon's book. Along with Martin, Clare's boyfriend, they set off from St Albans at two o'clock. On finally taking their seats just before half-time, Penny turned to Geoff Shreeves, another of our mates who would go on to become a familiar face on Sky. 'How are we doing?' Pen breathlessly asked. Geoff's face said it all. 'Not great, Pen. They haven't created much. It doesn't look good.'

The half-time whistle blew. Heads down. Disappointed faces. We trudged off the pitch a little downcast having failed to trouble Bruce Grobbelaar's goal. But the boss wasn't having any of that. 'Brilliant, lads. Well done. It's going according to plan. Now we just need to push on a bit. Lee, Nigel, I want you to get forward more, take a few more chances to give us some width. When we get a goal they'll become even more nervous. They're not themselves out there. They don't know how to play it. And we will get that goal, lads, believe me. Come on, boys. This is ours for the taking. The next forty-five minutes can put you in the history books. Don't let it slip by.'

Nigel Winterburn sums up the situation perfectly. 'How a manager can stand there at half-time and tell you what's going to happen and make you believe it. Absolutely sensational.'

As it turned out, this was the stuff of Nostradamus. George called it almost perfectly, whether he believed it or not. We nodded in agreement, on the one hand thinking he'd been on the brandy, on the other energised by his rousing words. Belief – so important in football. George gave us plenty on that famous night.

So out we went for the second half, praying a breakthrough would come fairly soon. Then it happened. The ref awards us a free-kick thirty yards out after Ronnie Whelan went in high on David Rocastle. Indirect, signals David Hutchinson, raising an arm. Rocky bares his teeth, clenches his fist and urges us on. I have so many memories of my dear mate but that one is a favourite, typical of his desire on a football pitch.

Straight away, we all knew our roles for this kind of free-kick, having gone through the drill countless times before. In training, George would have us rehearse this routine all the time even though it never seemed to work on a matchday. Nothing complicated. For a free-kick on the right, Nige would deliver an in-swinger towards me, Bouldy and Rodders (as Tony Adams was known due to his similarity to the dopey character in *Only Fools and Horses*). Bouldy would peel around the back, perhaps blocking off a marker on the way in trying to create space for me and Tone.

On this occasion, though, Tony went off piste by careering into the box to throw himself at the ball. Though he comically got nowhere near, the run and dive seemed to create a diversion to leave more room for me sneaking in at the far post just ahead of Bouldy. Ducking down, I glanced the ball into the corner, leaving Grobbelaar stranded. After crashing into Steve Staunton on the follow through, I carried on running towards the corner where our fans were going wild, some having even escaped the constabulary's clutches to dance about on the cinder track.

Only then did I turn to see the Liverpool lads surrounding the ref, furiously pointing and complaining about something they'd seen. Offside? No, surely not. The linesman never signalled. Handball? No chance. Did I not get a touch on the indirect free-kick? That could be their only complaint. Hutchinson calmly walked over to talk to his linesman, closely followed by a clutch of red shirts still arguing their point. For some reason, David O'Leary was our sole representative, the only one offering an alternative view. 'I kept saying to the ref and linesman, "Don't you get talked out of it. That's a goal."' A goal it may have been but I felt sure it would be disallowed. But no. After a brief discussion, the ref heroically pointed to the centre spot. Goal! Game on! Hutchinson has since revealed he never intended disallowing the goal, but went over to his linesman simply to placate the objectors. For my part, I can confirm I did indeed get a solid touch on that indirect free-kick, helping it on more than diverting its path. You can see that quite clearly on one particular replay and the mud on my left temple confirms the connection. Nevertheless, people still ask the question with a wry smile, especially when I venture into Merseyside.

That goal, furthermore, completely changed the atmosphere. If anything, the noise within Anfield got even louder, more as a result of nerves, I reckon, than outright excitement. The Liverpool fans didn't know quite how to play it. They desperately wanted a goal but, by the same token, didn't want their team piling forward willy-nilly to leave themselves short at the back. That way lay ruin. The upshot was a primeval yell of encouragement that went right through us. It actually gave us more energy to keep on pushing while inducing more apprehension in the Liverpool players.

Yet the pace of the game didn't slow down one bit. If anything, we cranked it up a notch in search of the second, chasing down the ball with added hunger. It's exhausting to watch, this frantic tempo, seeing as there's no let up right through the match. I know the game in general has got quicker down the years, what with improved fitness thanks to sports science. But I've rarely seen a game, before or since, conducted with such ferocity for ninety minutes.

In among all this, chances were few. When Liverpool did find an opening, they either messed up (John Aldridge's heavy touch) or missed the target (Ray Houghton's blaze). As for us, when Mickey hurriedly toe-poked a shot straight at Grobbelaar it was tempting to think that would be that. 'Oh no! That chance!' Mickey gasps now, still frustrated by the miss. 'I just felt I had no time with two players right beside me. I tried to toe-punt it in.'

By this point, the Kop had already started whistling for full-time, however optimistically. And without a clock in the stadium, our only other indication of how long was left was the frantic hand signals coming from our bench where the boss, Theo Foley, Pat Rice and Gary Lewin were becoming increasingly twitchy in waving us forward.

Cue the minute or so that changed our lives. Oh Barnesy. what can I say? Thank you so much for not taking that ball into the corner. Thank you for refusing to waste time by cutting inside to try and score. Oh, and thank you Kev Richardson for nicking the ball from Barnesy and passing back to Lukey. I know you were knackered, Kev, having collapsed with cramp only a minute before.

OK, here we go: that passage of play embedded in Arsenal folklore. The most famous moment in English club football history? Well, I think so. Tell me of another that tops this goal for spine-tingling drama. People talk about Sergio Agüero's last-gasp effort for Manchester City, the goal that won the title in 2012. Of course, it was sensational, the Premier League's standout moment, but that came against QPR, fighting relegation, not the champions of England in a straight shoot-out when everyone else had packed up and gone home. Because of those unique circumstances, there really is no contest. Agüero's winner doesn't even come close.

Lukey says he was shattered, lacking the strength to punt the ball upfield, so threw it out to Dicko, who didn't want it either. But with the ball at his feet, Lee couldn't understand why I showed for his pass, rather than spinning for a big hoof. But show I did, out of habit more than anything, knowing Lee would try and hit me, as he always did. And what a pass it was, fizzed in at pace. As it flew my way, I knew I simply had to take a chance by trying to turn first-time, otherwise run the risk of getting crowded out in a congested midfield. Luckily, this was one of those nights when everything came off, my ball control as good as it had ever been. As one Liverpool player flatteringly put it later, 'If they'd have fired a cannonball at Smith that night he would have brought it down first time.' Well, this wasn't a cannonball but it was a tricky pass all right. Thankfully, my first touch worked out perfectly, allowing me to swivel in one movement thirty-five yards out. A flash of yellow reared up in my peripheral vision. All I could do was try and find this shirt that, as it turned out, belonged to Mickey, making a run, going for broke. An instinctive poke fell into his path as Steve Nicol rushed across to cut it out. But a fortunate break of the ball saw it rebound right where he wanted.

'It was actually a crap touch by me,' Mickey told me years later. 'I knew Steve Nicol was the last man so I tried to dink it over his head and run round the other side. But I didn't get it right and the ball hit him.'

I know it sounds corny but everything, at this point, seemed to go into slow motion. I jogged helplessly behind, praying for Mickey to shoot, as Ray Houghton sprinted up from behind, unbearably close to making a tackle. I could see the whole picture and it didn't look pretty. Our last chance of glory was about to be smothered. We all knew what Mickey was like. As stubborn as they came. Never did anything in a hurry if it didn't suit and that trait to his character looked like costing us dearly.

With so much at stake, it turns out that our midfielder had decided to play cat and mouse with Grobbelaar.

'I'm just waiting for him to make a decision, to commit himself and go down,' Mickey says. 'Only when he made his decision was I going to make mine.'

Bloody hell. Talk about cool. In the event, Mickey's pig-headedness, his determination to do things in his own time, served him and us spectacularly well. As Bruce finally dived one way in their battle of wits, our hero flicked the ball the other way, his effort drifting over the keeper's legs to find the net. Cue pandemonium at that end of the ground. Cue deafening silence, absolute disbelief everywhere else.

The unthinkable scenario had just played out. I briefly ran up to Mickey, who was in the process of unfeasibly flicking himself up off the floor by his neck, before heading off to the corner where our fans were going wild. Funnily enough, we didn't spend long milking the moment. The ref told us to get back. Still time to play. We ran back to our half in a state of shock.

Time for one more Liverpool attack. A high ball into the box. It falls at Mickey's feet. Surrounded by red shirts, the calmest man in the stadium takes a sideways touch before passing back to Lukey. Good God. There must be ice in his veins. Right, I think. If I win this long kick, or at least stop my opponent from getting in a good header, we've won the bloody title. Here it comes. With Alan Hansen challenging, I just do enough. The ball runs towards the corner where Nicol nicks it past a lunging Grovesy. Too late. That's it. The whistle finally blows to end a remarkable contest.

* * *

How to describe moments like that? Impossible really. The pitch suddenly became very crowded as all sorts swarmed on. The gaffer marched across, hugging every one of us – another first for him. I stood with Lee Dixon, best mates off the pitch, trying to locate Penny, the only players' wife to make the trip. 'There she is, Smudge! Right there. Can't you see her?' No I couldn't, as hard as I tried. But I waved anyway, knowing she'd be waving back, immensely proud of her husband on his big night. I found out later that when Mickey's goal went in she'd been accidentally shunted and shoved all over the place by rapturous fans going absolutely crazy. If she'd have known she was pregnant with our first child, a worried frown might have replaced Penny's wide smile.

Down on the pitch, we started parading the trophy, unsure how Anfield would receive the lap of honour. But we needn't have worried. The Kop, nearly full still, warmly applauded as we walked past. That meant an awful lot. These were people who, following Hillsborough, had suffered so much in the last few weeks. It would have been so easy to walk out of the ground at the final whistle.

Back in the dressing room the champagne corks popped as we slumped back, exhausted and elated. Peter Beardsley popped his head round the door to say well done – a very nice gesture, much appreciated by all. The door opened again, followed by a crate of champagne from a home dressing room obviously not in need of the stuff. Liverpool's grace in defeat had touched us all. From the local police and stewards on duty that night, to the chap standing outside the players' lounge checking for tickets, they all said well done like they really meant it. No bitterness or bad blood. Totally the opposite, in fact. They seemed genuinely pleased for their conquerors.

I'm sure the horrors of Hillsborough had plenty to do with it. How can you get too upset at losing a football match when so many around you remain deep in despair? Perspective played a big part. It coloured everyone's mood, including ours.

That said, we couldn't help but feel ecstatic at the manner of triumph. And though achievements like this usually take time to fully appreciate, only really sinking in a year or more down the line, we all realised straight away that nothing could surpass this night.

'It's not going to get any better than this, lads!' someone shouted out. 'We might as well retire now!'

Nods and smiles all round. No matter how long we played for, how much we won during the rest of our careers, 26 May 1989 would always stand out. And so it proved, even for those who went on to win the double under Arsène Wenger.

The passage of time has done nothing to diminish the feat either. On the contrary, I think it has probably grown in stature as the years have gone by. For us players, it is a memory to be treasured, to be immensely proud of, knowing we stuck together and kept going till the end when very few people gave us a prayer.

On a personal level, I couldn't have asked for more. It had been one of those nights when everything went right. In terms of touches, it wasn't my busiest match, perhaps, but I felt confident out there, totally in charge of my actions, which doesn't always happen under lots of pressure. That's an incredibly satisfying feeling, knowing you responded to the challenge, stepped up to the plate if you'll forgive the cliché. It must have said something for my mental strength, as it did for everyone wearing yellow and blue.

Amidst the euphoria, I'd forgotten about the Golden Boot, the fact I'd now won it after all that confusion with Aldridge. Though this seemed incidental next to the incredible drama, the summer gave a good chance to reflect on my coup.

As for the images and words broadcast to millions that night, they are now enshrined in Arsenal legend. Steve McMahon, dripping with sweat, manically signalling 'one minute'. John Barnes surreptitiously shaking hands on a job seemingly well done. And then there's the commentary, which continues to tingle the spine to this very day.

'A good ball by Dixon, finding Smith . . . for Thomas, charging through the midfield. Thomas! It's up for grabs now! Thomas!! Right at the end! An unbelievable climax to the league season!'

Brian Moore wasn't wrong. A climax without compare. Unforgettable theatre never to be repeated.

THREE LIONS

During my time with England I played for two managers – Bobby Robson and Graham Taylor. In many ways they were similar, sharing a deep love for the game that shone through every word uttered. And boy could they talk. When it came to football, whether addressing the media or conducting a team meeting, neither ever struggled for something to say.

This trait, I suppose, is important in football management. You must find the right words in front of an audience. No good drying up, otherwise you look short on ideas and assurance. You've also got to convey passion and conviction to keep the listener engaged. With footballers, this is especially important, seeing as many will start to glaze over if you witter on for too long. Attention spans don't tend to last beyond fifteen minutes or so, after which the message fails to sink in, no matter how passionately delivered.

Speaking of messages, the one that disclosed your inclusion in an England squad was always a great thrill. In the 1980s, these announcements were a little different from today when the squad is officially revealed online.

'Alan! Alan!' George Graham called out one day as I walked over after training to the canteen. 'I've had Bobby Robson on the phone. You're in the England squad. He's coming to our game on Saturday but I don't want you worrying about that. Just play your normal game. That's why he's picked you.'

Mind you, it didn't always pan out like that. Quite often, if you wanted to find out straightaway, you'd have to rely on Ceefax, the old Teletext information service that involved calling up pages by pressing three numbers on the TV remote button.

'Put page 302 on!' someone would shout. 'Let's have a look at the England squad.'

After that, a formal letter arrived in the post detailing the squad and all the arrangements. For me, that letter lying on the mat, the Three Lions badge embossed on the envelope, was a very proud sight. I know Dad felt the same when reading it through. When coming down to stay, he'd ask to see the letter, reading every line a couple of times.

In November 1988, the postman delivered another, this time for a friendly in Saudi Arabia. By this stage, I'd already been included in a couple of squads without making my debut. That was fine. I didn't mind that, for the moment at least. As a rookie, just to be involved was exhilarating enough. But there was surely every chance now of winning a cap seeing as I'd been scoring bagfuls at the beginning of that 1988/89 campaign. If Robson didn't recognise those goals by giving me a run-out in this friendly, I was never going to win a cap.

So off I went, feeling pretty excited. Not just about the match either. We were flying on Concorde due to the game tying in with a British Aerospace trade trip. What a buzz, to travel on that plane after reading so much about its glamorous schedule hurtling Hollywood stars and supermodels across the Atlantic.

After settling into grey leather seats, uncannily similar to those in my beloved Ford Capri 2.8i, it was silver service all the way, haute cuisine accompanied by fine wine (well, for the FA blazers anyway). Up front, meanwhile, the figures on the digital display clicked steadily forward until we found ourselves zooming at twice the speed of sound. The old girl started to rattle, which drew some worried looks, but the stewardess reassured us this was entirely normal. Sat next to Gary Lineker, I knew this would be an experience to tell the grandkids; little knowing the sleek beauty wouldn't be around forever.

Talking of speed machines, this Middle East joust promised to win me a brand new Escort XR3i, something of a catch towards the end of the 1980s. The FA's tie up with Budget Rent-a-Car meant anyone making their England debut during this period would be handed the keys to the little racer. Sponsored cars among footballers were quite common back then. For Bentleys and Range Rovers, read a nice BMW if you were doing well. And it was regarded as a coup if the car company in question didn't insist on your name being plastered down the sides. As for the souped-up Escort, it might not have compared with my precious Capri, tennis racquet headrests and all, but we were talking about a free car here, an offer not to be sniffed at.

As a result, the Arsenal lads in the squad yet to make their debuts – Michael Thomas, Brian Marwood and me – were more excited than most in the hours leading up to this friendly in Riyadh's solid-gold-embossed King Fahd stadium.

In a window-less chamber next to the dressing room, Bobby Robson embarked on his pre-match team talk, aided by the usual flipchart detailing set-pieces and marking responsibilities.

Ten minutes went by, followed by another five as Bobby talked animatedly about the upcoming challenge.

'Lads, this is an important match for us. Don't take the opposition lightly. They've got some fast, tricky players. But if we play how we can – sharp passing, good movement – we'll beat them out there.'

I could see him warming to the theme, totally caught up in the moment, as the players did their best to stay on board.

'We've got one more friendly after this before a couple of World Cup qualifiers. There's still a lot to play for. Places are up for grabs. So those that play tonight have got a chance to impress.'

Half an hour must have passed before Robson finally turned to Don Howe, who'd been getting increasingly twitchy standing alongside.

'Anything to add, Don?'

'No, boss,' replied Robson's trusted assistant, nervously glancing at his watch. 'I think we'd better let the lads get changed. There's only forty minutes to kick-off.'

That was Robson for you. The game consumed his senses, including his sense of time. He could talk all day without taking a breath. Just a pity in this instance that his heartfelt soliloquy went to waste.

We just didn't perform against our pumped-up hosts, who were determined to claim a famous scalp. As expected, I got a run-out for the last twenty minutes, without being able to get near my Arsenal form. Even so, five days short of my twenty-sixth birthday, a full England cap had happily been won. Unaware at the time, this made me the only player in history to represent England at semi-pro and senior level. Leicester City's

Steve Guppy would later make it two. Still, that wasn't a bad feat, to straddle both set-ups. I walked off the pitch feeling pretty good.

The reporters upstairs, however, were in a different mood. A dismal 1–1 draw had provided more ammunition for the mounting attacks on a beleaguered Robson. The next day, this memorable headline dominated the *Daily Mirror*'s back page: GO! IN THE NAME OF ALLAH, GO! Robson was getting it from all angles. The press wanted him out. While I'm not sure you'd get away with that particular headline these days, it was a reflection of the growing frustration following England's dreadful showing in Euro 88.

Still, there's always a silver lining. My Arsenal teammates, Mickey Thomas and Brian Marwood, had also made their debuts – blazing a trail for Arsenal and now gaining England recognition. We were all pretty chuffed in Riyadh that night, and not just because brand new XR3is in brilliant white would shortly be turning up on our driveways.

Pleased as punch with the prize, I nearly lost it altogether only a few months later. Walking out of Burnham Beeches, England's hotel, heading for the bus to take us to training, I noticed my car wasn't where I'd parked it. That's funny, I thought, where has it gone? Maybe I was getting mixed up. It must be somewhere else in the car park. Anyway, I'd sort that out later. Training wasn't going to wait for me nor my trivial parking issues.

So off we set, down the leafy lane bound for Bisham Abbey fifteen minutes away. But we'd only gone a hundred yards when I saw it – my beloved white XR3i, abandoned on the verge. 'That's my car! Stop the bus!' Some little runt had obviously nicked it and gone for a short spin before jumping out. Not surprisingly, the lads thought this hilarious, even more so when they heard that all my cassette tapes had been left untouched in the glove box. The thief obviously didn't think much of my music. Spandau Ballet, ABC, Shalamar – what was there not to like? The tealeaf clearly had no taste.

As for Bobby Robson's taste, I'm not entirely sure he thought much of my abilities. People sometimes ask if he ever got my name wrong, as he tended to with some. Tony Adams, for instance, was often called Paul, a reference, apparently, to Paul Adams, a youngster at Ipswich during Robson's time there in the 1970s and early 1980s. But no, he didn't forget my name, mainly because he rarely tried to gain my attention.

This may be unfair. Perhaps he was just waiting for me to shine at this level. But I never got the feeling he believed I could cement a place in his team.

One day, Gary Lineker put it a little more succinctly. 'Your job, Smudge, is to make me look good,' he said over lunch. 'Make me look good and you'll look good.'

At the time, I wasn't quite sure how to take this comment. Was he being plain arrogant by implying my only role in the team was to serve his best interests? Never mind how I played. I might score a hat-trick but that would count for nothing if Gary hadn't looked happy. When I recalled the remark to a friend, he wasn't too impressed, taking a dim view.

'Cheeky bastard. Who does he think he is?'

Looking back, though, I can see what Gary meant. England, at the time, were on the lookout for someone who could dovetail nicely with their main striker, complement his game to bring out his best. If I managed to do that, my chances of staying in the team would get a real boost. Of course, I had to do my bit and play well myself. But if our respective styles clicked, just as they had at Leicester, that would go a long way to finding an answer.

In search of this harmony, Robson started me in the next international, a friendly with Greece in February 1989, a fairly lifeless affair in front of six thousand fans in Athens's huge Olympic stadium. Although we won 2–1 that day, I failed to make a real impression and got substituted towards the end.

Next up came Albania for a World Cup qualifier. What an experience, visiting the capital Tirana, a one-horse town with the same number of traffic lights, the country's only set.

As you might imagine, the team hotel was basic, the beds bending in the middle, the plumbing temperamental. But it was the local population that left the biggest mark with their fascination for this strange group of visitors. On arrival, we had to wait for ages on the coach outside the airport terminal. I don't know why. A problem with the paperwork perhaps? But for the length of that wait – an hour or more – a crowd of captivated locals, dressed in dusty old suits and dodgy tracksuits, stood there transfixed, staring up through the glass, rarely taking their eyes off their celebrated guests. It was a bit spooky really, the way they kept on looking, almost in a trance. Gazing back down, I wondered what life must be like for these hard-up folk. What did they do to earn a living?

Whatever it was, thousands found the time the next day to watch us train. Once the gates to a dilapidated stadium opened up, in they excitedly swarmed, quickly filling up the seats along one side.

Paul Gascoigne couldn't resist such a golden opportunity. He started clowning around, comically falling over, before grabbing Peter Shilton's gloves to go in goal, theatrically diving about during shooting practice. The fans lapped it all up, cheering Gazza's every move. Perhaps they saw similarities with Norman Wisdom, the madcap film star who was something of a legend in this part of the world.

A substitute for the match, I eventually got on, and should really have scored with a close-range effort. On such moments, England careers hinge. Lineker had found the net on his full debut, a friendly against the Republic of Ireland. After that, he rarely looked back, boosted by the realisation he could succeed at this level. In an Arsenal shirt, I'd have comfortably tucked away that chance in Tirana. For England, a bit of tension in the body made it more difficult, just as it did in the years to come. Luckily, that miss didn't cost us in a 2–0 win.

The Wembley return came along in late April, a mere month before our run-in with Liverpool on the final day of the season. Despite terrific club form that saw me making a charge for the Golden Boot, I was only on the bench, Peter Beardsley preferred as Lineker's partner. Gary, by the way, suffering a seven-match England goal drought, had faced calls to be dropped. In the BBC studio, Jimmy Hill felt the obvious solution was to play me, plus one other. If only Bobby Robson had listened to our Jim, a big voice in punditry usually hard to ignore . . .

In the event, Robson got it right for a game that came only eleven days after Hillsborough. With the country still in shock, and club football suspended, the FA quickly made changes to Wembley, modifying the fences so they could be quickly taken down should an emergency occur.

Following a minute's silence, a 5–0 thrashing of Albania saw Lineker end his goalless streak with an early header before setting up two for Beardsley. This was the partnership that had worked so well in the previous World Cup in Mexico, and the one that would also be used during Italia '90. As an option, I was flirting on the fringe, never making a loud enough claim for regular inclusion.

Having stayed on the bench all night, I returned to the dressing room feeling out of the loop. It was all happening around me, England's quest for the finals. I couldn't do enough to make Robson sit up. Gazza, on the other hand, most certainly had with a brilliant individual effort to make it five. He climbed into the big bath afterwards wearing nothing more than a huge grin.

'If I don't do anything else in my career,' he chirped in that broad Geordie accent, 'I've scored for England at Wembley. It doesn't get any better than that!' For once, he wasn't messing about. You could see immense satisfaction and pride in that cheeky face.

Ah, Gazza. A total one-off. 'Daft as a brush', according to Robson, who also recognised a quite unique talent. Funnily enough, I once roomed with the lad. Yes, I know – an unlikely pairing. Two more diverse personalities would be impossible to find. Whoever came up with the idea must have had a good sense of humour. What were they thinking? That my laidback demeanour would somehow rub off? Some chance . . .

I was and still am a fairly placid type, happy to lie on his bed and watch TV all afternoon. For some footballers, being confined to their rooms drives them round the bend. For me, it was no trouble at all. A bit of room service, some afternoon TV followed by half an hour's kip: what was there not to like? Before you knew it, the day had almost passed.

Gazza, on the other hand . . . well, I think we all know what Gazza was like. Couldn't sit still for a second. Always on the move. If there was a table-tennis match on offer, he'd be there like a shot. Snooker, tennis, darts, a game of cards – anything to stop him from getting bored.

Teamed up with Chris Waddle, his old Newcastle teammate, they'd come into the bedroom and chat for a while before heading down the corridor in search of entertainment. By the time I'd watched one episode of *EastEnders*, I think they'd got through four hands of poker, two frames of snooker and a table-tennis duel.

On the few occasions Gazza was actually in the room, he'd answer the phone pretending to be the fella in a Chinese take-away. 'Aah, herro, wha' you order? Number 53, 26 and 35?' My wife, more than once, thought she had dialled the wrong number. Hyperactive in the extreme, sleep didn't come easily.

I woke up one night disturbed by a noise. Gazza had the telly on, flicking through Ceefax.

'What are you doing, mate? It's bloody four in the morning.'

'Can't sleep,' he said, and carried on watching.

Of all Gazza's antics, a particular one starkly stands out. In April 1992 England travelled to Moscow with a large group of players. Two friendlies had been arranged with CIS (the Commonwealth of Independent States), an organisation formed during the dissolution of the Soviet Union. I got picked for the B team, as I had a few times with some success. A couple of years before, for instance, I scored the only two goals of the game to beat Czechoslovakia at Roker Park, Sunderland's old ground. And the month prior to this latest trip, I struck against the Czechs again, this time on a bumpy pitch in a place called České Budějovice to grab a 1–0 win. As a result, I went into this Moscow encounter feeling fairly chipper, an attitude that wasn't misplaced thanks to another goal, this time an equaliser in a one-all draw. It left me in a good mood as we took our seats the next day to watch the seniors.

After witnessing an eventful 2–2 draw, we boarded our coach outside the Lenin Stadium and waited for the first team. That was when the trouble began, since hanging around always made Gazza restless. You could see him getting fidgety as the minutes ticked by. Finally, to keep himself amused, our hero plucked a great wad of roubles out of his pocket and, wearing a big grin, reached up through the sunroof to place them on top of the bus. We were flying home the next day, so Gazza decided he didn't need the cash, which didn't amount to a lot anyway. By his reckoning, a bit of wealth distribution wouldn't do any harm.

Unfortunately, he didn't anticipate the near riot that broke out behind us when the coach eventually pulled away, causing the money to flutter into the air like alluring ticker-tape. Dozens of locals scrambled for a fistful, which inevitably led to one or two scuffles. That was it. The soldiers standing nearby weren't happy at all. Seeing the unfolding chaos, they stepped in front of the bus, demanding we stop. Now, it just so happened that I was sitting halfway down the bus in the seat right next to the steps that led down to the side door. It also just so happened that the furious soldier who marched on board came up through that door. He had the full kit on – long woollen khaki coat complete with epaulettes, oversized peaked cap and knee-length, shiny black boots.

Standing there with fire in his eyes and a rifle on his shoulder, he quickly turned to me, the nearest target, as the likely culprit. Yelling something in Russian, he gestured for me to stand up. Terrified, I jumped to my feet as he proceeded to issue the mother of all bollockings. You can forget about anything I had experienced in football, any tongue-lashings down the years from apoplectic managers. This was very different. I was convinced at one point he was going to yank me off the bus and frogmarch me off for interrogation. But after what seemed like an eternity, with me pathetically mumbling denials he didn't understand, the soldier eventually backed off, clearly still seething about our stupid prank.

Once he'd stomped off, you can imagine the reaction. The lads were in stitches, mainly because it hadn't happened to them. Gazza, meanwhile, had watched the whole scene unfold while crouched on the back seat. I turned around to see him uncontrollably sniggering.

The end of the 1988/89 season contained a few laughs too, seeing as it was dominated by club success, namely the hedonistic high of beating Liverpool to win the league. Everything else paled in comparison, even England's World Cup qualifier at home to Poland a week later on 3 June.

It is true that the days leading up to that Wembley tie were not entirely in line with proper preparation. After giving it plenty on that famous Friday night in Liverpool, spilling out of a snooker club in the early hours, I made the mistake of inviting all the boys and their partners to our house for a barbecue the following evening. To be honest, I didn't think many would come, but they all turned up, and wouldn't go home. Perry Groves, in particular, made his presence felt by rearranging everything in our bathroom and pouring bubble bath down the toilet. By this point, I had crept upstairs for a lie down, feeling pretty rough. The open-top bus procession on the Sunday involved more alcohol still, before some of us moved on to Langan's, a favourite West End restaurant, for yet more merrymaking.

As a result, I reported for England duty on Tuesday morning feeling slightly jaded, wondering how on earth I was going to start running about. Before training, the other players gathered round to say well done. They'd all watched the match in the England hotel ahead of playing Scotland at Hampden Park the very next day.

Terry Butcher, in particular, had enjoyed the climax. 'I nearly went through the ceiling when Mickey scored!' he beamed. 'Jumped so high I hit my head on the light shade. I so badly wanted you boys to win.'

Most felt the same, having seen Liverpool dominate for most of their careers. Just like with Manchester United in the following decade, everyone wanted the serial winners to get a bloody nose.

Maybe all the praise had produced some adrenalin. I somehow managed to get through the subsequent session without showing myself up. Even so, back at Burnham Beeches I was heading for only one place. Rushing to my room, I collapsed on the bed. Something had to be done if I was going to be in any fit state for the game on Saturday night. I called Dr John Crane, who wasn't just the England doctor but Arsenal's as well. The doc was a great bloke, a real gentleman who, with his blond hair and moustache, looked and sounded a lot like Leslie Phillips, famous for his suave bearing in the *Carry On* and *Doctor* films.

'I'm struggling here, doc. Don't feel well at all.'

After enquiring about my exploits over the previous few days, he quickly came to a conclusion.

'I think we've got an obvious case of alcoholic poisoning here,' he calmly said. 'A jab in the backside should bring you around.'

So out came the needle and down went my shorts. Whatever the doc injected that afternoon, it had the desired effect, allowing me to at least function in a near-normal way. Bobby Robson, of course, would have been briefed. Even if he had considered playing me against Poland from the start, my delicate condition surely made up his mind. Rocky and I started on the bench, coming on together for the last fifteen minutes of a 3–0 win.

Our friends, Clare and Martin, had come with Penny to the game and after having a drink in Wembley's vast players' lounge I suggested we have a quick tour of the stadium. Martin was and still is a big football fan. At Anfield in that May, he'd also been my ecstatic guest the year before to see his beloved Luton Town beat Arsenal in the Littlewoods Cup final. Getting a peek behind the scenes at the home of football appealed quite a bit, as you can imagine.

So down we went, heading straight for the dressing rooms where Martin looked around with great fascination. Then it was out on to the pitch to tread the hallowed turf and imagine scoring a goal.

But time was getting on. It had been more than two hours since the end of the game and Wembley felt deserted as we looked for a way out. No, that door was shut. Couldn't get out there. Best try another along the way. No joy here either. The Wembley staff, it appeared, had locked up and gone home. By this point, another chap had joined us to try and find an exit. He was as clueless as us about the right route. But then we finally pushed a door that dutifully opened. What a relief. Embarrassed laughs all round. We waved goodbye to the bloke and headed for the car park. Martin, however, couldn't contain himself. He couldn't believe who he'd just met.

'Clare! Clare!' he hissed. 'Do you know who that was?'

'No, darling. Who was it?'

'It was only Bobby Moore, that's who it was! It was only our World Cup winning captain. Oh my god. I need a lie down!'

Clare kept on walking, blissfully unaware of the man's stature.

Following that Poland game, it all went a bit quiet on the international front. Under Robson, the closest I came to winning another cap was huddling under a sleeping bag in freezing Katowice as a forty-year-old Peter Shilton brilliantly denied the same nation to secure World Cup qualification. That was it. We had made it, without conceding a goal in the qualifying group. All eyes now turned to those finals in Italy; more specifically, to the players in contention for the twenty-two-man squad.

Regretfully, the 1989/90 season had done little for my England claims, since Arsenal's form and my own had taken a noticeable dip. The portents weren't promising on the opening day when Manchester United thrashed us 4–1 in front of their prospective new owner, Michael Knighton, who'd trotted out beforehand in full United kit to show Old Trafford his ball-juggling skills.

From then on, I couldn't find any rhythm despite the team rallying over the next few weeks. Perhaps Brian Marwood's injury problems were a factor in my slump, with fewer good crosses heading into the box. Whatever the reasons, my goal ratio was poor compared to the season before. After the turn of the year, I went three months without finding the net before notching the winner at home to Everton. More generally, we really did struggle after the Lord Mayor's show, otherwise known as Anfield 89. In the end, we finished fourth, seventeen points behind champions Liverpool.

Despite all this, I remained optimistic about the World Cup. Surely my standing as a recent title winner, winning the Golden Boot along the way, would count for quite a bit when Robson got round to picking his squad? In terms of rivals, Steve Bull had emerged as a surprise contender, scoring against Scotland the day after Anfield and going on to grab a bucketload the following season for Wolverhampton Wanderers. But that, I reasoned, was in the Second Division. Bully had never played in the top flight.

The following April, I felt a bit more hopeful after scoring a brace for the England B side in that defeat of Czechoslovakia. That can't have done any harm, I thought. Pretty good timing, coming a month before the squad was due to be announced. Twenty-four hours later I didn't feel so positive. Bull replicated my feat, scoring two for the full side against the same country. The omens began to look worse when I didn't even make the bench for a home friendly with Denmark, the last game before the squad was named.

Still, nothing more could be done. Tony Adams, Rocky and I flew off with Arsenal to Singapore for an end-of-season tour, not knowing at the time that we'd be flying back early to join up with a provisional twenty-six-man squad. After a few days of training, Robson planned to whittle down the group to a final twenty-two.

So back we came, hoping for the best. Surely Robson wouldn't drag us back all this way if we weren't going to make the cut? On that thirteen-hour flight, we went through all sorts of scenarios. Tony, in all honesty, was lucky to be around anyway. Way over the limit, he'd badly crashed his car on the way to Heathrow, turning up late, looking a mess, complaining of a sore neck. In more ways than one, our captain was in no fit state to be representing his country at a World Cup.

Maybe that's why Robson ended up leaving him out. Whatever the reason, he made a big fuss of him on the morning in question. As roommates, we were walking down the corridor to breakfast when we saw the gaffer waiting ahead.

'Can I have a word, Tony?' Robson politely enquired.

It was an obvious sign for me to keep walking. So I left them to it, wondering what it all meant. Was this good news or bad, Robson talking to Tony and not to me? Did it mean I had won a seat on the plane?

Unfortunately not. Straight after breakfast, a team meeting was called in which a flipchart revealed the lucky twenty-two. Tony, Rocky and me – none of us had made it. I looked across at Rocky, clearly disappointed while putting on a brave face. Too polite to cause a fuss, he sat there in silence, absorbing the verdict. Along with QPR's David Seaman, Arsenal's trio would be going home that same day.

It turned out that Robson wanted to explain his reasons to Tony face-to-face. He wanted to let him down gently while assuring the defender he had a big part to play for England in the coming years. More than that, Robson told the press that Tony would captain his country one day. And everything he said did indeed come to pass.

None of this, however, much comforted Rocky and me, having found out our fate from a bloody flipchart. Once out of that meeting, our feelings ran free. How come Rodders got special treatment and we were ignored? It felt cruel and callous, the whole shebang. Hauled back from Singapore to suffer this? Having been fitted for our World Cup suits and assigned all the tournament gear, Rocky and I were absolutely gutted to come this close and still miss out.

Dodging the press on the way out, neither of us could wait to see our families and forget about football for a couple of months. Tony did it differently, launching into a gigantic bender lasting several weeks.

For me, the dejection intensified when England progressed all the way to the semi-finals. At the time, we were on holiday in Florida with our good friends, Lee and Jo Dixon. On the day of the semi-final with West Germany, Lee and I left the pool deck to watch it upstairs, fervently hoping England could make it to the final for the first time since 1966. Sitting there in our trunks, we kicked every ball, right the way through to the dreaded penalties. At the end, we returned to our families feeling pig sick.

Despite the huge disappointment, this tournament would be remembered for triggering a change in people's attitude to football. It became fashionable, hip, attractive to a section of the

British public that used to look down its nose at this hooligan-infested sport. Yes, Italia '90 was a special World Cup. All those involved tended to agree.

Steve Bull, for the record, was one of those players and Robson later explained in his autobiography that he had 'picked Bull's goals that season over Smith's lack of them'. Fair enough, I suppose. That was his prerogative. But that simple explanation didn't make his decision any easier to take. Maybe I'd have a bit more luck with Robson's successor.

GOLDEN BOOTS

'Win the Golden Boot? Me? Nah, I don't think so. I'm not the type to finish top scorer. Someone like Tony Cottee has got more of a chance. I see he got a hat-trick today as well.'

This was me at Wimbledon, talking to reporters after our 5–1 win on the opening day of the 1988/89 season. It wasn't false modesty either. I just couldn't see myself scoring more goals than serial predators like Everton's Cottee or Liverpool's Ian Rush. These lads lurked on the last line of defence, forever waiting to pounce, whereas I tended to play with my back to goal, linking the play more than seeking the main chance. That's how it had always been. That's why Gary Lineker, my old partner at Leicester, scored more goals than me; that, and the incidental fact he happened to be lightning quick with a deadly finish.

Those football hacks, however, couldn't quite see my point. Huddled in a narrow, concrete corridor under Plough Lane's ramshackle main stand, they really wanted their man to be a bit more bullish. This had been an impressive statement on the opening day, demolishing a streetwise Wimbledon side that had taken the lead through John Fashanu's header only for the Gunners to hit back in style. So satisfying, seeing as none of us were really looking forward to visiting this rundown corner of south London where the dressing rooms were bleak and the welcome hostile from a group of players that knew how to scrap.

So the fact we had met the challenge head-on to play some great football meant the reporters wanted to go big with their match reports. And a glowing description of potential champions needed a good headline to catch the eye. Something like PUT YOUR MONEY ON ME, BLASTS HAT-TRICK HERO SMITH. In the event, they got a few lukewarm quotes from a centre-forward quietly delighted with his day's work.

Form is a strange thing. One moment I was winning the Golden Boot and playing for England; the next I couldn't put a foot right. Most sportspeople will tell you that, when it comes to the crunch, they can't quite explain certain feats or disasters. Putting their finger on the secret is usually too much. I bet Jordan Spieth, for example, can't explain how he sank that thirty-five-foot putt for an eagle on the last day of the 2017 Open, when he had looked in desperate trouble but went on to win the championship. Come the key moment, when the pressure was on, he rose to the occasion to hit the middle of the hole. Why is that? How does it happen? Down to adrenalin maybe? A fierce will to win? Whatever the reason, this is the stuff of champions, what sets them apart.

Football, of course, is different to golf. Like many team sports involving a moving object, it is more about anticipation, getting there first. Those that master the art inevitably end up top of the tree.

In this regard, it was fascinating to read a section in Matthew Syed's highly acclaimed book, *Bounce*. The passage was about ice hockey, another team sport requiring great anticipation. Syed quotes an article in the *New York Times* magazine about Wayne Gretzky, arguably the greatest player to ever grace the ice.

> Gretzky doesn't look like a hockey player . . . Gretzky's gift, his genius even, is for seeing . . . To most fans, and sometimes even to the players on the ice, ice hockey frequently looks like chaos: sticks flailing, bodies falling, the puck ricocheting just out of reach.
>
> But amid the mayhem, Gretzky can discern the game's underlying pattern and flow, and anticipate what's going to happen faster and in more detail than anyone else in the building. Several times during a game you'll see him making what seems to be aimless circles on the other side of the rink from the traffic, and then, as if answering a signal, he'll dart ahead to spot where, an instant later, the puck turns up.

Asked to explain the knack, Gretzky keeps it simple. 'I wasn't naturally gifted in terms of size and speed,' he said. 'Everything I did in hockey I worked for . . . The highest compliment you can pay me is to say that I worked hard every day . . . That's how I came to know where the puck was going before it even got there.'

Here, there are valid parallels to be drawn with football, where the best strikers are adept at spotting the main chance before anyone else. Right place, right time. A natural eye for goal. Sniffs out chances superbly. We've all heard the clichés a thousand times over when it comes to describing prolific scorers. But how do they do it? Are they born with the skill?

Apparently not. Syed goes on to argue it's all about practice, putting in thousands of hours in your formative years so that movement and reactions, recognising pattern of play, become second nature. There's no such thing, he argues, as innate talent.

Thinking about it, I'm inclined to agree, having practised from dawn to dusk in my younger years and, vitally, maintained that work ethic as time went on. No short cuts. No secret formula. Impossible, I reckon, for someone to succeed by presumptuously counting on what they believe to be a natural gift. I've seen plenty come and go bearing this cocky attitude.

Now, I would never compare myself with Gretzky – he was an all-time great – but his ability to sense when the puck would skim into space is obviously similar to the bouncing ball in a crowded penalty box. My hat-trick at Wimbledon involved plenty of that, as did many others in that dramatic season when I won my first Golden Boot. An October 1988 brace at West Ham, for instance, saw me twice get to the ball ahead of everyone else. The second goal, particularly, involved sharp reactions among a mass of bodies. When the ball came in from a corner, it could have gone anywhere as players fought for a couple of headers. But in that situation you have to imagine the ball will come your way. Expect it. Prepare for it. If you do that, you will be in a better position to deal with the ball than a defender, who tends to react rather than anticipate. That's the key. That's what gives a striker the edge over his marker.

If anything summed up me at my best it would be those first few months of that campaign when everything came so naturally in front of goal. That was me at my sharpest, on a wonderful roll, instinctively taking chances without much thought.

Football felt easy, no effort at all. I was moving on to the ball with overflowing confidence to strike it cleanly with either foot or head.

In this regard, everyone needs an accomplice or two and Brian Marwood's service from the left was playing a big part. After joining from Sheffield Wednesday, we'd hit it off straight away, off the pitch too. As a lively personality, he had plenty of jokes, with some regular one-liners. 'Weighed in, Devon and Exeter!' Always a favourite when someone let rip with a fart.

With me in St Albans, Lee Dixon in Redbourn and Brian moving to Wheathampstead just up the road, the three of us grew close and had something in common as players moving south. The other lads, in fact, started calling us the Three Amigos and, for a bit of a laugh ahead of a trip to Spain, I even got some T-shirts printed with those words on the front.

As well as enjoying a laugh, Brian loved to tinker in business. He came in one day to announce a new fax machine was being delivered to his office. We all looked at each other a little non-plussed. 'Why the bloody hell does he need a fax machine? And what's the office all about?' I don't think we ever found out. To us, it all seemed a bit strange when we were getting paid to go out and play football. But that was Brian for you. He loved to keep busy.

Mind you, that seems to have served him well in his subsequent career, going on to become a great success, initially with Nike before moving to Manchester City where he has fulfilled several roles.

Whenever I see him, though, I can't help but think back to that glorious season when we combined to great effect. Not only was he chipping in with regular goals, the winger's crosses were creating plenty for me. We quickly clocked on to the same wavelength after I realised that Brian wouldn't always try to beat his man, often preferring to cut back inside and swing one in early with his stronger right foot. That was brilliant for me, knowing what was in his mind. I could time my runs off this uncomplicated approach. That great understanding lasted throughout the season, right up to the point when he got injured to unfortunately miss the grand finale. That must have been heart-breaking, given how things ended at Anfield.

No such disappointment for me, free of any long stretches without a goal. Three games was the longest, which meant I never lost momentum.

In that kind of form, you become a great favourite throughout the club. On the one hand, you'd expect that with coaches whose jobs are made a lot easier if we're winning and scoring. Whether it was Theo Foley or Stewart Houston, they'd come over and talk in a very relaxed way, happy to laugh and joke, content that the serious business was being looked after. But while I could feel their admiration, this was clearly something they didn't want to end, hence the constant urging to keep it up.

Other people at the club didn't look that deeply. Those working at Highbury – the ticket staff, the maintenance workers we all knew by name – they greeted you with a bigger smile than normal when things were going well. 'Here he comes, the hero of the day.' You felt like the favourite son of a large family dependent on results. Because if we were struggling, everyone's outlook was affected, right through the club. Most, in my experience, were Arsenal fans anyway. It made a big difference to see the team prosper.

So when it was thriving, and I was banging them in, it would be especially nice to chat with Highbury staff. That's when you could properly gauge the mood, when you went to the ground for training or for a bit of treatment in the afternoon. Rather than the bubble of London Colney, this would give you a better idea of what ordinary people were thinking.

Back then, turn right in the Marble Halls and walk up the corridor towards the dressing rooms and you'd find a pokey chamber tucked in on the left where you'd usually come across one of the chaps who seemed to spend their whole lives down Avenell Road. One was Paddy Galligan, a wee Irishman practically married to the club who actually lived for a time in the West Stand. He did the lot, responsible for everything from climbing on top of the stands to hoist the flags on matchday to changing the 'next game' signage around the ground. Firing out thoughts in a thick Limerick accent, Paddy could be hard to understand if you didn't concentrate. But our ruddy-faced mate was proud as punch when we won, despite a strong allegiance to Manchester United. Knowing this, George Graham once invited him to travel on the coach with us to Old Trafford, sitting up front as guest of honour.

Then there was Pat O'Connor, a more quietly spoken character forever wandering around fixing bits and bobs, a screwdriver and hammer hanging from his belt. I think he was an electrician by trade but could easily turn his hand to all sorts of jobs. With the kettle always on the boil in that little room, one or both would be on hand to pass the time of day over a cuppa. And if we weren't doing well, like we weren't in the 1989/90 season, there'd be no sugar-coating.

On a personal level, there was certainly no room for bullshit at the start of the 1990/91 season, either. All thoughts of ever winning another Golden Boot were gone when a nine-game drought had my confidence on the floor. This was the ugly flipside to those prolific runs, the side that robbed me of energy and any trace of self-belief. After the first four games of goalless toil, George left me out, no doubt hoping the jolt would do the trick. It didn't. Once reinstated, I still couldn't find the spark. In fact, I couldn't find anything, including the lungs to run about. Things came to a head in Graham Rix's testimonial against Tottenham when some of Arsenal's old boys turned out for the cause, among them Liam Brady.

Jinking away in midfield, waving that famous left foot like a wand, Brady was reminding the crowd why he was regarded as one of Arsenal's greatest ever players. For some reason, though, this had an adverse effect on the club's present-day centre-forward who kept tensing up and losing the ball when Brady rolled one in. Eager to link smoothly with the great Irishman, I couldn't put a foot right in that wretched game. God knows what he thought of this lanky incompetent unable to control the simplest of passes. A run-out that was supposed to be a bit of relaxed fun to honour Rixy turned into a total embarrassment for one participant.

That was it. I had to see the manager to try and explain, which gives an indication of how desperate I felt. Over the course of eight years at the club, hardly ever did I seek a one-to-one chat about performance, tending to just get on with it and leave the boss to draw his own conclusions. But this was different, partly because I felt horribly unfit, unable to get about the pitch in my usual way. Coupled with dreadful form, this needed sorting.

'Can I have a word, boss?' I said to Graham before training following that benefit match. He took me out to the front where no one could hear. 'What's the problem, Alan?' 'Look, I've got to apologise for my form, boss. I don't know what's wrong. The ball feels like a stranger at the moment. I just can't get going. I mean, I don't know if something's wrong because my legs feel like lead.'

'Look, Alan,' the gaffer calmly replied. 'We're winning games at the moment so don't worry too much. If we weren't, it'd be different but we are so just keep going and the goals will come.'

It was true. We were in the process of winning four on the trot without conceding a goal, including a 1–0 victory at Old Trafford featuring the infamous twenty-man brawl. The time to start panicking was when results dipped. That's when the boss would have to look at taking more drastic action.

Nevertheless, to put my mind at rest about fitness, it was decided I should go up to Lilleshall, the national sports centre, to have a check-up, make sure nothing was wrong from a physical aspect. This side of my game had never been a problem, a good engine in a sleek frame always serving me well. Hopefully nothing had changed.

So off I went to Lilleshall, a former country estate in Shropshire, where they did all sorts of tests, including the one on the treadmill wearing a mask when, to test lung capacity, you ran till you dropped. The results thankfully showed there was nothing physically wrong. Although I'd felt exhausted at times on the pitch, this must have been more of a psychological thing, a lack of confidence draining my legs. I knew that could happen after suffering this kind of thing before to a lesser extent. When nothing is going right, your body tightens up, you just can't relax, and that takes away strength. Well, that was something, at least. No need to worry too much. Get back on the goal trail and all would hopefully be cured.

And this is the crazy thing about football. That's exactly what happened when, finally, on 17 November, a full thirteen games into the league season, I grabbed a couple against Southampton to end the agony. What a huge relief. You can see it in my face as I jog back to the halfway line, hoping this brace would mark the start of something new.

More generally, the result definitely made a strong statement to our title rivals. A few days before, an FA tribunal decided we should be docked two points for that Old Trafford scrap. Two points – that seemed a bit harsh on top of a £50,000 fine, especially as Manchester United were only docked one. With the punishment leaving Liverpool eight points clear at the top of the table, we felt the FA had practically handed the title to Kenny Dalglish's side.

Mind you, I have to admit some proper punches were thrown in that mad melee, unlike most spats when a bit of push and shove is the worst it gets. It started when Gary Pallister rose above me to win a header. With the ball bouncing around, Nigel Winterburn flew in high on Denis Irwin with, let's face it, a scandalous challenge, a real leg-breaker. Not surprisingly, Irwin lashed out in retaliation, kicking Nige on the ground as Brian McClair joined in.

Watching the replays, it's funny to see Mickey Thomas and David Rocastle sprinting past me to get involved without even thinking – tough south London lads taking no shit. They saw a mate in trouble and didn't hesitate. Let's just say I was a little more considered, vainly appealing for calm amid the mayhem.

So violent was the dust-up that Alex Ferguson and the boss ran up the line to try and make peace, as did some subs in a chaotic scene. Finally, a harassed Keith Hackett, ref on the day, restored some order, booking who he reckoned were the main culprits.

In the dressing room afterwards, Anders Limpar, in particular, was buzzing, claiming he landed a great right-hander on McClair. 'I got him just behind the ear. He was bleeding I think.' Our little magician had not only thrown a punch, he had scored the only goal of this tempestuous affair. Not bad going for a player some thought would find our league too tough. Yet the signing from Cremonese had settled in straight away, quickly getting to grips with the pace and aggression. None of us had heard of him when he arrived but by the end of his first training session, when those size-six feet had bamboozled and baffled, we were all convinced of the rumoured talent.

'Did you see how quick those feet moved?' someone piped up in the showers. 'Never seen anything like it!'

Soon to become roomies, we clicked straight away. Our very own super Swede had a cheeky sense of humour, with a slightly wacky side that led to some unusual moves. Shaving off all his pubic hair, for one, got us all laughing. 'Madeleine likes it like this,' he said with a grin one day, referring to his wife as he showed off his work.

Following slightly more aggressive work at Old Trafford, Anders was one of three players to get fined two weeks' wages by Arsenal, along with George Graham for failing to control his players. These were testing times, a crisis of sorts, with the club's reputation getting dragged through the mud.

Yet my own reputation was thankfully on the mend after breaking my duck against Southampton. I was off. Couldn't stop scoring, much like that opening spree two years before. Eight goals in eight games had me forgetting all about those earlier woes when mind and body fell into a stupor. Full of running once more, my reactions, previously lethargic, now felt razor sharp.

One of many highlights was a rasping drive against Liverpool, a match televised live at the beginning of December 1990, after Paul Merson cheekily found me with a back heel. That made it 3–0 to confirm a conclusive win over our main title rivals. The goal clip, what's more, would find its way onto the opening credits of *Saint and Greavsie*, the popular show on Saturday lunchtimes. Oddly enough, that meant quite a lot. It felt like public recognition from a world sometimes slow to grant it.

Not long after that match, another seismic shock hit the football club. It came on the news one weekday morning: Tony Adams had been sentenced to four months in prison for a serious drink-driving offence. No, surely not. This couldn't be happening. Nobody expected this, even though we could all remember Tone in a dishevelled state turning up late at the airport, holding his neck, for that pre-season trip to Singapore. Four times over the limit after a boozy barbecue, our captain had ploughed his sponsored Ford Sierra into someone's front wall. Several months on, his chickens had come home to roost. The judiciary was sending a message by making an example of this high-profile sportsman.

By coincidence, we were due to have our Christmas party on the day of Tony's sentencing. When I say party, nothing much was ever organised, just an agreement to go into town for a festive piss-up. On this occasion, several of us had arranged to meet at Steve Bould's house, just up the road from me in the centre of St Albans. Sitting in his lounge, reeling at the news, we wondered what to do – cancel or continue. After a brief discussion, we decided to crack on. 'It's what Tone would have wanted,' someone breezily quipped.

Can you imagine that happening now? The captain of a top club gets sent to prison for drink driving and, on that same day, his teammates decide to go on the lash? Incredible. But that's how it was. We went into London and, in those easy-going days before camera phones and social media, had a good laugh in relative privacy without ending up in the morning papers.

Of more concern was the prospect of coping on matchdays without Rodders. He was our captain, after all, the loudest voice in the dressing room and on the pitch. Not only that, Tony was obviously a very fine defender whose partnership with Bouldy formed the team's bedrock. Could we get by without him? Granted, George had bought Andy Linighan the previous summer as an alternative in that position. But Andy had yet to settle in an Arsenal shirt, often appearing nervous and accident-prone when called upon. Still, not much choice now. Andy it was for the next few months until the law decided Tony had served his time. In the event, those matches over Christmas and the New Year went pretty smoothly, with goalless draws at Aston Villa and Tottenham being our only points dropped. Tony's dad would often come into the dressing room to wish us good luck, which we thought a little strange given the gaffer's reluctance to let anyone in. 'Hello, Mr Adams,' went the usual greeting. 'How's Tony getting on?'

By this point, talk had inevitably turned to us going the whole season without being beaten. Because the papers were discussing it, so were we, albeit on the quiet, out of the boss's earshot. Why not? We were looking really strong, still tight at the back, with a marvellous goalie in David Seaman, who had joined us from QPR in summer 1990. Given a bit of luck, it wasn't out of the question, as long as we kept focused.

Looking back, I don't think focus was the reason for our run finally ending. Maybe luck played a part – the bad kind – when we went to Chelsea at the start of February. Nil-nil at half-time, Bouldy was forced off through injury, leaving Dave Hillier as a makeshift centre-half. The writing, at that point, was scratched boldly on the walls of Stamford Bridge. A couple of mistakes and Chelsea pounced, going two-up with only seconds left. That was it. Our London rivals had killed the dream and, despite my late reply, we returned to the dressing room feeling pretty down.

Not for the first time, George Graham found the right words. 'Lads, all I've got to say is well done on such a great run. You've been brilliant! But it had to end some time. Now we've got to brush ourselves down and go again, go on another run. Come on, pick yourselves up. Let's get showered quickly and get ourselves off home.' There you have it. No blame being laid, no finger-pointing. The message that day was to kick on again.

And kick on we did, thrashing Crystal Palace at Highbury before, crucially, pipping Liverpool 1–0 on their own patch. From then on, you could hardly call us rampant, drawing five of the last twelve, but it was certainly effective in preventing Liverpool from closing the gap. For that, our magnificent defence, Dave Seaman included, deserved great credit. With or without Tony Adams, they remained wonderfully defiant to end up conceding a mere eighteen goals all season, twenty-two less than anyone else.

The loss of Tony apart, that campaign featured one other setback that still hurts to this day.

We were already established at the top of the league when, on a sunny Monday morning in April, George sat us down on the freshly mown grass at London Colney. Here we go, an early team talk ahead of Sunday's FA Cup semi-final against Tottenham, the first semi in history to be played at Wembley. From the start, none of us were especially keen on that idea. We thought it might detract from the actual final. Still, that was hardly at the forefront of our minds under the circumstances. We were playing the old enemy. The pressure was on. Even though we had only lost that single game to Chelsea in the league, our fans would be gutted if Spurs came out on top. After all, this was a great chance to win the double and emulate our predecessors from 1971.

Nobody knew that better than George, a key component of that Bertie Mee side. Imagine winning the double both as a player and manager. Nobody had ever achieved that before. It would propel our boss into a select group of one, which would naturally appeal to anyone's ego. Maybe that's why he seemed more edgy than usual in discussing our strategy for this distinctive derby.

'Lads, I want to know what you think.' Straight away, this was unusual. Normally, the gaffer couldn't give a monkey's about our opinion. 'Just do as I say' – that was his way, rarely consulting on tactical matters. For some reason, though, he wanted to know what we thought this time.

'I'm wondering whether we should man-mark Gazza, get someone to follow him wherever he goes.'

This too was virtually unprecedented. I couldn't remember the last time he had even considered such drastic action, never mind implemented it. Paul Gascoigne, however, seemed to be spooking him. Maybe it was his match-winning heroics on the way to this semi, which had the whole country cooing about Tottenham's flamboyant playmaker. Maybe George deemed it too much of a risk to let Gazza run free on Wembley's wide meadow. That said, he wasn't entirely sure, hence the consultation.

'Or do we keep our shape and leave the job of marking him to whoever is closest, whether it's Mickey or Davo?'

I know what Mickey Thomas and Paul Davis thought. Here we were, top of the table, favourites to win the league, and our manager wanted one of them, preferably Mickey, to sacrifice his game in order to smother an opponent. Our talented central midfielders not only thought this idea demeaning, they feared the ploy could easily disrupt our game to prove counter-productive.

They were right too. In the end, George went with the man-marking option, which resulted in Mickey blindly following Gazza all over the pitch, so preventing our man from playing his own game. It was a total disaster, one of the very few times George made the wrong tactical call.

To be honest, we may have lost anyway, for Spurs were sharper than us in every department. Even in the tunnel beforehand, they were incredibly pumped up, especially Gazza who kept on shouting something about cup-final suits. At the time, getting ready to walk out into the Wembley sunshine, we didn't know what he was talking about. Only afterwards did the rumour reach us – totally false – that we had been measured up for our final suits. God knows where that one came from. As if any club would be so stupid to jump the gun. Still, that whisper had the desired effect, galvanising Gazza, to inspire one of the great Wembley displays, as much as it hurt the red half of north London.

That free-kick from Gazza – what an absolute belter. I can still feel it whistling past all these years on. Granted, Dave Seaman might have done a bit better. He apologised at half-time, explaining how his studs had got caught in the lush turf to inhibit his dive. But nobody was blaming our majestic keeper, largely flawless that season. He certainly couldn't do much about Tottenham's second, a classic poacher's effort by Gary Lineker after the ball had bounced off my unwitting hip.

A more useful contribution came on the stroke of half-time, my header giving us hope that the tide could be turned. It couldn't. In fact, the waves kept on coming, Lineker sealing the result with twelve minutes left.

Tottenham's day, no doubt about that. In Arsenal's season of highs ending in triumph just a few weeks later, this marked our low point by quite some distance.

Looking back now, and especially considering my early season form, it still feels a bit odd that I won the Golden Boot again that season, putting me in a select band of two-time winners.

I don't seem to be alone either. People often look surprised when they hear of the feat, as if it never occurred to them such a thing could be possible. 'Wow, you won it twice? Didn't know that.' Well, I've never been the sort to shout from the rooftops. And I suppose that kind of attitude transfers to the wider arena, particularly to the media.

As an example, I'll never forget a Nike advert published in football magazines after the end of the 1990/91 campaign. I was back on form, following the disappointments of 1989/90. We had cruised through the year, losing only one game, with me banging them in at a pleasing rate. My England career may have seemingly waned, but I was flying, in the form of my life in winning a second Golden Boot in the space of three years. So I was slightly put out when leafing through a magazine to come across a full-page spread of Ian Rush underneath a headline that went something like this: CAN RUSH WIN BACK THE GOLDEN BOOT FROM ALAN SMITH NEXT SEASON? Eh? Why have they gone down that road? Nike had made it all about Rush and his chances of reclaiming the high ground, when it was actually me on top of the hill.

I'm not knocking Rushy, a true legend of the game. He was Nike's star man, the main figure used to shift merchandise. Not only that, the Welshman was a bigger name than me, having pulled up trees at Liverpool for quite some time. So in normal circumstances I would have understood Nike's stance. But for one thing: I'd knocked in all those goals wearing the swoosh: I was also a client of Nike at the time! So why hadn't they celebrated my achievement, given it a big splash, rather than focus on a runner-up? Great. Typical, that. Even when I come out on top someone else gets the treatment.

Looking back now, I can see that was down to me as much as anyone else. If I had pushed myself forward a bit more, not been so reticent in furthering my cause, maybe more recognition would have come my way.

Even George Graham wished I would put myself out there more to get the credit he thought I deserved. For instance, we had more than one conversation about my reluctance to take penalties.

'Why don't you take them, Alan?' he asked quizzically. 'It would give you another six or seven goals a season, give you an even better chance of finishing top scorer.'

'I just don't fancy them, boss,' I shrugged. 'Never have. Some people are suited to them and some aren't. And if it's good enough for Kenny Dalglish then it's good enough for me!'

Dalglish never went near penalties. And he was top man in my eyes. Even so, the gaffer couldn't understand why I would turn down the chance to grab more goals. I suppose it was in his best interests as well as mine to have a striker leading the list of scorers. It reflected well on his team, made it look exciting and attractive at a time when some criticised our style for being too functional.

Funnily enough, the only time I stepped forward to take a penalty in a match rather than a shoot-out was for the express reason of finishing top scorer. It helped, I suppose, that we had already won the league when Manchester United came to Highbury for our penultimate game of that 1990/91 campaign. The party hats were on (quite literally for some during the warm-up) after Nottingham Forest had ended Liverpool's title hopes earlier that day.

It also helped that I had already grabbed two when the ref generously pointed to the spot for handball. Lee Dixon, our normal and very reliable penalty taker, nodded across straight away. As very good mates, we'd already had a chat in the dressing room beforehand about this scenario. I could have the pen, not only for my hat-trick but in my attempts to win another Golden Boot. In a close-run race for the award with Lee Chapman at Leeds and my old teammate Niall Quinn, now at Manchester City, this penalty could be important. Thankfully, I tucked it away high and left without any nerves, thinking it might have been very different in a tight match that actually meant something.

That wasn't the end of the matter, though. Another match still remained which could change everything. Going into that game, Coventry City at home, I badly wanted to score, knowing one goal would probably be enough to clinch the prize. I therefore felt a bit miffed when a close-range header clearly crossed the line only for the ref to boldly wave play on. It would be twenty-five years before Hawk-Eye's goal-line technology avoided such injustice. For now, I had to accept the decision and simply plough on. Luckily, we were comfortably on top of a Coventry side playing for nothing when Dave Hillier chipped a ball into my path. Taking it in my stride, I sprinted away before steadying myself to confidently clip it past Steve Ogrizovic. That made it twenty-seven goals in all, twenty-three in the league, a very satisfying total in a masterly team effort over the whole piece.

Fitting that it should be capped by a 6–1 rout, with Super Swede Anders Limpar – sensational that season – claiming a hat-trick. We walked in afterwards to get a breather before going back out for the trophy presentation. I asked straight away about the other scores, particularly keen to find out how Leeds had got on at Nottingham Forest. It turned out that, in a 4–3 thriller, Chapman had grabbed two to finish on twenty-one, leaving me clear by a couple. That made the title celebrations all the more special. First and foremost, I felt incredibly proud of our achievement. To lose one game all season took a bit of doing. We had suffered the fewest defeats for over a century, only bettered by Preston North End in the 1880s. That thought stood out the most as we messed about in front of the North Bank, saluting the fans, kissing the trophy. But it was also immensely satisfying to come out on top in the goalscoring stakes. Wearing number nine for Arsenal brings great expectation and pressure, as Steve Burtenshaw memorably said when showing me around that day. Yet here I was, lapping up the acclaim, the crowd singing my name. I had come through, not just unscathed, but with flying colours.

For me, the achievement capped a memorable three years that, as it turned out, marked my professional peak. To win two league titles was thrilling enough. Never did I think that would be remotely possible during those simple, happy days playing for Alvechurch. Back then, to even be in a situation where I was in a top team challenging for the big prize seemed wildly optimistic.

But to claim two Golden Boots along the way . . . well, that was quite something, comic-book stuff. From the foot of the pyramid, I had reached the very summit of English football, both from a team and individual perspective. I'd done it, what's more, with a famous old club that looked set to dominate for several more years. Not yet twenty-nine, I could surely continue in this same vein for a good while yet – a comforting thought over the summer of 1991. Only a few months later, however, that spell was cruelly broken. The leaves were still falling when misgivings and mishaps began to creep in.

RETURN TO NATIONAL SERVICE

In July 1990, Graham Taylor's appointment looked like very good news. As Aston Villa's manager, he'd always been complimentary, never slow to publicly admire my talents as a striker. As a result, I came back into the England fold towards the end of the 1990/91 season. You could say I was his sort – a big centre-forward comfortable handling long balls and all the aerial stuff attached. Taylor, after all, had made his name at Watford with a direct approach. Although he modified that style at Villa, this honest son of Worksop essentially favoured the no-nonsense route.

A shock tactic in Poland later in 1991 highlighted that doctrine. It was England's final group game in European Championship qualifying when a point in Poznan would see the team through to the finals in Sweden. For such a high-pressure occasion, Graham bravely decided to award a debut to Andy Gray, the marauding midfielder from Crystal Palace. Quite a call. Most people thought Andy had done well to make the squad in the first place, never mind be handed such responsibility. But that was Taylor for you. He tended to veer away from gifted technicians in favour of more prosaic performers.

And if the Londoner was nervous beforehand, his manager's instructions wouldn't have helped matters.

'Right, Andy,' Taylor began, turning towards his man the day before. We were going through a few moves on the training ground and this one, it turned out, heavily involved the new boy. 'If we win the toss, we'll choose to kick off. And when we do I want the ball knocked back to you on the edge of the centre circle. Your job then is to find touch as far up the pitch as you possibly can. That will allow us to squeeze up and box in the Poles as they take the throw-in deep in their own half. It puts them under pressure straight away.'

We all glanced at Andy, who looked a little unsure. This was his debut, his first game for England, and he was being asked to hump the ball out of play with his first touch. You had to feel sorry for the lad. He might be following orders but those hard-bitten reporters up in the press box wouldn't know that. They'd be moaning and groaning as the ball sailed out. 'Told you he wasn't good enough!' 'What a nightmare start!' There'd be plenty of that coming from the hacks.

Still, our man did as he was told. Or tried to anyway. If memory serves, the ball fell slightly short of its intended target. Maybe that moment put him off. Maybe this level was all a bit much, but for the rest of that first half Andy struggled to settle down. Towards the end, with us trailing 1–0, Taylor turned to me on the substitutes bench. 'Get ready, Alan. You're going on for the second half.' Off came the debutant, never to play for England again.

As for the match, we qualified for Euro 92 thanks to an acrobatic equaliser from Lineker, our habitual go-to man. Shortly before that, I'd hoisted a great chance high over the bar. Although the offside flag went up, that wasn't the point. This was yet another example of me snatching at the ball in an

England shirt, unable to find the composure so abundant at Arsenal. If only I'd been able to even partially emulate Gary in this sort of match. My England career would have taken a very different path.

Mind you, this tie in Poland came at the end of a very decent run that saw me start five games on the trot, much better than anything managed under Robson. It started on 1 May with a scrappy away win in a qualifier against Turkey thanks to Dennis Wise's goal. Shortly after that strike, I hit the bar from close range after a good near-post run. Head in hands, I couldn't believe it. Another chance wasted to further my cause.

Later that month, I did a lot better in the England Challenge Cup, a three-team tournament involving the USSR and Argentina. Presented with a much harder chance than the one in Izmir, I reacted quickly against the Russians to redirect a Geoff Thomas shot into the top corner. I hadn't had time to think about this one. It was just an instinctive flick. Still, my first goal for England – what a fantastic moment – which helped us win the game. Could this be the springboard for better things?

Maybe so, because four days later I put in an accomplished performance against Argentina, arguably my best in an England shirt. My movement was good, touches assured and, perhaps most importantly of all, I linked well with Lineker who scored the opening goal. What was that Gary once said about making him look good? This was what he meant. And although we let a two-goal lead slip to end up drawing 2–2, I walked off the pitch satisfied with my contribution.

Sadly, four months later I walked off that same Wembley pitch totally deflated having struggled to get a kick against

Germany. Even though we ended up losing this friendly 1–0, the team played OK, creating plenty of chances against the world champions. Despite this, I simply couldn't escape the smothering attentions of Guido Buchwald and Jürgen Kohler. These two were something else – frustratingly sharp, abnormally strong and, if that wasn't enough, acute readers of the game. They just wouldn't let go, these oppressive centre-halves. In fairness, they'd seen off much better opponents than me. Kohler ended up winning more than a hundred caps while Buchwald was still revelling in the glory of marking Diego Maradona out of the game in the 1990 World Cup final. No shame in struggling against this pair.

Even so, I still felt disheartened, doubly so when, in his post-match press conference, Graham Taylor expressed disappointment in my performance. Blimey, I must have been bad. Graham was normally a fan. The whole sobering experience, in fact, brought home the importance of real pace at international level. Either that or an ability – à la Peter Beardsley – to move the ball cleverly in very tight spaces. If you can't do either, top-class defenders will often gain the upper hand. I wasn't slow. But neither was I quick. That shortfall may have played some part in preventing my England career from taking off.

But hold on a tick. Better was soon to come. Despite that criticism, Taylor picked me again for the European Championship qualifier at home to Turkey in October 1991. And what do you know? I got the only goal. It was far from spectacular, a close-range header from Stuart Pearce's cross. But who cared about that? If it meant a lot to England, securing three points in a tight group, it meant an awful lot more to the goalscorer. I had notched for my country at Wembley in an important match. Just as Gazza gleefully remarked after that Albania game, it doesn't get any better than that. With my parents in the stand to witness this day, I felt incredibly proud at the final whistle. It didn't even matter that we got loudly booed off following a second half Turkey dominated with some clever football. This was a night to remember, one to dearly cherish. They don't come around too often for most mortal souls.

As a result, my England career was back on track, and I did enough over the course of twelve months to make it into the squad for the 1992 European Championships in Sweden. Unfortunately, one person who wouldn't be on the plane was Steve Harrison, who had long been Taylor's number two for both club and country. 'Harry' was a born comedian, someone who loved to mess about to entertain the troops. He'd do it night and day, no matter the occasion or audience. I don't know what the FA bigwigs thought, for instance, when the bloke on the opposite table pretended to fall asleep in his dinner, face covered in peas and gravy when he sat up.

And heaven knows what the gathering Wembley crowd thought one night when Harry launched into one of his favourite routines. We were warming up before the game when our coach emerged from the tunnel dragging his leg, holding his arm at an awkward angle and pulling a face. Because we were up the other end, he limped half the length of the pitch in character, weaving his way through the opposition. God knows what they thought. For our part, we chuckled away, not because it made fun of people with impairments, but because Harry was prepared to do something so outrageous on the grand stage. This was an important occasion attended by the great and the good at the famous home of English football, and here was our coach pushing the boundaries of taste in an attempt to relax the players. That's what it was all about – making the team laugh in a pressurised environment.

His good friend Graham Taylor knew that well enough. He'd seen it work at Watford and Aston Villa before trying out the tactic on the national side. But Taylor wasn't just employing a likeable clown. Harrison could coach with the best of them, particularly when it came to the defensive side. Early on in his England spell, one of Steve's sessions blew everyone away. He spoke clearly and concisely with knowledge and authority while explaining the desired defensive shape with and without the ball. The lads walked off at the end hugely impressed. Up until then, we'd only really seen the practical joker, the bloke who revelled in an audience laughing at his antics. The only ones not laughing where those at the FA.

Like Bobby Robson, Graham Taylor loved to chat. We used to joke that he'd call a meeting to arrange a meeting, so fond was he of these get-togethers. And once Graham got going, there was no stopping him. It all came so naturally to this confident speaker.

One example came at the end of the last training session at Bisham Abbey before we left for the European Championship, when Graham sat us down on the grass to go through a few things before we checked out that afternoon. With the sun shining down on this lovely spring day, none of us were too bothered if the boss decided to launch into one of his rambles. And he did, covering everything in detail from that morning's training to our plans for the next few weeks when we would hopefully make a mark in the upcoming tournament. It was all delivered in that cheery, good-humoured fashion that made him difficult to dislike. I had a lot of time for Graham, and not just because he rated me as a player. There was an inherent decency to the man you had to admire.

After twenty minutes of information and instruction, he did what most managers do at this point, what Robson did in Saudi Arabia after rattling on for ages – he turned to his assistant, in this case Lawrie McMenemy, who was effectively Harrison's successor. 'Have I missed anything, Lawrie? Do you want to say something?' Lawrie nodded sagely before looking down at the squad. 'Make sure ya tidy ya rooms,' he said in that deep Geordie voice, the one that must have carried weight during National Service when he served with distinction in the Coldstream Guards.

Tidy ya rooms? That got us going. Really made us laugh. What about the football? No bits of advice from the number two? Lawrie seemed more concerned with making sure we left the hotel in good order than addressing any issues on the pitch. That must have been old habits kicking in – sort out your kit, make your bed before marching out.

He was a great bloke, Lawrie. A proper person with a knack for understanding different characters and getting them to perform. You only have to look at his memorable spell at Southampton where Kevin Keegan, Alan Ball, Peter Osgood and Mick Channon, big names with big opinions, lit up the Dell. I can imagine him trusting their experience and letting these old heads sort things out on the pitch. Lawrie's career as a footballer was modest at best. He wasn't going to try and tell this lot how to play the game. They already knew. No, man-management – that was more his thing, getting to the bottom of someone's personality to treat them in a way that would produce results.

I got a brief taste of his methods during those Euros in Sweden. A training session had just finished when I crisply half-volleyed a ball half the length of the pitch into the top corner. It was just one of those things that players tend to do when they see a ball bouncing about. Lawrie, however, saw more in it than that. Watching nearby, he strolled over, hands behind his back. 'You're better than you think you are, you know,' he said, deadly serious, nodding at the far goal where the ball had nestled.

Although I didn't say much at the time, responding with a smile, the remark stuck in my head. He was probably right. After achieving what I had at this stage of my career – two league titles, two Golden Boots – I really should have been strutting about with a lot more assurance. Don't get me wrong, I was hardly skulking around, head down, feeling out of place. But neither did I pump out my chest and command the environment. That just wasn't me, unlike a young lad in that England squad, just on the cusp of making his name.

I didn't really know what to make of Alan Shearer when he first made the breakthrough from promising Southampton youngster to full international. He was quiet around the England camp, a little aloof I thought, sticking close to those he knew. Not in any way intimidated, though. For one so young, he moved about with a natural confidence bordering on conceit.

I'd seen that solid self-belief the day he scored a hat-trick on his full debut against Arsenal in 1988. Sitting in the away dressing room afterwards, we talked about the unknown seventeen-year-old who had just taken us apart, albeit against a makeshift defence featuring Mickey Thomas and Gus Caesar as bemused centre-halves. Not everyone was totally convinced, thinking this might have been just a fluke. 'What do you think, Smudge?'

someone shouted across, interested to get the view of a fellow centre-forward. Without wishing to sound like Harry Hindsight here, I quickly came back with a ringing endorsement. 'Very good. Nice technique. Holds the ball up well. I think he's going to be a very good player.' In the years to come, as Shearer set about breaking all sorts of records, I would smugly remind the lads of my shrewd prediction.

In 1992, though, the smart money certainly wasn't on England to shine in Sweden. Fair to say, this wasn't the finest squad to ever leave these shores, thanks to a number of absentees. John Barnes, for instance, ruptured his Achilles tendon in Finland only a week before the serious stuff began. In that same match, Gary Stevens of Glasgow Rangers, himself a late replacement for my injured clubmate Lee Dixon, sustained a stress fracture in his right foot, which left the final squad without a recognised right-back.

Taylor had already discarded Chris Waddle and Peter Beardsley, two longstanding creative forces, while Ian Wright somehow missed out despite finishing top scorer in the First Division. In addition, Paul Gascoigne had long since been unavailable after a reckless challenge on Gary Charles in the 1991 FA Cup final.

Just to add a bit of farce to the mix, on the day of departure we were sitting on the coach outside our hotel when a head count revealed one person missing. 'Where's Mark Wright?' Taylor impatiently shouted down the bus. 'Where the bloody hell is he? It's time we were leaving!' The coaching staff withdrew to make some enquiries. It turned out Mark hadn't even been at the hotel. Having aggravated an old Achilles injury in that Finland game, the Liverpool captain, unbeknown to Taylor, hadn't travelled down to join the squad. We couldn't believe it. This felt more like the Dog and Duck than the Three Lions. Incredible goings-on before a major tournament. Even worse, because the withdrawal came so late, Taylor wasn't allowed to call up a replacement, leaving us with nineteen players instead of twenty.

So the omens from the start weren't particularly promising. Not only that, we knew that in a group containing France and the hosts, Sweden, we'd have to play pretty well to go any further. Our opening game, in fact, looked the easiest on paper, seeing as Denmark weren't even supposed to be there. Included only after the very late disqualification of war-ravaged Yugoslavia, the Danes had been forced to hurriedly prepare. If we couldn't beat this lot, well, what chance did we have?

As for me, I had been chosen to start alongside Lineker up front. With my old mate Paul Merson cutting in from the left, Trevor Steven on the right and David Platt making runs from central midfield, this was quite an attacking line-up selected by Taylor, one we all hoped could do the job. But on a warm night in Malmo, chances were few. I came as close as anyone in an England shirt, connecting cleanly on the volley with Merse's cross to force a sharp save from Peter Schmeichel. Later on, John Jensen nearly snatched it for Denmark by hitting the inside of our post, the ball rolling agonisingly back across goal for Chris Woods to gather. Although no one could have possibly guessed it at the time, this was a precursor to Jensen's heroics in the final when a spectacular winning goal against Germany led to his Arsenal move.

Yes, the Danes only ended up winning the bloody competition, having sneaked in by default at the last minute. In hindsight, then, this wasn't a bad point against the eventual champions, even though it felt at the time like a missed opportunity. We returned to our hotel knowing the France game was going to be crucial.

For that one, alas, I didn't make the cut, a young Alan Shearer preferred in my place. Taylor took me aside to explain his reasons, as he tended to do, being a decent sort. To be honest, I couldn't really tell you what he said that day. Once you know you're dropped, the words of explanation rarely sink in. He's talking, but you're not listening. Who really wants to hear why they're not needed? In any case, the manager gets paid to make these kinds of calls. If he'd made up his mind, there wasn't much I could do. Earlier that year Shearer had scored against France on his debut. Perhaps that played a part in Taylor's thinking.

In the event, the selection proved incidental in a tight tussle that didn't involve much good football or, indeed, either goalkeeper. Michel Platini's swashbuckling outfit boasting Laurent Blanc, Didier Deschamps, Eric Cantona and the prolific Jean-Pierre Papin struggled to create chances against our newly formed five-man rearguard. The most notable moment revolved around Basile Boli, France's badass centre-half, who, for some crazy reason, laid the nut on Stuart Pearce following a corner. Pearcey collapsed to the turf clutching his face. What was Boli thinking? He could have been sent off. But the officials didn't see it and our doughty left-back, never one to make a fuss, picked himself up and trotted over to the touchline where our physio, Fred Street, applied the magic sponge to his bleeding face. Later on, Pearcey nearly got revenge with a fizzing free-kick that crashed off the underside of the bar. That was it.

Another dull, goalless draw, meaning we'd have to beat Sweden in our last game. In theory, a high-scoring draw would also do the trick, but that looked decidedly unlikely given our record in front of goal.

This time, for the shoot-out in Stockholm, neither Shearer nor I made the starting eleven, Taylor deciding to play Lineker through the middle on his own, with Tony Daley introduced to bring speed on the flank. And this tactic looked inspired when David Platt hooked home after only four minutes. Buoyed by the breakthrough, we really took the game to Sweden in that first half, without being able to find the finishing touch that surely would have decided the tie. Taylor was getting increasingly animated on the bench, annoyed that these chances were being passed up. Like any experienced football person, he must have feared his side would come to regret these wasted openings. That said, a goal lead at half-time wasn't bad at all. Retaining the initiative must now be our aim. Mind you, that was always going to be difficult against a host nation in front of their fans. I think we all knew a fightback was imminent.

And so it proved. After the break Sweden started to produce what their manager, Tommy Svensson, would later describe as 'the best I have seen Sweden play for years'. Recognising the turnaround, Taylor kept jumping up and down, moaning to his coaches, McMenemy and Alan Ball. Gary Lineker, in particular, was coming in for some stick for failing, in Taylor's eyes, to keep hold of the ball.

'Oh, fucking hell!' he'd yell, nudging McMenemy in the ribs. 'Look at him! Look at him! He's lost it again! Keep hold of it, Gary, for fuck's sake!'

Patience was wearing thin even before Sweden equalised through Jan Eriksson's towering header. It came from a corner, a bloody corner no less. Of all the ways to concede, that wasn't how we expected to let our opponents back in, opponents that didn't look back from that moment on.

This was too much. The signs looked ominous. In response, Shearer and I were told to warm up. Off we jogged up the line, knowing one of us at least would soon be going on. For me, it was a nerve-wracking few minutes, going through my stretches and sprints in the Råsunda Stadium. If Taylor called on me, it would be a golden chance to make a mark on the international stage in a way that had, up till now, proved frustratingly elusive.

To step up in these finals, in this game especially, would mean an awful lot. It wouldn't just get everyone talking back home, get them really excited at the prospect of England playing in a semi-final, it would elevate my standing in a way only international success could. Having come close on a few occasions to making a proper splash, coming up trumps here would definitely seal it.

Out on the pitch, Lineker knew something was coming. 'I remember seeing you and Shearer warming up and I thought, "Oh, that's good, they're going to get someone to play up with me." But then I thought, "Actually, I've got a feeling he's going to take me off." I knew I was never really his type.'

Then came the call. The familiar wave. Taylor had chosen me to try and turn the tide. Off with the tracksuit top as team-mates on the bench wished me good luck. A few quick words of advice from Taylor before the fourth official held up his cards (yes, this was before the advent of the electronic board). Only at that point did I realise Gary was going to be culled. Seeing as we needed a goal, that came as a shock. I had naturally assumed I'd be going on to join my former clubmate – rekindle the old magic and all that – not replace a household name on the verge of equalling Bobby Charlton's goalscoring record. Penny told me later that up in the stand Gary's wife, Michelle, a good friend from our time together at Leicester, had shed a tear when her husband was subbed. You could understand that, even if it made Penny awkwardly fidget in her seat.

Down on the pitch, I didn't have time to think about any fallout from the substitution. This was about me making a difference in a huge game. A quick shake of the hands with Gary and on I trotted to try and get involved in a contest turning worryingly one-sided as Sweden knocked the ball about with impressive pace and intent. If a goal was going to come it would come at our end where Woodsy was having to fling himself all over the place. And then it happened – a rapid one-two, followed by another, before Tomas Brolin, so sharp on the night, hooked a marvellous effort past our goalie. After that we never looked like responding. It was all a bit chaotic, far too panicky, as we chased a game moving further away. As hard as I tried, my impact was minimal during those last few minutes. The final whistle blew to signal England's limp exit from a tournament in which we had never got going.

Back in the dressing room someone triggered a round of applause to acknowledge Lineker's marvellous England career, one that had just shuddered to an undignified halt. You could see the frustration and anger in Gary's face and maybe a little awkwardness in Taylor's demeanour as he launched into a post mortem few wanted to hear. Those two had never really hit it off, even though Graham had made Gary captain. There was always something there, perhaps a clash of ideals, a contrast in philosophy that created a distance.

At that precise moment, however, I wasn't too bothered about that. We were going home and I'd failed to make a mark. On the plus side, at least I'd achieved an ambition of representing my country in a major tournament. After Italia '90 rejection, that meant something. Just a pity our campaign had turned out to be so lifeless. To be fair, it would have felt even worse if I had known at that moment I would never again pull on the England shirt.

We woke up the next morning to predictable disgust, the papers going to town on our demise. Looking back, there's no doubt Taylor made a mistake in allowing English newspapers into the team hotel. We would go down to breakfast and there they were, laid out on a table, rarely too flattering with their observations. The boss used to get particularly wound up by all this. You'd hear him complaining to anyone willing to listen about what he saw as a lack of support. On one occasion, he even lost his rag during a live TV interview, snapping at the presenter for his perceived negativity.

With that as a backdrop, we all knew what was coming straight after that Stockholm defeat. The tabloids, in particular, weren't going to hold back. 'Swedes 2 Turnips 1'. On opening the *Sun*, you couldn't help chuckling. But with Taylor cast as the unfortunate root vegetable, our Swedish sojourn had turned thoroughly rotten.

Back at Luton airport, a 'welcome party' started yelling insults. Heads down, we couldn't wait to get out and leave behind an experience none of us would remember with too much affection.

That was it then. With me struggling for goals the following season, Taylor looked elsewhere for attacking talent. Thirteen caps, 7 starts, 784 minutes and 2 goals: hardly the stuff of legend. My England career had never reached a gallop, more also-ran than winner's enclosure.

Then again, this was nothing to be sniffed at. How many people would happily part with their life savings to turn out for England for just a few minutes? Plenty, I'd imagine. In all my time with the squad, I never lost sight of that fact. But as proud as I always felt in pulling on that shirt, the actual reality never truly hit home, only sinking in at the end of my time.

And here it is: lined up at Wembley or indeed anywhere in the world before an international, you are the country's first choice for that particular position. On that day, at that moment, you are deemed to be better than any other living Englishman. In my case, no other centre-forward was better equipped to do the job. Written down in black and white, all this might sound obvious. But caught up in the challenge, you never distil the situation into such simple terms.

Thinking about it now, though, I can see it for what it is – a fantastic achievement. The best centre-forward this football-mad country could possibly produce: seven times, I pulled off this feat. Seven times I stood alongside ten colleagues singing the national anthem. So while a little bit of regret definitely plays a part in my England story, how can I possibly moan about the end result?

CUPS AND DOWNS

On hearing the news that Ian Wright was signing for Arsenal in September 1991, I felt really excited. This was going to be great. Wrighty's style would surely go hand-in-hand with mine. For the past few years I'd watched on in admiration as he tore about for Crystal Palace, banging in some fantastic goals. He looked perfect for me. That busy way of his, all pace and aggression, should work a treat next to my target-man qualities. Such a mix, after all, had gone down a bomb at Selhurst Park where Mark Bright, an old Leicester teammate roughly sharing my style, had brought out the best in his effervescent sidekick. It was the classic big man/small man routine, both profiting from the partnership, and it should be no different across the river at Highbury.

Not that I thought we needed him at the time. After all, we had just won the league, losing only one game, with Kevin Campbell emerging as a powerful prospect. After a slow start to the 1991/92 season, the team had picked up to put in some fantastic performances, including a 4–1 win at Wrighty's Palace, a memorable 6–1 thrashing of Austria Vienna in the European Cup (when I scored four) and a 5–2 thumping of Sheffield United. That was the last game before Ian's arrival, and we got a proper bollocking at the end for easing off the gas. Four-nil up at half-time, George Graham was far from happy with what he saw as a lack of concentration in the second half. Although we all thought he was going over the top a bit, that was the gaffer for you. He never let up.

And with regard to Wrighty, who became the club's record signing, I suppose George made the move with an aim to taking the team forward. He hadn't forgotten what happened after the heroics of 1989. With no one of note coming in to freshen up the squad, the atmosphere in the dressing room grew a little stale and we went on to struggle with the mantle of reigning champs. The boss wasn't about to make the same mistake again. Even though we had started knocking in goals for fun, George obviously felt Wrighty could take things even further with his infectious attitude and insatiable appetite for goals. We could see his point, too. With all due respect, this was closer to proven talent than Kev Campbell's potential.

That became obvious straight away as the new boy set about delivering with startling success. I watched injured from the stand at Leicester as he scored on his debut in the League Cup before grabbing a hat-trick at Southampton to really make his mark. An Arsenal legend was born in double-quick time. The fans absolutely loved this super-talented, passionate, sometimes explosive character with a variety of celebrations for his constant stream of goals. As a supporter, how could you not worship the sheer flamboyance on show, not to mention the prolific output? It was all markedly different to what had come before when the team ethic tended to overshadow any individual.

Of course, we had Merse who could always produce the unexpected – a cheeky chip or pass – and someone like Rocky with his dazzling feet and Hollywood smile. But Wrighty took things further: he brought showbusiness to Highbury with the way he went about his everyday life, whether through his latest car, something expensively cool, or his fashion sense, slightly different from the norm. Such was the size of that extrovert personality, his arrival quickly changed the tone of the dressing room.

In tandem, his maverick style also had an effect on how things were done on the training pitch. Up until that point, George had always been a stickler for running through team shape to nail down where everyone should be at any given time. Quite often, we'd go through some shadow play, which meant lining up without any opposition and rehearsing various moves until they became second nature. Yet it soon became apparent this was going to be difficult with Wrighty. Try as he might, the gaffer couldn't get the new man to fall into line, to follow strict instructions in terms of where he should run when, say, Lee Dixon had the ball in the full-back position. Wrighty would just follow his instincts and do what came naturally, which usually ended up with the ball in the back of the net. After several weeks trying to rein him in, George eventually gave up and just let Wrighty get on with it, realising he was never going to tame this gifted free spirit.

In one respect that was great. Ian was given carte blanche to play off the cuff. You could hardly complain when he did what he did. For me, though, this total change around in practice knocked me off my stride. It left me confused, unsure of my movement, seeing as I just couldn't tell what Wrighty was going to do next. I'd show for the ball, only to see my new strike partner dash across my path in a way that would just never have happened with Paul Merson, Kev Campbell or Perry Groves, who all adhered to the structure laid down by Graham. The upshot was that I ended up simply reacting to Wrighty, by taking up positions to try and complement his, rather than sticking to the movement with which I was so familiar.

That wasn't the worst of it, though. For some reason, my confidence in front of goal started to plummet. I began snatching at chances I would normally tuck away without even thinking. Next to Wrighty's lethal marksmanship, my miskicks and fumbles felt totally embarrassing. I wanted the ground to open up and swallow this shadow of a striker who started to dread the prospect of finishing practice. Watching on, Wrighty must have wondered how on earth this bloke had managed to win two Golden Boots. He'd obviously seen me on telly knocking them in for fun and perhaps imagined we would make a deadly double act. I couldn't blame him because I had felt exactly the same. But now this was happening, the dream-team scenario quickly turning to dust. And the harder I tried the worse it got.

I'll be honest. I privately blamed Wrighty for this. From my angle, he had burst through the doors to upset the status quo. Where before, Merse might have passed to me, Wrighty let fly. I let what I regarded as a selfish attitude badly affect me, to the extent that when a chance did come my way I couldn't relax so made a real hash of it.

Looking back, I should have had a private word with Ian to try and sort things out; explain to him that his improvised, unpredictable style was not what I was used to; try to find common ground, a way forward, so we could both flourish instead of just him. But to my eternal regret, I didn't have that chat, which, in fairness, is typical me. A bit like Arsène Wenger, I have always hated confrontation, any kind of situation that might get a bit awkward, never mind one that could turn into an argument. I tend to shy away from those situations, even if it means the problem getting worse.

I am not particularly proud of this side to my character. I see it as a weakness, a flaw that has occasionally let me down over the years. And this was definitely one of those times when I should have got everything out into the open instead of bottling up a growing frustration. But because I didn't, an unspoken distance grew between Ian and me. It's not as if we didn't get on – there was always mutual respect – but I could feel a certain awkwardness there and I know Ian could, too, judging by how he spoke to me compared to others.

I don't know whether the gaffer could see any of this. If he couldn't, he must have noticed our partnership on the pitch failing to click. Should I have a word with him? Explain the situation? I decided against, feeling this would have looked like going behind Wrighty's back. And I didn't want to do that, even though the problem was getting steadily worse. In any case, I can imagine what the boss would have said: 'Ian is doing his job. You've got to start doing yours again.'

Feeling increasingly desperate, I took what was quite a drastic step for me – going to see a sports psychologist to talk things through. With my goals drying up, with training fast descending into a miserable chore, I simply had to do something to try and turn things around. If I didn't start enjoying my football again by rediscovering some form, my career was heading only one way. As the records clearly show, my goal return slowed down to a sad trickle once Ian turned up. With eleven to my name after that Sheffield United game in September 1991, I only got another six over the course of that season. Wrighty, meanwhile, went on a thrilling goal spree to win the Golden Boot, an award I had proudly claimed only a year before.

So off I went, up to the Midlands, to have a chat with Dr John Gardner who I knew from my time with England under

Graham Taylor. In the early 1990s, Graham had taken what was a fairly unusual step back then of bringing a psychologist into the camp. And because this was new, the lads were inevitably wary. When John spoke to us as a group, there were a few furtive sniggers and nudges, much of it down to embarrassment and scepticism of a science that had yet to be widely used in our traditionalist, sometimes cynical sport.

On the other hand, Dr Gardner's one-to-one sessions were probably an entirely different story. Get them on their own and footballers, like most people, will open up. Although at the time I didn't feel the need to book an appointment myself (why, I don't know), I'm sure John's confidential chats helped a good few England players over that period.

But now I did want to see him. I couldn't think of anything else that might fix the problem. Sitting in his living room among the potted plants, I explained the situation as best I could; how my game had degenerated, particularly my finishing, since this boisterous extrovert had burst into my world. What can I do? How do I get round this? John listened carefully, asked a few questions, before getting me to practise a certain mental drill. In truth, I can't remember what it was exactly – something about squeezing my thumb and forefinger together to trigger a thought so that I could go back to that thought at any given time. I did the best I could, concentrating hard on the task in hand, hoping it would be the first step on the road to repair. For whatever reason, though, I came away that day feeling no more optimistic than when I arrived. Perhaps I hadn't properly bought in to John's methods. Perhaps I didn't truly believe anything could be done.

As a result, I returned to London Colney no better off. The same pattern continued as if nothing had happened and I grew

Golden Boot? Nah, don't put your money on me. *(author's collection)*

nost invincible. Celebrating our 1991 title win with Alan 'Maxi' Miller. *(author's collection)*

Arsenal 4, Spurs 1. *(Bob Thomas/Getty Images)*

Two legends called Robson, and me. *(Mirrorpix)*

A dispiriting night against World Champions Germany. *(Frank Tewksbury/ANL/REX/Shutterstock)*

Sticking my tongue out at Argentina in my best game for England. *(Colorsport)*

eplacing Gary in Sweden. To no avail. *(Colorsport)*

Make that 4–1. The best of my four goals v Austria Vienna. *(Colorsport)*

Rolling back the years with my winner v Parma. *(Colorsport)*

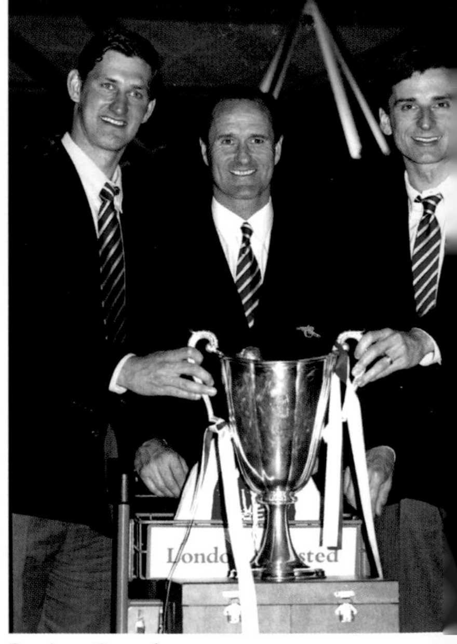

Precious Copenhagen cargo. *(John Stillwell/PA Archive/PA Images)*

eeting the great man in Johannesburg in 1993. *(Phil O'Brien/EMPICS Sport)*

the tourist trail in China with soon-to-become ex-teammates. *(author's collection)*

My benefit match agai
Sampdoria with my
daughters Jess and Em,
9th November 1995.
(Mark Thompsn / ALLSPORT
Getty Images)

'He'll be disappointed with that, Martin.'
(author's collection)

Talking nonsense with Geoff Shreeves, a close
family friend. *(Geoff Shreeves)*

ıom and Dad. *(author's collection)*

Christmas with the Rocastles, very special friends. *(author's collection)*

e wonderful Clare and Mart. *(author's collection)*

Linda: more a mate than a mother-in-law. *(author's collection)*

The Core Four – my family. *(author's collection)*

There she is, the love of my life. *(author's collection)*

Two rum punches down with my fabulous Emily. *(author's collection)*

Jessie: beautiful in every way. *(author's collection)*

more disenchanted with each passing week. Inevitably, this led to me getting dropped more frequently than ever before. Nearly always a starter if fit in my first four years at the club, I now had to get used to the indignity of occasionally sitting on the bench, with Kevin Campbell preferred as Wrighty's strike partner.

The screw painfully turned further the day Kev turned up in a brand new Mercedes convertible with the number plate KEV 9. Hold on a minute. What was this? Nine was always my number. Does my teammate now think he has taken over as Arsenal's first-choice centre-forward? Whatever the reason for that plate, this felt like a dig, another wound to my pride. To me, it summed up my humiliating fall from grace. No longer the main man, the balance of power was shifting in a worrying direction.

My uncomfortable relationship with Ian rarely flared up into anything visible. He got on with the business of scoring while I huffed and puffed, doing my very best to stay in the team by contributing something useful other than goals. If I couldn't do that, then what was the point? I might as well pack up.

Looking back on that whole period, I think I became intimidated by Wrighty's soaring self-assurance. For some reason, his dominant personality had a negative effect when, for most of my teammates, it had the opposite one. This is an embarrassing thing to admit. Even now. I shouldn't have felt the least bit daunted by Ian's arrival. We had just won the league, for heaven's sake, losing only one game. And I had topped the scoring charts for the second time. What was there to worry about? If anything, the outsider from Crystal Palace with limited experience of the top flight should have been the one harbouring self-doubt, wondering whether he was good enough to add something to a team that had been so successful.

In the event, I ended up blaming Ian for my own struggles. Not to his face, mind. It was all bubbling up inside, the resentment increasing as the months passed. It was great before, I reasoned. Why the bloody hell did the gaffer have to change it? Because even though Ian was banging in goals left, right and centre, we had turned into a cup team rather than the title-challenging one of previous seasons. In my mind, too much emphasis was placed on hitting our goal-getter early with balls over the top. That tactic bypassed yours truly who had always depended on service from the flanks, an aspect of our game that noticeably suffered without genuine wide men.

In truth, I made too many excuses for my own problems, too quick to point the finger rather than look in the mirror. While it was certainly true that the team had declined in terms of quality and balance, I shouldn't have been affected to such an alarming extent. Granted, goal-scoring opportunities weren't coming along anywhere near as regularly as before. And when they did, you could be sure that Wrighty would usually be in pole position to snaffle them up. But I did still get chances, only to waste them with a hesitant touch. You couldn't blame anyone else for that. The buck stopped with me. I should have done more to reverse a trend that was not only harming my reputation as a reliable goalscorer, but casting a shadow over my day-to-day life.

Going home to Penny and the girls, the *joie de vivre* of old had been compromised. Whenever conversation turned to my job, Penny could see the dejection in everything I said. To be honest, I tried to avoid the subject as much as possible, fearing my wife would think less of me if I admitted to what I regarded as a weakness in character. Along with the angst there was a deep disappointment about letting this happen. What the hell was wrong? Why had my confidence crumbled to such an extent?

Desperately searching for a cure, I reluctantly decided to ask for a transfer, a drastic step I could never have envisaged taking just a few years before. But I didn't really know what else to do. If matters were showing no sign of improvement, the only alternative seemed to be a move away. George Graham, however, thought it a bad idea for two reasons. For a start, he wasn't prepared to let me go before finding a suitable replacement. His pursuit of Norwich City's Chris Sutton was all over the papers. Secondly, he pointed out that I wouldn't be entitled to an upcoming loyalty payment after putting in an official transfer request. But such was my determination to bring about change, I went ahead anyway, handing the board a handwritten letter. As George predicted, it did no good whatsoever. The bid for Sutton came to nothing as I continued to flounder in the same miserable vein. Consequently, I decided to withdraw my heartfelt request, reasoning that there was no point losing money as well as dignity. Best to soldier on and hope for an eventual resolution.

In the meantime, I had to make sure I was contributing something on the occasions our boss felt me worthy of a starting place. In the 1992/93 season, that amounted to twenty-seven league games out of forty-two. Though some were missed through injury, this was still something of a come-down from those halcyon days of being automatic choice.

A rare highlight came in the fourth-round FA Cup replay that had us travelling up to Leeds on a misty February evening. Without a goal in nine matches since returning from injury, I opened the scoring in our eventual 3–2 win by skipping ahead of David Weatherall at the near post to clip a first-time shot above John Lukic. It was my type of finish, a sharp poacher's effort, the sort I'd regularly snap up when playing well. More promising still, Wrighty had provided the cross. Perhaps our partnership could work after all.

Four days later, that prospect gained legs when I pinched two goals at Selhurst Park in a convincing 3–1 defeat of Crystal Palace in the first leg of the League Cup semi-final. This was more like it, the Smudger of old. Could I possibly kick on to put the bad times behind me?

Unfortunately not. The following couple of months passed by unremarkably, my form mediocre, my spirits low, with niggling injuries, never a problem before, now playing their part. As a result, despite that brace against Palace, it wasn't a huge surprise to only make the substitutes' bench for the League Cup final, the first of two Wembley duels with Sheffield Wednesday towards the end of the 1992/93 season.

On the plus side, our gradual transformation from title challengers to cup team meant that if I was going to suffer, and suffer I did, at least it would be at a club where something good was happening. Here was a chance to do what no English team had managed before – win both domestics cups in the same season. History in the making. A great opportunity.

Pleasingly, the first part of that opportunity was grasped with both hands. Less enjoyably, I watched the entire ninety minutes with my tracksuit on. I'd like to say that League Cup final was dull, lacking real excitement and remembered more for the unfortunate accident that saw match-winner Stevie Morrow break his arm after Tony Adams hoisted him up and clumsily dropped him in the post-match celebrations.

Yes, I'd like to say that because as an unused sub you tend to view proceedings through a negative lens. It can't have been any good if I wasn't playing. That sort of thing. But I've got to be honest. This was a lively affair, full of goalmouth incident. Wednesday played some slick football and so did we. It had most things you'd want from a major final.

So on to the big one – the mother of all matches for those of a certain age, for those growing up in the 1960s and 1970s. FA Cup finals were always a huge event, the most important date in the football calendar. At about ten in the morning, I'd claim a spot on the carpet in front of the telly and lie there all day, glued to the build-up – so comprehensive back then – that took you into the team hotels, let you meet the players' wives and girlfriends (long before WAGS) and even encompassed a ride on the team coaches bound for Wembley Stadium. It was magical, watching all this unfold. I dreamed of the day I'd get there myself. Oh, to tread those sacred pastures on a sunny May afternoon before climbing, as victors, the thirty-nine steps leading to the Royal Box and that famous trophy. That would be a major highlight in anyone's book.

Well, that's what I thought at the time anyway. It's funny how reality can turn out so differently, how it stubbornly refuses to conform to expectations. The script had already drastically diverted from the ideal path in the months leading up to these showpiece affairs.

For instance, by the time the much-anticipated FA Cup semi-final with Tottenham came around in early April 1993, I had amassed the grand total of two league goals. Pathetic; certainly no kind of form for an occasion like this – an obvious chance to exact revenge for the old enemy's 3–1 victory at the same stage two years before. George Graham, it seemed, wholeheartedly agreed.

Sat on the second row of Wembley's old bench, I had to crane my neck to see Tony Adams head home a free-kick for the only goal of a sterile game. 'The Donkey Won the Derby': that's how it was coined, a reference to the insults long since endured by our steadfast skipper. Rushing across at the end to congratulate Tone, I couldn't help feeling empty, downcast with the situation. Yes, we had reached the FA Cup final, a fantastic achievement, but I was in no mood to relish the big day.

Again, the gaffer concurred. Kev Campbell was chosen once more to partner Ian Wright. I couldn't complain. To be honest, I didn't want to complain, such was my state of mind around that time. These two cup finals, in truth, had just happened to pop up during the worst period of my career when self-belief had dipped to an all-time low. It followed that I wasn't in the mood to be questioning the manager's judgement. In any case, I knew that any banging on doors, demanding to know why I wasn't starting, would be met with short shrift by our hard-headed boss. My long-awaited cup final wasn't going to pan out quite how I had imagined.

Mind you, I didn't miss much in that game on 15 May. Unlike our earlier encounter with Wednesday, this final interminably dragged on bereft of excitement, save a couple of goals, one for either side. Wrighty's excellent header laid down a first-half marker before David Hirst eventually replied after the break. In the event, I got to run around for quite some time, replacing Ray Parlour just after the hour to lead the line right through to the end of extra time.

A replay: not what anyone wanted. As players, we shook

hands at the end with something of a weary sigh, knowing we'd have to go through all this again the following Thursday night. As for the country in general, we suspected that plenty of people were getting a bit bored of this drawn-out saga between the same clubs.

That said, once the Thursday rolled around a buzz of excitement returned to our ranks. This was, after all, the FA Cup final, an event still ardently watched by millions around the world. Nobody wanted to miss out and I, among others, badly wanted that medal to complete my set of domestic trophies. David O'Leary had always regaled us with stories about the time Arsenal reached the final three years in a row. A winner in 1979 thanks to Alan Sunderland's iconic last-gasp goal against Manchester United, David also started in the 1–0 defeats either side to Ipswich Town and West Ham United. Imagine that – reaching three finals on the trot. Apparently, the financial rewards from various sources were quite something back then.

Yet few were preoccupied with money this time, since our official bonus was hardly a life-changer. If you started the final, an appearance fee of £3000 was due, with the subs getting half that amount. And if we ended up winning the cup, £400 would be paid for every appearance made along the way, which came to £2400 if you played in every tie, discounting replays. Even in 1993 that wasn't anything to be getting excited about if you were a top player. We strongly suspected other clubs paid a little more. Still, there was nothing we could do about that now. Our minds had to be focused on finishing the job for football reasons, rather than fixating on the Spanish holiday home you could have bought with the proceeds.

More immediately for me, it was about hoping I'd make the

team this time. Missing out twice was bad enough. I didn't want to make it a hat-trick of substitute appearances. And, praise be to God, that mercifully didn't happen. George came to his senses by naming me in the side to face Trevor Francis's lot.

On the night, the skies opened up, torrential rain lending a much different feel to this famous event. On top of that, kick-off was put back thirty minutes after a bad accident on the M1 had delayed thousands of Wednesday fans travelling south. All in all, circumstances were stacking up to make this occasion far removed from the one of childhood dreams when you lifted the cup, knackered and sweaty, following a classic on a roasting Saturday afternoon.

Still, no time to be getting caught up in emotional clichés. There was a game to be played, hopefully won, and I had a chance to make a mark. Granted, the portents weren't good in terms of my form, but that didn't mean I was on to a sure-fire loser. I reasoned anything could happen on the big day.

And plenty did happen, including me getting booked for the one and only time in my career. But first to a more useful contribution. On the twenty-minute mark, I flicked a first-time volley between two defenders to release Ian Wright for a chance that – surprise, surprise – he coolly finished.

I was happy with that. If I couldn't do the business as a goalscorer, assisting our main threat was the next best donation. Strange really, because I wasn't struggling for confidence when it came to the kind of deft touch that created that chance, only the more decisive ones in front of goal. No matter. George Graham's decision to pick me had been partly vindicated. Pacing the touchline, he must have been fairly pleased.

Mind you, it didn't take long for his mood to change as my contribution took a turn for the worse. Every time I failed to get hold of the ball, every time a Wednesday defender nicked it away, George would be up on his feet, bawling angrily my way, gesturing for me to be stronger in these important duels. That was always a bugbear of our manager's – seeing his centre-forward lose the ball this way. Of all the criticisms I received off him over the years, this was the most common. It really wound him up.

Yet there was an element to this I felt George never fully understood. Either that or he chose to ignore it in favour of fury. The thing about retaining possession in these circumstances, when you've got an opponent aggressively biting away from close behind, is that it's vital you stay nice and relaxed as the ball approaches. If you're not, if you start feeling anxious about the whole situation, knowing a bollocking will result from poor control, the body tenses up. And when that happens, producing a cushioned first touch becomes very difficult indeed. It's a vicious circle. The harder you try, the worse it gets, the ball bouncing off a stiff torso. Not that our boss, going crazy on the touchline, was going to consider that. It seemed like he didn't stop yelling for most of the match.

Oh God, I wish he'd just shut up, I thought, fretfully toiling away. *Yes, I bloody know I've got to get hold of the ball. Can't you see I'm trying?*

But it was no good. George didn't let go and I continued to suffer in an endless tussle that, thanks to Chris Waddle's deflected equaliser, went into extra time for the second time. It was during this period that my scandalous booking occurred following a brief tangle with their substitute midfielder, Graham Hyde. When we both ended up on the deck, referee Keren Barratt awarded a free-kick Wednesday's way. Perched on my hands and knees with the ball sat temptingly in front, I instinctively knocked it away with my hand, just to buy a little time, to get back into position.

Oh no, Keren wasn't having that. Out came the book, to my astonishment and mild amusement. Eleven years it had taken to get on the wrong side of the law. All those games, all those skirmishes, some of which had actually done serious damage.

One night at Luton, for instance, Steve Foster, their forthright centre-half, had to go off to have stitches after an aerial challenge saw my sharp elbow cut through the scar tissue just above his eye. Not even Fossie's famous headband could shield the blow.

'You fuckin' did me there, Smudge,' he spat on his return, jabbing a finger my way. 'I'll have you for that.'

Whether I 'did him' or not, it was purely accidental. In the rough-and-tumble 1980s, you could get away with a flailing elbow. The 1990s, however, didn't seem so keen on petty infringements, judging by the reason for that yellow card.

'I administered an official caution for Ungentlemanly Conduct to the No. 9 of Arsenal FC Alan Smith,' so explained Barratt on the FA's official report players receive in the post. 'This was after he had blatantly and most deliberately knocked the ball away with his hand after a free kick had been awarded to the opposing team in an attempt to delay the taking of the free kick.'

Fair enough. Guilty as charged. As the ref doled out his punishment, I'm sure I heard a faint gasp seep from the Arsenal end. 'Smudge getting booked? You can't do that!'

Well, he could. And to be honest, I was quite glad I'd blotted my copybook. Nobody wants to be called goody-two-shoes, do they? Now I could be known as a hard-hitting tough guy who takes no shit. Well, something like that anyway.

As for extra time, I could have erased all the anguish that came before with a goal that would have surely secured the FA Cup. Made one, scored one. Forget about a few poor touches along the way, such a record could have easily clinched the man-of-the-match award.

But that opportunity went begging when, faced with a one-on-one against Chris Woods in goal, my tentative flick lacked power and precision, clipping off Woods to trickle wide of the far post. Turning away, my face screwed up in frustration. 'That was it, Smudge,' I angrily muttered to myself. 'That was your chance to score the winner in an FA Cup final.'

Thankfully, Andy Linighan would soon render that miss totally irrelevant, to the team at least. Our centre-half would finally end a well-matched contest that, in a minute or so, would have been decided by penalties for the first time in the competition's history.

But we had won a corner so, in the 119th minute, everyone moved into their assigned positions. On the night, George had put me at the near post, which hadn't always been my role. In the fruitful years, I'd start on the edge of the box with Tony Adams, charging in to try and meet Bouldy's attempted flick on. Not tonight though. George had other plans.

Paul Merson swung one in. It flew over my head and that of a few others before firmly meeting the forehead of the towering Linighan, nursing a broken nose after a dubious first-half challenge by Mark Bright who, perhaps fittingly, was marking Andy at this corner. The resulting header was strong, if not brilliantly directed, arrowing straight towards Woods, ready on the goal line. That looked to be that – our final chance gone to seal the deal and avoid penalties. But no. For some reason Woods let the ball slip from his grasp like a bar of soap and it crossed the line before my mate Hyde, positioned on the post, could do much about it.

No way back now. Wednesday's Thursday was ruined. We'd won the FA Cup after a compelling contest so much more enthralling than the drab original. That said, I felt pretty crap. It had been a match to forget in terms of performance. So when the boss marched over, I thought it best to say something before he got in first.

'I'd just like to apologise for that performance, boss. Couldn't do anything right tonight.'

In the event, I needn't have bothered. In the wake of glory, George had forgotten all about his earlier complaints. He batted off my apology with a wide smile and hug, much more concerned with the end result than any small details along the way.

Maybe there was a lesson to be learned here, one I should have taken on board. Don't be too hard on yourself. Don't be so self-critical. You certainly aren't pulling up trees just now but neither have you hit rock bottom. Look at the facts. You've just created a goal for the winning side in an FA Cup final. Things can't be too bad. Lighten up a little. Keep things in perspective. Plenty out there would love to be in your place as a double league winner with two Golden Boots and both domestic cups now in the bag. So cheer up. Enjoy the moment. After all, it isn't every day you parade the FA Cup around Wembley, even if the occasion didn't quite match that dizzy dream you harboured as a boy.

In any case, there was still time for all that, though I could never have guessed. Twelve months on from this soggy evening, my part in a final would bring those comic-book fantasies spectacularly to life.

SLICING UP PARMA

It started with tears – those of Ian Wright. He got booked in the first half of our tussle with Paris Saint-Germain in the semi-final second leg of the European Cup Winners' Cup, the competition we'd qualified for by winning the FA Cup. Ian was now going to miss the final through suspension. If we got there, that is. 'Where's Wrighty?' George Graham impatiently asked at half-time. With us leading 1–0 through Kevin Campbell's early header, this was going to be an important team talk. Everyone looked nonplussed. Our striker was nowhere to be seen. Wrighty had actually taken himself off to the shower area where he was pacing up and down, bursting with frustration at the cold reality. Having done so much to get us this far, the prospect of missing the best bit cut him to the bone. Among others, Tony Adams and the boss tried to calm Wrighty down, urging him to concentrate for the next forty-five minutes, otherwise nobody would be flying to Copenhagen. And to his eternal credit, Wrighty did just that. Wracked with remorse for a silly tackle that earned that fateful yellow card, he managed to regain his composure to put in a disciplined performance that helped see us through.

Time to celebrate. This was some achievement, to reach the final of a strong competition that featured Real Madrid, Ajax,

Benfica and Bayer Leverkusen. Not only that, Arsenal had only ever won one European competition – the Inter-Cities Fairs Cup back in 1970. Adding a second would mean a lot to the club.

And it was no mean feat to come through all the tactical tests that any European adventure throws up. I think George Graham, in particular, felt incredibly chuffed. On a personal front, he saw it as a valuable addition to his managerial CV, having changed his approach to these continental ties after learning a lot from our European Cup experience in 1991.

That campaign started so promisingly, when a 6–1 thrashing of Austria Vienna included four goals in quick succession from Arsenal's number 9. Everything fell for me that night. Of the four, you would probably describe three as poacher's efforts. But not my hat-trick goal, a spectacular diving header beautifully set up by the outside of Paul Merson's right boot. It was some night. I mean, who scores four goals in the European Cup? Well, Dean Saunders for a start. The man who nearly ruined our title chances with Derby in 1989 had also grabbed four that same night in Liverpool's UEFA Cup trouncing of Finnish side Kuusysi Lahti. Deano, don't try and steal my thunder, old son. It's never going to work.

That Austria Vienna game also sticks out for something I had never done before and never did again – intentionally dive to win a penalty. Don't ask me why I did it. It was a spur of the moment thing as I saw the tackle coming in. Looking at the replays now, it wasn't a bad effort at all, even if you measure it against the expert simulation we now see in this country on a weekly basis. In real time, it looks for all the world like my opponent chopped me down when, in reality, he missed me completely as I tumbled to the turf. In the TV studio that evening, even Kenny Dalglish, with the benefit of replays, thought it a penalty, reasoning that, though contact was minimal, I had to take evasive action to avoid the challenge. I knew differently though. Picking myself up, I felt a bit sheepish. This was new territory – trying to deceive the ref. Even worse, I had succeeded in winning a penalty at a crucial stage (it was still 0–0 at the time) in such a big game. Thoughtfully, Lee Dixon made me feel a bit better by crashing his effort against the crossbar. And come the end of the match, I had almost forgotten about the aberration amid all the talk of my heroics.

Some time later, however, it got dragged up again and there was no one to blame but myself. Jerome Anderson, my agent at the time, thought I should raise my profile with a big newspaper interview. I might have recently won two league titles and two Golden Boots, but my quiet nature, my aversion to the limelight, meant my profile wasn't as high as some others at the time. Jerome thought it a good idea to change that, for commercial purposes more than anything else. Though this felt a bit awkward, putting myself out there, I reluctantly agreed so we set up a meeting with Bob Harris, a very well-known journalist with one of the tabloids.

When we met at Jerome's modest office in Edgware, Bob came straight to the point. 'If we're going to do this, Alan, you need to have something quite newsworthy to say. There's no point otherwise.' Right, I thought. What can I give him? Then it occurred to me – that dive against Austria Vienna. So I recounted in detail exactly how I conned the ref to win the penalty, how it was so out of character and filled me with guilt. This seemed to do the trick. Bob's shorthand got quicker. I could almost hear his brain ticking over. *'Squeaky clean Alan Smith, yet to be booked in his career, shockingly admits to cheating.* Yes, they'll be happy with that in the office. We can make a nice splash.' Bob shut his notebook soon afterwards, pleased with our chat.

I, on the other hand, didn't feel entirely comfortable, knowing the upcoming article would cause a fuss. I could see the headline now. It filled me with dread. On the upside, I was satisfied that I had made it clear this sort of simulation was a one-off, that I would never consider doing it again. If this is what it takes to boost my sponsorship earnings, then so be it. I'll just have to stomach it. It might go against the grain but, hey, you've got to make hay while the sun shines, haven't you? It's a very short career. Now this might sound like someone desperately trying to convince themselves. And you'd be right. Against my better judgement, I went down a road that didn't suit. As if to prove that point, the boss pulled me aside a few days after the article was published to say the FA were less than impressed with my confession. They might have to take action, he said. Admitting to diving? It brings the game into disrepute. Oh, God. Wouldn't you know it? The one time I try to be vaguely outspoken, the authorities come crashing down. But much to my relief, nothing happened in the end. Just like the accused standing in the dock for a first offence, previous good behaviour may have been taken into account.

Time to move on. Having seen off the Austrians with no little élan, Benfica were next in the second round. Managed by Sven-Göran Eriksson, they looked a decent team, though nothing to be getting overly worried about. A 1–1 draw over there in their cavernous old stadium seemed to confirm that impression. We flew back from Lisbon feeling fairly confident of finishing the job at Highbury. Unfortunately, it didn't quite work out that way. Though we went a goal up through the unlikely figure of Colin Pates, Benfica outmanoeuvred us with their pace and tactical nous. That said, I missed a sitter, so did Tony Adams during the course of a tussle that went to extra time. Then came the kill when Vasili Kulkov and Isaias, a very lively Brazilian who had tormented us all night, delivered the fatal blows. We could have no complaints. It had been a harsh lesson in the necessities and nuances of European football. George Graham, I know, was absolutely gutted, not just about going out of the competition but getting outwitted from a tactical standpoint. I think he saw it as a personal slight, a black mark on his coaching reputation, something that wasn't going to happen again on his watch if he could possibly help it. And it didn't, as proved by us reaching two European finals on the trot.

That first campaign, which ended in glory, involved some very tight tussles along the way. From Odense to Torino to PSG, none of them made it easy over two legs. Only Standard Liège, whipped 10–0 on aggregate, allowed us to play free of tension and pressure. The Torino tie, in particular, proved a really hard slog, especially out there in the Stadio delle Alpi, a huge, charmless bowl devoid of atmosphere where, four years before, England had fallen to West Germany in the World Cup semi-final. Talk about a dull game. Man-marked by the dogged Angelo Gregucci, I hardly got sight of goal over ninety rain-soaked minutes. Not even the great Enzo Francescoli, starring for the Italians, could add any colour to this monochrome affair. Not that we were all that bothered. A goalless draw in Turin set us up nicely for the home leg where we scraped through 1–0 thanks to a Tony Adams header.

So on to the semi-final and a trip to Paris where George Weah and David Ginola were leading the charge. Taming that pair was surely the key. And we did for fifty minutes. At the Parc des Princes, Lee Dixon began a feisty, entertaining scrap with Ginola that would continue for years, right through the flamboyant Frenchman's time in England with Newcastle, Tottenham and Aston Villa. With that duel as an interesting sideshow, we went about the business of trying to grab a precious away goal. And when I was fouled in the right-hand channel, Ian Wright brilliantly headed home Paul Davis's free-kick.

One–nil up at half-time, that interval has since passed into Arsenal folklore. There seem to be several stories of what exactly happened, how a new chant came about, but the most popular version goes like this: when the stadium PA system started blasting out *Go West* by The Pet Shop Boys, a big hit at the time, the Arsenal fans joyously put their own words to the tune. '1–0 to the Arsenal!' was born, a song that, thanks to the result, reached a crescendo in Copenhagen and a song that can be heard to this day when the score line demands.

On this occasion, however, it didn't finish 1–0. And I will never forget Ginola's equaliser that night, a glancing near-post header from a well-worked corner. Tony and Bouldy had been in Ginola's ear all match, winding him up, trying to put him off. Merse joined in the fun at that particular corner, laughing over his shoulder as he stood in front, charged with stopping the cross from reaching the danger man. So good was the delivery, though, that Merse could do nothing to prevent Ginola from scoring with a really cute flick from a tight angle. Wheeling away in celebration, he suddenly remembered all the stick he'd been getting, so quickly turned back to give his tormentors a mouthful. Tony and Bouldy could only suck it up.

Sat in the dressing room afterwards, though, none of us could be too upset with the draw and an away goal against a very dangerous team. The only doubt in our minds was that we'd been here before when that draw on Benfica's patch felt like a great result. But surely we were wiser this time thanks to that experience? George definitely thought so, having changed our shape for these European ties in an effort to become more solid in midfield where continental sides can absolutely kill you. As a result, we were using 4–3–3 this time, with two from Ian Wright, Paul Merson and Kevin Campbell lining up either side of me. 4–4–2 on a Saturday. 4–3–3 in the week. It took a fair bit of work on the training ground to successfully make the switch. But the boss was determined not to get caught out again, hence a lot of laborious shadow play – who goes where and when – in the days leading up to every match. For us lot, it was a bit of a pain, walking through various situations for an hour or so. But we certainly knew, as did the gaffer, that without good preparation the new system could fall flat on its face.

With that painful Benfica experience in mind, then, the challenge was clear. A clean sheet in north London would do the job. And that's exactly what we got, just about anyway, after our talented visitors, on a wet and windy night, tried everything possible with some very slick stuff.

When the final whistle blew, Highbury erupted. Arsenal were through to a European final for the first time in fourteen years. And so to Denmark, home of Hans Christian Andersen, a fella who knew a thing or two about fairy tales.

Some things seem very important at the time, only to appear insignificant when looking back. On this particular occasion, an extremely big one for everyone concerned, the Arsenal lads were disappointed in the quality of our hotel, a fairly basic affair just outside Copenhagen. The rooms were quite sparse, with very few frills, just a low single bed, a simple bedside table and wardrobe in the corner. It was like somewhere you'd stay for pre-season training, when it's more about the outdoor facilities than anything inside. There were a few moans and groans about the club being tight. For a European final couldn't they afford something better than this?

Under the circumstances, we thought a bit of five-star luxury wouldn't have gone amiss, something to reflect the grandeur of the occasion. In fairness, though, I think the club had chosen this hotel for its location, a quiet suburban district where we could prepare in peace, rather than having inebriated fans keeping us up all night.

On the plus side, the food was pretty good, which is always important. Few things are guaranteed to get footballers moaning more than dodgy meals leading up to a match. And once we had settled down, accepted our surroundings, thoughts quickly turned to the job in hand.

On the night of the match John Jensen hobbled across to my wife. On crutches after tearing cruciate ligaments, he growled his prediction with that lovable grin. 'Penny, we will win 1–0 tonight and Smudger will get the goal. I'm telling you. I've just got a feeling.' At the time, Pen thought nothing of it. JJ was just being JJ, one of the most popular members of the squad, a really good lad who, in the best British tradition, loved a beer and a fag. He might not have set the world alight at Arsenal, having arrived with a big reputation following his spectacular winning goal for Denmark in the 1992 European Championship final, but the midfielder settled quickly in the dressing room. We all loved JJ so felt for him when that serious knee injury ruled him out of this final in his home city. It wasn't like we could afford to lose experienced players from a midfield department that wasn't the strongest to begin with. It got further depleted on the day of the game when Dave Hillier and Martin Keown failed fitness tests. Martin was the closest of the two but, used as a midfield destroyer at the time, he couldn't be persuaded to give it a go.

With all due respect to Stevie Morrow and Ian Selley (both excellent on the night), these weren't names that would have Parma quaking in their boots.

Mind you, I don't suppose the Italians were impressed with many in our team. They certainly didn't look it as our paths crossed the night before. We had just finished our stint on the pitch, an hour of light work getting used to the surface and surroundings. I always loved those sessions. Short and sharp, they were a chance to imagine all the good things that might happen the following night. Our work done, we trudged off, laughing and joking as usual, perhaps not looking the smartest in our training kit. The Parma lads, on the other hand, looked absolutely immaculate as only Italian teams can, waiting by the corner flag for us to leave. These impromptu meetings are always intriguing. It's a chance to get a close look, to size up opponents by examining small details – boots, shinpads, haircuts, the lot. On this occasion, the Parma players looked us up and down with what we interpreted, rightly or wrongly, as a look of disdain, a look that said, 'Who the hell are you? You don't deserve to be on the same pitch'. As you can imagine, that perceived insult got our dander up. 'Did you see that lot? Cocky bastards! Think they're the dog's bollocks. We'll show 'em.'

In their defence, this was a more than useful Parma outfit. As holders of the trophy, they clearly regarded themselves as favourites and, looking at the star-studded line-up, it was hard to disagree. As well as the usual names mentioned – Gianfranco Zola, Tomas Brolin and Faustino Asprilla – half of Italy's World Cup squad seemed to be there, the squad that would go on that summer to reach the final in the US, only losing to Brazil after penalties. As well as Zola, Luca Bucci, the goalie, Antonio Benarrivo, Luigi Apolloni and Lorenzo Minotti all appeared in Los Angeles on the Azzurri teamsheet. Quite a challenge, then. Especially without Ian Wright, our go-to match winner.

What we did have, however, was fantastic support on the night. Jogging out for the warm-up, the noise hit us straight away. All the lads were amazed at the number of flags and banners around three-quarters of a ground decked in red and white. This was going to be like a home game. We returned to the dressing room a little more confident than when we had left.

Adding to the armoury was a back four in its pomp. Tony Adams has since said that the defensive unit formed in 1988 reached its peak that night in the Parken Stadium. The know-how, understanding and fitness within that quartet was as good as it ever got, even though they all continued at the top for several more years. Not only that, Dave Seaman was one of the best keepers around, as proved by some fantastic saves that night, despite a cracked rib requiring painkilling injections

If the Parma players, the forwards in particular, were unaware quite how good that defence had become, Nevio Scala, their manager, must have had a clue. Scala, after all, came with a great reputation for being a talented coach with a sharp eye for detail. Mind you, he had Zola, Brolin and Asprilla up front. With such quality, you could forgive him for believing that, at some point, a way through would be found.

And they very nearly succeeded after only twenty seconds when Asprilla raced clear. It looked like only Seaman could stop the Colombian, until Bouldy's long leg came out of nowhere to execute a brilliant sliding tackle. Shortly afterwards, Brolin's diving header landed on top of the net, before the same player hit the post after a swift counterattack. All this and only thirteen minutes gone. We were gasping for breath, searching for our second wind as Parma went for the kill. This bore all the hallmarks of a very long night for the hassled back-pedallers wearing red and white.

But then a goal came out of nothing in the twentieth minute. Showing for Lee Dixon's throw-in, the regular drill, I laid the ball back before spinning into space. Lee then tried to find Merse with a swinging left leg, but his attempt fell short and found Lorenzo Minotti instead. At this point, any hint of danger should have disappeared. As Parma's captain, Minotti was a top-class defender, fast and versatile, not one known for making silly mistakes. For some reason, however, he made the wrong choice that night by going for a risky overhead kick that – would you believe it? – headed straight my way. There was only one thing for it. Taking the ball on my chest, I had to act fast. With opponents quickly converging, I dared not wait until the bouncing ball dropped to a perfect height, so took it early, jumping to catch it cleanly with my left instep. For a second, Bucci's desperate dive masked my view of the outcome. But when the keeper crashed to the ground I could see the ball had rebounded off the inside of the right-hand post and was happily rolling along in the back of the net.

Cue pandemonium as I ran to the corner screaming with joy. I had never been one to think ahead about goal celebrations, preferring to let my emotions take care of the moment. That approach usually led to pretty standard fare – two arms aloft, maybe an embarrassing high five. This one certainly had the second bit as I twisted around to celebrate with Merse, first on the scene. But it also contained an outpouring of emotion that I hadn't experienced for a very long time. This goal, after all, felt like a port in a storm after so many testing days when the whole business of football lost its appeal. To most on the outside, this may sound way over the top. He's a professional footballer, playing for Arsenal. How bad can things be, for God's sake? A friend once said exactly that. Champagne Phil, so-called because he used to crack open a bottle of bubbly up in the East Stand when Arsenal scored, couldn't quite sympathise with my lowly mood. As a leading expert in mental health, more qualified than most to understand the challenges of everyday life, my situation was nothing compared to the problems he tackled in the wider community. As a rabid Arsenal fan, Phil would have given anything to take my place, whatever the ups and downs along the way.

Even he couldn't see that it isn't so simple when you are caught up in the middle. Perspective goes missing as problems get heavier. As much as you tell yourself this really isn't important, that it's only a game, it doesn't do much good. You cannot get out of the rut. And, the odd bright spot apart, it had been that way for two or three years.

Mind you, Nelson Mandela wasn't to know, which feels like a very strange sentence to write at this particular point. To explain: we'd met the great man only nine months before during a pre-season tour of South Africa. Manchester United completed a line-up including the country's two most famous teams, Orlando Pirates and Kaizer Chiefs.

And it was at the beginning of our final friendly with the Chiefs in Johannesburg that Mandela's motorcade eased into the stadium to be met by huge roars from the sell-out crowd. Quite a moment. Released three years before from his 27-year incarceration, Mandela was a living legend amongst his people, soon to become President the following year.

Walking along the line, he had a friendly word for everyone, that famous, beaming smile never leaving his face. Coming to me, he said, 'Ah, you're the one who scores all the goals.' A smartarse might say he'd been away for too long.

Because when that ball hit the net in Copenhagen, it was like turning back the clock to 1991, a much happier time when these kinds of moments, these sorts of feelings, regularly came around.

Mind you, I hadn't experienced anything like this: a European final, a different story altogether from domestic triumphs. To come good on this stage added something valuable to your CV, confirming you as a player capable of adjusting to and thriving against a different style of football. In short, it meant a great deal.

We had to win first, though, otherwise, in years to come, my goal would be reduced to a tiny footnote. And the prospects of victory began to look bleak when Parma continued where they had left off. In other words, throwing everything at it. Zola was at the forefront, first going close with a free-kick before forcing Dave Seaman to pull off his best save of the night.

After that, there were several nervy moments that could have gone the other way – offside decisions and last-ditch tackles. Lee Dixon, for instance, can't help laughing when remembering a scything challenge in the box that poleaxed his man. Somehow, the ref waved play on. In the end, then, a combination of acute defensive nous, sheer determination and a bit of luck saw our heroic back four emerge unscathed. Against all the odds, we had come out on top. When the final whistle blew, the Arsenal flags waved, the fans went ballistic and the players jumped around, struggling to believe we had actually done it.

My emotions were a jumble as teammates rushed across to say well done. Of course, I was happy, but at the same time something held me back. This couldn't compensate for the lack of enjoyment over the last few seasons. I would have swapped this moment in a flash for scoring fifteen to twenty goals in each of those campaigns, for returning to the confident figure of years gone by. I looked up to the stand, trying to pick out Penny, just as I had at Anfield in 1989. In moments like this, you desperately want to see loved ones that have lived through the tough times as well as the good. Penny had been my sounding board, someone willing to listen. Among all the faces, I couldn't pick her out.

The trophy handed over, a scrum of photographers yelled for me to hold it aloft. OK by me, for a short time anyway, but after a bit I felt uncomfortable, standing there taking the glory.

Back in the dressing room, I slumped down next to Bouldy. 'You've done it all now, Smudge,' he grinned. 'A goal at Anfield, two Golden Boots and now this.' I looked across at my mate, happy to just smile. In the short time since the final whistle, I hadn't given a thought to the broader context – for all of us really, not just me. Since the majority came together in 1988, this group had won every domestic honour going. This felt like the icing on the cake, only Arsenal's second European trophy in history.

More than enough reason to celebrate, then. Well, it would have been, if the club hadn't arranged to fly us straight back that night, knowing the last game of the season, Newcastle away, would have been vital for European qualification if we hadn't won here. So after joining the gaffer in the post-match press conference, I quickly showered and changed to join the lads on the coach. All the wives and girlfriends were waiting on the plane. Once on board, Penny quickly told me what JJ had said, his prediction I would score in a 1–0 win. I couldn't believe it. What made him think that? Not only that, she described the look on my dad's face when she jumped on the coach that was taking him and her own dad back to the airport. They'd clearly had an amazing time, enjoying lunch in Tivoli Gardens before a couple of beers in a sunny town square full of Arsenal fans. For them, having it end like this was an absolute dream. Sitting on the back seat of the bus next to my equally merry father-in-law, Penny said Dad's flushed face beamed with overwhelming pride.

'Schoey had us standing on our seats at the end!' my dad said, laughing.

'I feel like a celebrity!' Allan shot back. 'Everyone keeps coming up to say well done.'

It brought a tear to Penny's eye, seeing them like this, her father and father-in-law joined at the hip, lapping up every second of this special day. She loved my mom and dad dearly, having known them for so long. She knew how much it meant to 'Bobby Dazzler' (her nickname for Dad) to see his son shine on the big stage. Not only that, Penny's own dad, Allan, had always been a football nut. Once a regular at Villa Park, Schoey turned his attention to non-league Alvechurch and became the lynchpin at the Southern League club. And if that hadn't happened, I would never have met the girl who became my wife. Listening to the events of the day, then, I was so pleased that our dads had made the trip, to sample the atmosphere on a quite wonderful night in Copenhagen.

The short flight home was filled with champagne and song, including a chant to salute my contribution. Much to my embarrassment, 'Walking in a Smudger Wonderland!' rang out several times. Being the centre of attention has never sat right. Mind you, more was to come. After walking through customs at Stansted in the early hours, Tony Adams, the boss and I stood posing for photos with the shiny trophy, looking a little dishevelled in our Arsenal blazers.

Less than forty-eight hours later, we travelled to Newcastle for a match that, in the players' eyes at least, had become a dead rubber. Mentally, we were already on the beach, with a Cup Winners' Cup medal tucked down our trunks. Unsurprisingly, though, George Graham did not see it that way. He wanted a strong finish, a good performance at St James' Park, to round off a league season that, in the end, saw us finish fourth, twenty-one points behind champions Manchester United.

Now, George had been the kind of player who enjoyed a good drink. He knew the score, especially at times like this when focus, let's say, was not at its peak. For him, the alarm bells probably rang louder when, on checking in to our hotel on the Friday afternoon, we heard that a wedding reception was taking place that night. Ooh, really? Sounds interesting. A few of the lads fancied poking their heads round the door. So as part of his plans to keep the squad in check, George asked Stewart Houston to go around our rooms that evening, just to make sure everyone was behaving. Stewart's tactic was to knock on our rooms and, when the door opened, poke in his nose to smell for anything suspicious. As bad luck would have it, when he came to us, my roommate, goalkeeper Alan Miller, and I had just taken delivery of four Budweisers to toast the achievement of two days before. Stewart walked in, surveying the scene. 'Just a couple of beers,' we said. 'Nothing to get excited about.' Under the circumstances, we felt this was the least we deserved, especially as some of our teammates had sneaked downstairs to say hello to the bride. I'm not sure if Stewart or the gaffer ever found out about that. For Stewart, this was embarrassing enough – having to warn people like me and 'Maxi'. 'Just make sure that's all you have then, lads,' he said, sheepishly. 'Big game tomorrow.'

It wasn't of course, as clearly shown by our half-hearted efforts in a 2–0 defeat. Still, it had been quite a week, one we would always remember with tremendous pride.

THE MAN WHO WOULD BE KING

He wasn't there when I signed, which only added to the mystique. Away with the team in Portugal on a mid-season break in March 1987, he would remain a stranger for a few weeks yet. Only a year into the job, George Graham was already building a reputation as a stickler for discipline in the old Arsenal way he first encountered as a player under Bertie Mee and Don Howe back in the 1970s.

I was just about old enough to remember those days when an elegant style and, so it was said, a certain aversion to hard work earned him the nickname of 'Stroller'. But he scored some important goals, did George, in playing a key part in the 1970/71 double triumph. Though he moved on to Manchester United in 1972, his six years at Highbury clearly left a profound mark that would go on to shape his personality and management philosophy.

'*Remember who you are, what you are and who you represent.*' While this longstanding club maxim is thought to have originated with Mee, George carried the baton with zeal, forever reminding his players about their responsibilities as an Arsenal employee.

Until I joined Arsenal, I could only go on the stuff I'd seen on telly, when the suave Scot invariably spoke with authority and charisma. The day he took charge at Arsenal was a case in point. Full of self-assurance, he strode on to the pitch, looking every inch the part in a smart Prince of Wales check suit to mark his first TV appearance in his new role. Towards the end, the interviewer asked about the perils of football management.

'One of my old managers once said that this is the only job when you know you're going to get the sack,' he said, smiling. 'The only thing not on the contract is the date it will happen! I thought it quite funny at the time. Maybe I won't think it's funny in the future.'

No, he certainly wouldn't. On that sunny spring day in 1986, George could never have foreseen the circumstances involved in his dramatic dismissal eight-and-a-half years later.

As for me, I was immediately struck by the confident demeanour, which probably played a large part in my decision to join the Gunners. This was clearly a man going places in charge of a team full of youthful promise.

Always immaculately suited and booted on matchdays in his Arsenal blazer, gold cannon on the breast, George rarely missed the chance on other days to pull on his tracksuit. Actually, that's not strictly accurate. Weather permitting, he loved to wear shorts, regarding his legs, I suspect, as a prime feature. With that unmistakable trot, you could see him coming a mile off.

Seeing this figure approach, everyone stopped messing about. We knew the upcoming session would be intense. If we weren't practising team shape, we'd be working on closing down in a long rectangular area divided into three. The boxes either end saw two people trying to nick the ball off four or more opponents who chipped it to the other square once they'd strung ten passes together. Though a very demanding drill for those chasing the ball, it forged a great understanding between those grafting in tandem.

But we were used to all this. It was par for the course, with George omnipresent throughout. In fact, I can think of only a handful of occasions during his tenure when he left the training to one of his coaches. It may have been a funeral, a family matter perhaps, but rare were the times he didn't turn up. On those odd days we would naturally relax a little, maybe take a few liberties with Theo Foley or Stewart Houston, George's assistants. One morning, Niall Quinn launched himself at Theo, rugby tackling his countryman during the warm-up, with both ending up at the bottom of a grassy ditch. Thankfully, Theo wasn't the sort to get on his high horse. Both had a good laugh before brushing themselves down to continue the jog. I think everyone accepted these days were a chance to step off the gas, knowing the gaffer would soon be back to turn up the heat.

Our manager loved it on that training ground, marshalling movement, barking instructions, sometimes emphasising a point by showing you how it was done. Still relatively young in his mid-forties, more than capable of joining in, he'd stroke the ball wide towards a winger with extravagant style, arms out, holding the pose. We thought he was just as bothered by how he looked as where the ball went. True or not, we'd sneakily take the piss behind his back.

As a former striker himself, George would regularly give me lessons on heading the ball – again, using an exaggerated movement, this time to indicate the importance of using neck muscles.

'It's like this, Alan,' he'd say, drawing the head back, before jutting it forward like an excitable chicken, blowing through pursed lips at the same time. 'It's all about timing and power, using those neck muscles. And keep your eye on the ball until the last second. The maker's name. Keep looking at the maker's name.'

There was no getting away from the fact that George could head the ball. I'd seen him score some great goals that way in TV clips. It was just the way he showed us that brought on the giggles, that bobbing motion as he walked along.

Joking apart, George taught me a lot about movement around the box. We'd go through shadow play to nail down where he wanted us at particular times. And when it came to attacking a cross, the boss was full of good advice about timing your run.

'Once you're in, you can't get back out,' he'd shout, jogging towards the middle of the goal as a ball flew over his head. 'But even if you start a fraction late you still have a chance of getting on the end of a cross. So don't be too quick to dash in when the ball goes out wide. That makes it easier for defenders who can see where you are. Stay out of their eyeline. Learn to time your run.'

For me, a tall centre-forward adept in the air, this was invaluable advice. It was the same with backing into an opponent, a favourite topic. George would spend ages demonstrating the best technique. 'Try to stay side on,' he'd urge, bumping into a defender used as a guinea pig. 'That way you can hold out your arm, feel where your man is and keep more distance between him and the ball as it's played in. If you just barge in backwards, it's easier for the defender to poke round a leg.'

At the time, coaching like this felt a little laborious. I'd rather get on with some crossing and shooting. Yet when it became second nature and worked in a match, I really did appreciate the effort involved. George was an excellent teacher. So much has rightly been written about his endless work with the back four, but his input on the striker's art was also invaluable.

Away from the pitch, he was a more distant figure. This was a manager, after all, whose first rule of thumb was to keep players at arm's length, make sure business and pleasure never overlapped. For instance, I'll never forget his face on walking into a bar in Puerto Banús in Spain, only to see several of us swaying on the stage drunkenly singing 'Georgie, Georgie, stand by me . . .!' As we murdered our version of the Ben E. King classic, George quickly turned on his heels to find another watering hole.

As a player, of course, you would have probably found him up on that stage. Everyone knew George used to love a drink and a good time, never once showing an interest in the coaching side. His best mate, Frank McLintock, Arsenal's inspirational captain of the 1970/71 double-winning side, firmly backs this up.

'We'd be there after training, discussing some aspect of the game,' Frank once told me. 'You know, how we were going to handle the opposition's centre-forward that Saturday or something. But George wouldn't be interested at all. He'd never get involved. "Ah, put the ball away, will yer? Let's go and have a drink!" That was George for you. I couldn't believe it later when he got into coaching.'

Terry Venables, in truth, had plenty to do with that, persuading his close friend and former Chelsea teammate to do some stuff at QPR. As an avid student of the game, perhaps Venables's enthusiasm became infectious at a time when George needed to earn a living. From our perspective, we saw a man who'd done plenty of partying in the Swinging Sixties. As such, he knew all the tricks, every excuse, which maybe accounted for his tolerance of drinkers like Tony Adams and Paul Merson.

Ah, yes, the skipper. You know politicians often talk of the 'special relationship' between Britain and the US? Well, there was a similar understanding in north London. Tony could do no wrong in George's eyes. And when he did, when he caused a scene, say, on one of his benders, the matter would be sorted behind closed doors, with the gaffer, we assumed, gently urging Tone to go a bit easier on the socialising front.

Those meetings became regular occurrences at London Colney where the gaffer's changing room, shared with his coaches, doubled up as an office for tête-à-têtes. Situated at the top of the narrow breeze-block corridor, measuring no more than three metres square, the room would be cleared for one of Tony's visits.

As our captain, we would regularly ask him to have a word on our behalf, whether about travel arrangements, timekeeping or something more significant, invariably concerning money. Prior to the 1988/89 season, we weren't happy about bonuses, what we received for a win or draw and what we'd get for winning a trophy. It always seemed to be a bone of contention, agreeing on figures for a part of our earnings that were quite important back then. A successful season would noticeably bump up your wages, unlike today when bonuses seem incidental compared to huge salaries and signing-on fees. These bonus sheets, what's more, had to be agreed before a certain date otherwise we'd remain on the old terms until the next season, so making it vital a good deal was struck early.

'Go on, Tone, go and sort it out. Tell him we're not happy. We want a bit more.'

So in marched our representative, full of good intentions. We waited for ages outside, unable to start training until the pair had finished. What are they doing in there? Half an hour went by. Maybe forty-five minutes. Finally, our skipper emerged, looking content.

'How did it go, Tone? Have you sorted it out?'

His expression changed a bit, a sterner look accompanying the verdict.

'No, sorry, lads. The boss won't go any further. We've got to accept those figures. Take it or leave it. But I've got some good news. I've just agreed a new contract!'

'Oh, great! Really pleased for you, Tone. Glad you sorted yourself out. Don't worry about us!'

Tony took all this stick in his stride with a huge grin, never feeling too bad about us having the hump. But it was easy to forget Rodders was only in his early twenties. Made captain at twenty-one, off-the-pitch responsibilities came with the job, irrespective of whether or not he was suited to the task. He was just a boy really; admittedly blessed with natural leadership skills but a boy nonetheless, ill prepared to negotiate on behalf of the team.

George knew this. Maybe took advantage. Tony was everything he wanted from a captain – inspirational on the pitch as a marvellous defender getting the right message across, and doing it without any of the drawbacks that may come with an older player who would be more resilient in representing the team.

In this regard, Brian Marwood offered a perfect example. For a time, he was our union representative for the Professional Footballers' Association, a role he took seriously as a conscientious sort. So, when it came around again at the start of the 1989/90 season to complain about bonuses, we asked Brian to bat for us rather than Rodders.

We were adamant. The terms had to be better. We were champions of England now – that should surely be reflected in our pay packet. Although it never came to a threat of withdrawing labour, a rebellious mood hung in the air. So Brian faithfully and forcefully stated our case, insisting there would be no backing down this time.

The gaffer was furious. On the cusp of a new season, having just won the league at Anfield in sensational style, a revolt in the camp was the last thing he needed. All momentum could be lost over this matter.

In response, he called a meeting at Highbury, got the entire first team squad to squeeze into Pat Rice's tiny office opposite the home dressing room. It was packed in there. You could hardly move as George launched into his tirade, threatening to freeze out anyone who failed to fall into line.

'Right,' he said finally, looking around the group. 'Hands up those who aren't going to sign the bonus sheet.'

Silence. Nobody moved, apart from Brian who instinctively put up his hand, no doubt expecting everyone else to follow suit. But we didn't. Heads bowed, browbeaten by the lecture, all but one of the squad had crumbled under pressure. Not surprisingly, Brian wasn't happy afterwards. He thought quite rightly he'd been stitched up, hung out to dry by us caving in.

And that's how it turned out. A fall guy was born. A key component in the 1988/89 title-winning season, pivotal to our success, Brian fell out of favour, with a succession of niggly injuries further damaging his chances. When Anders Limpar turned up in the summer of 1990, Brian was soon moved on to Sheffield United. Although it took a while, George had cleared the dressing room of what he regarded as a barrack-room lawyer with a little too much to say for himself. Brian wasn't the first to be frozen out and he wouldn't be the last.

Only a month after Brian's departure, the infamous Old Trafford brawl tested the boss in a completely different way. This wasn't about bullying people into submission, it was about rallying the troops at a turbulent time for the whole club.

Once again, he called us all together, this time at the training ground to address a situation that left us two points worse off following the FA's sanction. With him and five players getting fined two weeks' wages by the board, these were unprecedented times requiring decisive action. In response, George delivered a pep talk that, because it was filmed, has since gone down in Arsenal folklore.

'The media are enjoying it, the majority of fans are enjoying it as nothing usually comes out of Highbury,' he said, smacking some rolled up notes into the palm of his hand. 'It seems fashionable just now to jump on the bandwagon and lay into Arsenal. But we're not second bottom, we're second top. We're second in the league. That's the best start we've had for over forty years. So keep thinking about football all the time. You should all be proud of yourselves . . . We're all professional people. You've all got responsibilities to yourselves and your families so keep that in mind at all times.'

It was stirring stuff from a fine orator whose Lanarkshire tones perfectly suited both bollockings and motivational addresses. When George spoke, you tended to listen, or else risk being ostracised by the hardnosed Scot. As proof, Paul Merson recounts an incident in training. When the gaffer barked at him for not tracking back, he instinctively giggled, giving the impression he wasn't taking things seriously.

'He didn't say a word,' Merse recalls. 'Not a word. Didn't pull me in. Saturday, the teamsheet goes up. I'm not in the team. I never played again for about two months.'

That was George for you. He strived to ensure his authority was never undermined. That said, he took things too far when it came to Paul Davis, who had become unhappy with the way he was being asked to play. Davo's side of the story knocked me back when, some years later, we revisited the incident.

'Yeah, I just grew disillusioned,' our elegant midfielder recalled. 'The ball was just going long and it didn't suit me. I went to see him about it but what really got his back up was when I spoke to a newspaper. That was it. I didn't play for eighteen months after that.'

Me: 'Eighteen months? Bloody hell, I didn't realise it was that long!'

Paul: 'Yeah, it just spiralled out of control. I thought at the start that he'd leave me out for a couple of weeks but it just went on and on.'

Me: 'You got changed next to me, Davo. I can see you now, stoically putting on your kit and jogging over to a distant pitch to train with the youth team. We were all upset to see you being treated this way. Not only that, to see a talent like yours being wasted. But that's how it was back then, eh?'

Paul: 'Yeah, it was. But after about six months of this, I went in to see the boss and said, "Well, if you're not going to pick me I might as well put in a transfer request and leave." He said, "You can put in a transfer request but you're not going anywhere." So he was really turning the screw, making an example of me. You know what it was like, Smudge, once you got on the wrong side of George that was it. It was a horrendous time. I still think about it now all these years later. He didn't need to do that, to rob someone of eighteen months of their career. That's quite a severe thing to do.'

It certainly was. That was the side of George none of us liked, the side everyone feared. Don't mess with the gaffer. He'll tear you in two.

Mind you, he wasn't unique. Plenty of managers used to go the same way, if not quite so far. They would send you to Coventry, make you train with the stiffs, secure in the knowledge no one higher up would ask awkward questions. It was the manager's prerogative, making these calls. Try something similar now and the club's chief executive would doubtless be straight on the phone asking why a player getting paid 100k a week is not being used. 'If you don't want him, we are going to sell him' would surely be the message. Not then though. George had carte blanche to do as he pleased.

'Gaddafi' – I think Kevin Richardson came up with the nickname in response to the gaffer's despotic leadership. As Libya's longstanding dictator, Colonel Gaddafi was forever in the news with an oppressive approach to his subjects. As George liked to rule with a rod of iron, the moniker seemed appropriate and stuck for a while.

Fortunately, I stayed in Gaddafi's good books for my first five years at the club, scoring goals and playing well as the silverware gathered. On a personal level, what was not to like? I never gave him any trouble, was always committed in training, always followed instructions. Moreover, he knew I looked after myself away from the club, a family man conscientious about his work.

Even when the goals started drying up in 1992, a level of respect remained. Yes, a bit more criticism came my way – that was to be expected – but George delivered it in a way that took into account my standing at the club, my previous achievements. That said, I knew he had virtually given up on me, a suspicion confirmed after one of Tony's meetings. Our captain emerged to relay what was discussed, listing a series of points about the team's travails. 'And he says you're past your sell-by date,' Tony nonchalantly added, turning to me. That casual aside hit me like a brick, even though I knew my star was falling. Eventually, matters came to a head: the denouement landed after the game when John Jensen finally broke his scoring duck. At the ninety-eighth time of asking, JJ curled in a beauty from the edge of the box to not only level the scores against QPR but send the North Bank wild in hailing a cult hero. Those 'I Was There When Jensen Scored' T-shirts would soon be doing brisk business on the merchandising stalls all around Highbury. Just a pity that, on that bitterly cold New Year's Eve afternoon of 1994, we ended up losing 3–1.

In truth, it had been a shoddy all-round display, following on from plenty of the same in a season now remembered for our narrow failure to retain the European Cup Winners' Cup. Real Zaragoza had pipped us in the final this time, courtesy of Nayim's last-gasp extra-time goal from forty-five yards in Paris. Injured for that one, I sat up in the Parc des Princes stand that night with Bouldy and a few others. As the end of extra time approached with the score locked at 1–1, we decided to go down and watch the penalty shoot-out from the side of the pitch. Nobody wanted to be stuck up here for such an important moment. Once we got there, though, the scene differed markedly from the one expected. All our mates had collapsed, distraught on the ground.

'What's happened? What did we miss?'

Someone quickly filled us in, describing the freak goal. Back in the dressing room, David Seaman took it hard, having been beaten from such a distance. Bob Wilson, our goalkeeping coach, quickly walked across to offer support.

Despite this result, that had become our strength – progressing in cup competitions. No longer good enough to challenge for the title, our superb defence, in conjunction with a goal-scoring machine called Ian Wright, made for a very effective weapon in one-off duels.

Unfortunately, we were anything but effective against QPR. And I was probably one of the worst, powerless to get in the game never mind threaten goal. With fifteen minutes left, George had seen enough and hauled me off to hand young Adrian Clarke his debut. I could hardly complain. With only two goals to my name, the season had turned into another washout. Nothing was happening, no matter how hard I tried.

In the dressing room afterwards, Graham flipped his lid, which, despite his tough reputation, only happened every now and again. Absolutely furious with the performance, he started going round the room laying into everyone with more vitriol than usual, jabbing a forceful finger, spitting with rage. And then he came to me.

'And you, yer c★★★, you're always on the treatment table! Never fit! And when you are you put in a performance like that!'

I couldn't believe what I'd just heard. He called me a c***. He just called me a c***, the manager with whom I'd shared so many good times, the manager who brought me to the club, trusted my worth and reaped the rewards. This was the man who marched over at Anfield to give me a hug after our sensational victory in 1989. The same man who, two years later, shared a laugh and a joke with me in front of the North Bank when we were cavorting about with another championship trophy. Yes, it was the bloke who, only seven months earlier, had sat next to me up on the press conference dais after we'd beaten Parma in the Cup Winners' Cup. So much history. So much glory. So much respect. Or so I thought.

'Don't call me a c***!'

I was angry but hadn't exactly leapt up from the bench aggressively to strike back. It was more a staunch protest at the manner of the bollocking as teammates looked across to gauge my reaction. They knew this was extraordinary, a departure from the norm – savagely insulting one of the old guard. It had always taken a lot to get me riled but this . . . this was too much. The gaffer, in my book, had overstepped the mark in questioning my value in such a ferocious way. But being the person I was then, the person I am now, I didn't respond in the way that perhaps I should have. Far too placid? Not nasty enough? This side to my character, offered up as a weakness sometimes in the past, meant I didn't fiercely hit back in the way others might have. And then, as so often happens in this kind of incident, in the days that followed I thought of all the right things I should have said, remarks that maybe would have hurt him, possibly shut him up. I kicked myself that those words didn't come out in the heat of the moment.

Something like this perhaps:

How dare you speak to me like that after all I've achieved at this club! I don't WANT to be injured. It's not something I enjoy. I hardly missed a game in my first six years here and now you're having a go about a few niggles. You should look at yourself. You've turned this team into a shit one with all your crap signings. We were the best team in the league and now we're nowhere near.

I'd have been on solid ground with that last accusation, since some players in the squad should have never got near an Arsenal shirt. The sharp dip in quality confused me for one. Why was George buying players way off the pace? Pål Lydersen, for one, was especially poor. A very bright lad with a background in shipbroking, he just wasn't cut out for this level of football. For a start, he was simply too cumbersome. The full-back would stomp around in training, clearly short of agility for that particular role. Maybe we caught him at a bad time, seeing as Pål ended up winning twenty caps for Norway. As far as Arsenal were concerned, though, it just didn't happen.

In terms of my riposte, the mortal blow, the *pièce de résistance* could have been a cutting reference to the swirling rumours:

We've all heard about the bungs. You've had your hand in the till. So don't try and lecture me about anything. It's you who's let the club down, not me!

Of course, I would never have dared go this far. For one thing, I didn't know for sure that the gaffer was guilty. Whispers are one thing, hard facts quite another. It was Lee Dixon who first made us aware of the story, saying he'd heard on very good authority that the gaffer had been caught taking a bung and was heading for the high jump. Lee was insistent that it wasn't just hearsay. To be fair, Dicko wasn't the type to be spreading salacious gossip in the way that some others mischievously did, which made his revelation all the more shocking. Even then, though, I couldn't quite believe the news was true. It didn't seem real, such a sensational development, despite bungs having been part of football since the year dot. Various managers down the years had a reputation for taking backhanders, without the authorities ever finding proof.

So could they in this case make an example of Arsenal's manager? If so, that would be momentous, naming and shaming such a famous figure. For now, however, the truth had yet to come out. So imagine if I'd launched into an angry tirade only to later find out he was innocent. That really would have been the end of me at Arsenal. George would never have spoken to me again.

In hindsight, this emerging scandal must have been the reason for a noticeable change in George's behaviour. During those months at the end of 1994 and leading up to his February dismissal, the man was a lot more short-tempered, more scathing generally, not just that day when I copped an earful. Partly to blame for the transformation would have been our lacklustre form, a world away from the vibrant stuff of old. Seeing standards slip this far could not have been easy for him to take, enough to send anyone into a foul mood, let alone the person ultimately responsible for the poor displays. The bond with the players had also weakened as, by his own admission, he became jaded and, in turn, we grew immune to familiar methods.

All that must have been nothing, however, compared to the other matter – the sword of Damocles hovering over his head. For someone embedded in the club as a successful player and even more successful manager, the approaching storm surely filled him with dread. If found to have transgressed, the sack was inevitable, as was heavy punishment from the FA, thus trashing a reputation he'd worked so hard to build up. It later transpired George had agreed to leave that coming summer after admitting to Arsenal that he had accepted what he described as 'unsolicited gifts' totalling hundreds of thousands of pounds from Rune Hauge, the Norwegian agent involved in several transfers, Lydersen's included. The resignation letter had been signed, with manager and board hoping a parting of ways would do the trick. But events were moving too fast to be bypassed. The net was closing in, with George looking vunerable, hanging from a hook. The club had to act before the FA, and impending humiliation on that scale cannot be easy to handle. It must tear you apart, change everything. I can only guess at the stress as the day of reckoning approached.

Still, that's no excuse in my book. To call me out that way in front of my teammates was totally out of order. I regarded it as a betrayal of a relationship I thought had been built on mutual respect. Even today, my hackles still rise thinking about it. How could he talk to me that way? He knew I was suffering from a collapse in confidence. There was nothing dishonest about my troubles, like pretending to be injured just to stay out of the firing line, as some have been known to do. After eight years together, he should have known me better. No, after eight years together, he should have *treated* me better. Look, nobody should be exempt from a harsh bollocking. That comes with the territory when performances plummet. But to do it this way really cut to the quick. Given our shared history, I thought I deserved more.

It seems George thought the same about the board, having transformed the team into a trophy-winning machine, unrecognisable from the underperforming outfit he had inherited. But rather than unqualified support, he felt some directors were becoming distant, embarrassed at the growing scandal, eager for his resignation. At the start of December 1994, in an effort to smooth the waters, he had handed the club a huge cheque to cover Hauge's payments. The club later promised to let him leave with dignity, planning to announce a termination of contract by mutual consent, complete with a generous financial package to reflect his achievements.

In the dressing room, meanwhile, we knew none of this. We could only go on an increasing amount of damning reports in the papers, some of which claimed George had taken a 'bung' from Hauge for the Jensen and Lydersen deals. You can imagine the chatter every morning as another story broke. Footballers love a bit of gossip and this was as juicy as it came.

'Seen that about the gaffer in the *Sun* today?' someone would say. 'It's not looking good. I reckon he'll be gone in a week.'

This growing possibility made us all think. Many of us, after all, had been with George for a very long time. He was the only manager we'd ever known in London N5. Consequently, the questions naturally fermenting in everyone's mind took on added significance. If he does get the sack, who will come in? More importantly, what will that mean for me? As a player, you immediately think of yourself in these situations. Self-preservation becomes the order of the day rather than any concern for the bloke facing the chop. *If the gaffer has been a bit naughty, that's his fault. Nothing to do with me. I've got a living to earn whoever's in charge.* So sympathy was scarce in those daily conversations. Nobody shed any tears for the man in the dock.

Quite often, I'd be listening to the escalating chit-chat lying on a mat in the small entrance area at London Colney, having gone under the knife in early January 1995. Those walking through the door had to step over as you tried to concentrate on rehabilitation exercises set by Gary Lewin. That's what happened back then. The walking wounded would be dotted around in spare bits of space outside the treatment room.

'How's it going, Smudge?' the lads would routinely ask. 'Yeah, not bad,' I'd wearily reply in the middle of a hundred straight-leg lifts, a weight wrapped around my ankle to work the muscles harder. If this wasn't tedious enough, my mood wasn't helped by the £2.5 million arrival from Luton of John Hartson, a young, promising centre-forward leading the line in my absence with some success. He was a good lad, John. Very respectful. I think he felt a bit awkward taking my shirt.

The team as a whole remained anything but buoyant, sinking to thirteenth in the table in the middle of January. Just to confirm how far we'd fallen, at the start of February Fabio Capello's superb AC Milan side completely took us apart over two legs in the European Super Cup. Even worse, George didn't seem to have an answer, and was buying more players – Chris Kiwomya and Glenn Helder – who would never have been good enough to wear an Arsenal shirt in the title-winning years. His mojo had disappeared. In that following week he looked weary and stressed.

They do say that after a certain amount of time either the manager must go or he must totally overhaul the playing staff – with quality first-team replacements – to prevent staleness setting in. Neither had happened. A good seven or eight of us had heard every George-style bollocking. We knew his methods inside out, his training regime, his strong-arm tactics to try and produce a performance. Likewise, he'd probably grown tired of us, seeing the same faces staring back every day.

I think both parties knew the end was in sight. The relationship had run its natural course. Time for a change to move the club forward. All that said, when the axe fell it still felt like a huge loss, made all the more dramatic by the scandal involved.

On the day in question, 21 February 1995, I was meeting Gary Lewin in an hotel car park just off the M25. Gaz was taking me to hospital, the London Independent, for a check-up on my knee, the initial injury sustained only a week after that bollocking. Though the chairman had already told Gary before it went public, our physio was still visibly shocked when we met up. So was I, after hearing the news on the car radio on the way down. Yes, I knew he was in trouble, that his job was under threat, but it still hit me hard when finally confirmed.

The gaffer, unceremoniously sacked, told to clear his desk, practically ushered out of the building, persona non grata – this was the man with Arsenal in his blood, who'd brought the title back to Highbury after an eighteen-year wait; the man who had delivered six major trophies over eight-and-a-half years to re-establish the club as a serious force. For it all to end this way stunned the football world, never mind people much closer to hand.

We drove into town feeling quite numb, wondering what would happen, what the club would do next. George's personality had totally dominated Highbury. It was going to be strange not having him around.

And despite our falling out after the QPR game, I was gutted to miss him when he slipped back to say his goodbyes at the training ground. Off having treatment, I missed the opportunity to say thanks face-to-face, thanks for some times neither of us would forget. The lads subsequently told me it was quite an emotional meeting, his final farewell. Everyone stood transfixed as he said a few last words, the sentiments not new but extremely accurate. The boss had always maintained that we wouldn't always enjoy working under him, it might be laborious and painful, but come the end of our careers, with plenty of medals in the cabinet, we would realise all the effort had been worthwhile. That day, he repeated this conviction in front of the group, reminding everyone that the memories would more than compensate for all the sweat and suffering. Looking back, he was absolutely right. How satisfying to know your career didn't pass by in an uneventful blur devoid of special moments. Yes, of course there were hard times but, in hindsight, they are much easier to accept when countered by glory. That's what George meant. And that's what George brought.

For that, all the players involved owed him a debt of gratitude. Of course, he couldn't have done it without us. The route to success must be a two-way street. But George single-handedly built that team, earmarking every transfer target himself, unlike today when it can so often be a group effort. Not only that, he put his faith in talent emerging from the ranks, often at the expense of proven experience. Following on, he worked with great devotion to mould a proper unit that defended as a team, attacked with panache and, perhaps most importantly, stuck resolutely together when the going got tough. That was his hallmark. George Graham sides rarely rolled over, the southern softy tag never sticking here.

Football teams, you hear, are invariably a reflection of their manager's character and personality. So it was that Arsenal under George were steely and stubborn, hardworking and committed, with a ruthless streak running right through the middle. Difficult to argue with that. Like 'Gorgeous George', however, they also bore a certain style, which could turn into a swagger when the mood took. For that, all Arsenal fans should be grateful. He brought back the good times to a famous institution, provided rich memories to last a lifetime. Longer term, the boy from Bargeddie laid the sturdy foundations that enabled Arsène Wenger to flourish. When the Frenchman arrived, a culture of success was already in place, with a magnificent back five still around to pass on good habits. Legacies like that cannot be denied. Despite the inauspicious ending, despite his flaws, my old manager should be remembered as an Arsenal all-time great.

CROSSING THE LINE

It was Michael Hart who opened the door. He offered a pathway when I seemed to be staring at a dead end. Just a few months after George Graham's dismissal, my own career suffered a mortal blow. That injury at Millwall on 7 January 1995 had cruelly produced another ex-footballer. What was I going to do with the rest of my life?

Fortunately, Michael had a suggestion. As the London *Evening Standard*'s longstanding chief football writer, he had got to know me well over the years. He or Ken Dyer, another top bloke from the paper, would hang around the Arsenal canteen after training to have a word with one or more of the players. It was agreed with the gaffer. No press officers back then. George would arrange the best days to come. And because these were familiar faces, you tended to trust them much more than you would someone from a national newspaper, especially a tabloid. Because they had to keep coming back, the chaps from the *Standard* weren't about to tuck you up with a dodgy story, unlike a stranger who might never have to see you again. So when you spotted Michael or Ken sipping tea in the canteen, you'd go over for a chat even if, on that particular day, they were seeing someone else. A relationship developed that, because of the barriers, doesn't tend to happen so much with reporters these days.

Thank goodness it did then, though. And I had long since told Michael that I quite fancied having a bash at writing. My background in languages – my general level of education, in fact – would surely help. Make a success of this, I thought, and it would be a decent niche. Something to keep me involved with the game and bring in a bit of dough.

So when push came to shove, and the retirement axe fell, he suggested I compose some words about the whole affair, including the ordeal of going to the training ground to pick up my boots and say my farewells.

'Describe the emotions involved,' he said. 'Tell us what it feels like. If your story comes up to scratch we'll print it in the paper.'

And print it they did, as well as several other columns during that first season on the outside, all of which led to writing for the *Daily Telegraph*. This was a big thing for me, seeing my words in such well-respected outlets. It gave me a buzz. Admittedly, nothing like scoring a goal in front of the North Bank but a buzz nonetheless. I was learning a new trade at a high level, doing something meaningful that stretched the brain to take my mind off the recent loss.

I was spurred on by the fact that very few other footballers had actually written for themselves. This was unusual, a former top-flight player sitting in front of a keyboard himself to bang out the words. It put me in virtually a minority of one, whether penning a column at home or writing at a game while trying to master the art of keeping tabs on the action. The evening kick-offs were worst, since the sports desk needed copy for the first editions by the final whistle. Under those conditions, producing something thoughtful isn't easy at all.

For skilled, seasoned journalists, it's different. It becomes second nature. For me, it was a scary experience, this race against time, head bobbing up and down from pitch to laptop, fingers furiously typing as the dreaded deadline approached. Eventually, the mobile rings.

'Any idea when your copy will arrive, Alan?' A hint of mild panic crackles down the line.

'Yes, sorry, won't be long now.'

That became a regular two-way between me and the desk on nights when inspiration came in short supply. After the game, it wasn't so bad. I had an hour or so to tweak my stuff for the later editions.

Then there were the technical issues of filing from stadiums where the internet connection proved a little haphazard. Finishing your article was one thing, getting it back to London another altogether.

For various reasons, one episode stands out. Six years on from our European Cup Winners' Cup glory in Copenhagen, Arsène Wenger's Arsenal returned to the very same Parken Stadium for the 2000 UEFA Cup final against Galatasaray. For me, this obviously brought back special memories – scoring the only goal of the game to defeat strong favourites Parma. This time, however, I was there to write rather than wrestle. And it wasn't an easy game to cover, eventually ending with Galatasaray winning on penalties after 120 minutes of goalless toil. So with deadlines even tighter than usual due to extra time, a sense of relief prevailed as I pressed 'send' on the laptop. But something was wrong. I wasn't online. It appeared that my phone point was not playing ball.

Feeling a little stressed, I fell to my hands and knees to pull out the wire. I'd have to see if someone else could spare their line for a minute or two. Sitting in front, the highly respected journalist Martin Samuel kindly obliged, so I crawled under his desk to reconnect. Clambering to my feet, I dusted down my trousers, by now a bit dirty, which made Martin laugh given the circumstances.

'Smudge, six years ago you were down on that pitch lifting a cup. Now you're up here scrambling in the dust!'

I could see his point. The Parken Stadium wasn't treating me quite so kindly this time. Funnily enough, though, that didn't bother me one bit. I was simply pleased to get the job done, just as I was previously against the Italians. And I'd like to think that episodes like this, when I got my hands dirty in the name of journalism, earned the respect of my new peers. They could see I was having a go, that I was serious about doing it properly.

Yet earning the respect of players was another matter altogether. With my involvement at Sky growing alongside the writing, my emergence as a 'pundit' (not my favourite word) quickly gathered pace. Looking back, I do wonder how on earth this all happened. It just goes to show the unpredictability of life. An understated character, I was surely never cut out for this kind of thing – publicly analysing, praising and, more awkwardly, criticising footballers, including former teammates. It was like turning traitor after serving in the same regiment, pledging your allegiance to the other side. Like most players, I used to take a dim view of former professionals having a swipe. Even if they were right in what they said, you found it hard to accept, this public naming and shaming by figures who, in your eyes, should know better.

You didn't forget either. A critical comment on the telly or a wrong word in print would get stashed away in the memory bank, ready to use if the occasion arose. Not many are immune to the slings and arrows that come with performing on the big stage. Some footballers go as far as to claim they would never stoop so low as to make a living out of punditry. Even Frank Lampard, that most eloquent and elegant of characters, once used the word 'bargepole' in this respect. When his playing career finished, Frank clearly saw things differently.

I see some old pros who want it both ways. On the one hand happy to criticise on TV or in ghost-written columns, they also want to be mates, all smiles and high-fives when bumping into their victims. My advice would be to let it go. Take a step back. You're not a player any more so don't pretend to be one. If you want to do your new job properly, put some distance between the past and present. That means no more visits to your old training ground to try and glean juicy gossip and tactical info that make you sound in the loop when next on the telly. A wrench it may be, but put it this way – those present-day players see you as an outsider anyway, someone not to be trusted with anything sensitive. The moment you walk away from that club to become an ex-footballer, the circle of trust quickly closes behind. Nothing wrong with that. That's how it should be. Accepting that fact right away avoids an awful lot of angst.

I speak from experience, having fallen out with Arsenal following that infamous ruck at Old Trafford on 21 September 2003. I was there to write for the *Telegraph*, alongside Paul Hayward and Henry Winter, when Sky asked me to fill in for Alan Shearer who, for some reason, had been forced to pull out. Yes, OK, I said. This was the company, after all, paying the bulk of my income. Though I have never been one of Sky's stars – a safe pair of hands, that has always been me – you hope this kind of reliability goes a long way. As Woody Allen once said, 80 per cent of success is just showing up. So that's what I did, agreed to fill in, even though the extra commitment would add to the pressure by squeezing the time I had to file my *Telegraph* piece. Yet that was just part of the media game. Plenty of other ex-sportsmen, cricketers particularly, regularly manage to write their stuff after stints in the studio. It wasn't new to me either. I found that the extra pressure concentrates the mind in a positive way.

That said, ammunition for my column looked in short supply after eighty uneventful minutes of a tetchy contest. Up in the studio, presenter Richard Keys wondered what on earth we were going to talk about. It had been a disappointing spectacle between United and Arsenal, the two title contenders, neither side managing to hit their stride. A forgettable goalless draw looked the most likely outcome. Well, it did end up goalless, but it certainly wasn't forgettable after Patrick Vieira and Ruud van Nistelrooy lit the blue touch paper with a little contretemps that ended with Vieira getting sent off following a second yellow card. With the temperature rising between two sets of players that didn't like each other to begin with, Martin Keown gave away a penalty in the last minute.

It looked as if Manchester United would nick the points to bring to an end Arsenal's run of being unbeaten all season. Van Nistelrooy, however, slammed his effort against the bar, much to the delight of a snarling Keown, convinced that the Dutchman had got his teammate sent off. And when, seconds later, the final whistle blew, all hell broke loose. Keown jumped up in celebration and crashed down on van Nistelrooy without really trying to make it look accidental. Lauren followed up with a hefty shove in the back. The scuffling continued as Roy Keane led his man away.

Watching from that studio, I was quite shocked by Arsenal's behaviour, especially the way they had ganged up on van Nistelrooy. I knew the striker was no saint but, to me, he seemed like the innocent party on this occasion. In the commercial break that immediately followed the match, Keys turned to me and asked if I'd be happy to tackle the argy-bargy, seeing as it would be awkward for our other guest, Steve Bruce, manager of Birmingham City at the time, to get involved.

Well, what choice did I have? As a Sky man, I had to step forward and speak my mind, no matter who it upset. And it certainly upset Arsenal when I suggested that my old club had gone too far, had stepped over the line at the final whistle. The FA, I predicted, were sure to get involved. Standing up at the end, hurriedly unclipping my microphone to make a quick getaway, Keysey congratulated me on being so forthright. That comment worried me slightly. Had I gone too far in the heat of the moment? Though not outspoken by nature, I always like to be honest when answering questions.

On this, I always think of something Vic Wakeling once said about me. As the managing director of Sky Sports, Vic's opinion carried weight. 'He might have a boring voice but he always tells you something.' Chuckling at the first bit, I was chuffed with the punchline. When Vic sadly passed away, I thought of those words. In the business of punditry, you cannot hedge your bets or constantly sit on the fence.

Yes, this was my old club, the one I held so much affection for, but this was also my job. Arsenal weren't paying me now.

As a result, similar sentiments were expressed in my *Telegraph* column, once I'd rushed out of the studio and down to the press box. As I opened my laptop and took a deep breath, Rob Shepherd, a well-known newspaper journalist sitting alongside, took the trouble to say he disagreed with my comments on telly. 'I'll explain why another time.' Don't bother, Rob. It didn't really matter what anyone else thought. For me, Arsenal were the main villains on that highly fractious afternoon.

In the days that followed, as the dust settled, my position on the matter got praised in some quarters. For someone closely connected with the Gunners to come out so critical of them was viewed as a sign of journalistic integrity. Martin Samuel even went so far as to say in his column that he thought I should win sports writer of the year. Not sure about that, Martin, but thanks for your support. During a turbulent time, it meant a great deal to get the nod from someone at the peak of his profession. It eased some misgivings that were beginning to creep in. I have never been the sort to thrive on controversy. It instinctively feels foreign, unsuited to my temperament. What's more, the hostility shown by some Arsenal fans, feeling betrayed by my firm stance, was difficult to take.

It did make me wonder how all this would affect my relationship with Arsenal, up until now a very happy one; more specifically, my agreement with the club magazine, which involved popping along to interview a player every month. Well, nobody rang so I thought all was good. It was only when the weeks passed with no news about my next assignment that I began to suspect something was up. Picking up the phone, I spoke to the magazine editor who had to awkwardly explain that the lads didn't think I could come down to the training ground and be all friendly one minute and then have a pop on TV the next.

Patrick Vieira, I learned, was particularly adamant. As a result, it was best to end the arrangement, he said. Fair comment. I could see the players' point. I hadn't been retired so long that I couldn't put myself in their shoes. Soon after, stories started circulating about me being banned from the training ground – not strictly true but close enough. If that was the price to pay for being honest, then so be it. I felt further vindicated when Arsène Wenger later issued an unqualified apology for the actions of his players at Old Trafford that day. By that time, however, a line had been drawn. My connection with Arsenal had now moved away from friendly ex-player to impartial commentator. In hindsight, it was the best thing that could happen. The episode served to separate my two careers, lending welcome credibility to the second one.

Yet players can't usually see it from your standpoint. One night at Southampton, I had a row with Martin Keown when he chose to bring up my Old Trafford comments. Stood in the St Mary's tunnel a couple of hours before kick-off, he just couldn't understand why I said what I did. As a former Arsenal player, he thought I should have been more supportive. An old teammate with whom I got on quite well thought me bang out of order on this particular subject. It got fairly heated – that can happen with Martin – as I defended my corner and he argued his. In the end, Geoff Shreeves, Sky's reporter on the night, intervened to calm things down. Not the ideal way to prepare for co-commentary.

Mind you, Martin hasn't been the only one to get the hump. Though you don't hear about the vast majority, sometimes a grievance finds its way back.

This once happened with Sami Hyppiä when I asked the Liverpool press office if I could talk to their redoubtable centre-half for the *Daily Telegraph*. It was for my weekly interview, a thousand-word spread published on Saturdays. That was hard work, I can tell you – trying to secure a decent name, someone relevant to the upcoming fixtures. Not only was it difficult trying to get an answer from the respective press offices, you were often in competition with several other newspapers for the same player.

After a few days of silence from Anfield, word eventually came back that, no, Sami didn't want to do it.

'Is there a reason?' I asked.

'Yes,' came the embarrassed reply. 'He says he didn't like something you once wrote about him.'

At that point I wracked my brains to remember the comment. What could I possibly have said to upset the big Finn? It was no good. I just couldn't recall. To be fair, at least Hyppiä was honest. He could easily have knocked back the request without giving a reason.

Ashley Cole, I assume, harboured a similar grudge, the only difference being we were attending the same event when his annoyance became clear. In August 2005, Arsenal announced they would be adopting the David Rocastle Trust as the club's charity for the forthcoming season. Four years before, non-Hodgkin's lymphoma had tragically taken my very close friend. And Rocky had always been a favourite of Cole's, ever since the day our classy midfielder chatted to the ten-year-old prospect in Highbury's treatment room. From that moment on, the youngster strived to be like his hero and it was a nice touch when Arsenal's left-back came along to this official announcement.

As the only two footballers present at the small gathering, it would have been natural to say hello, perhaps chat for a few minutes. But Ashley was having none of it, steadfastly refusing to make eye contact, no matter how many times I looked across. Oh dear. It soon became obvious he'd got the raving needle with something I'd said on telly or maybe in print. Strange, because I could only remember praising the talent and determination of the youth product now excelling for club and country. Yet that implacable expression, seen so often on the pitch, was emphatically telling me to keep my distance. *That's a shame,* I thought. *In Rocky, we have something in common. It would be nice to talk about the great man.* Still, I was under no illusions. Footballers take criticism to heart. For years to come, it sticks in their gut as well as their head.

During the course of my work, people often ask if I miss playing, if I would love to be out there still instead of holding a microphone up on the gantry. The answer is always the same.

'No, not at all. I've had my time. I enjoy what I'm doing now.'

And that's not just me putting on a brave face. It's the truth. Going right back to the day my playing career ended, I've never once yearned to be back in that dressing room, pulling on my shirt, tying up those boots. Don't get me wrong, nothing after football can get anywhere near the incredible high of scoring a goal, particularly an important one in a big match. Anfield, Copenhagen – those adrenalin rushes will never leave me. For a second or two, it feels like the world is all about you. And I definitely missed the lads, the dressing-room spirit.

In a wider sense, though, I've never hankered for the adulation, the roar of the crowd. Perhaps it helps that I've never really felt comfortable being the centre of attention. As much as I enjoy being recognised these days, signing autographs and chatting to fans, my character suits a slightly lower profile than the one that came with wearing number nine for Arsenal. As a result, the change in circumstance didn't hit hard in the sense that I desperately missed all the fame and attention.

In any case, perhaps my career had run its natural course, despite it being unexpectedly cut short. I'd won the medals, had a laugh, created some wonderful memories. Now it was time to head somewhere else. Well, not somewhere else entirely, because in my job, in the co-commentary role specifically, you are constantly thinking back to how you felt as a player in certain situations that crop up in a match. Putting yourself in someone else's shoes – a big part of the craft. *What was he thinking when hitting that ball early from a tight angle? Why did he dive in to give away a penalty?* It isn't always easy, reading the mind of someone who is effectively a stranger, but the ex-pro stands more chance than most.

On that subject, one nugget of advice has always stuck. It referred specifically to co-commentary, a job I was initially reluctant to try when Tony Mills, Sky's highly respected lead match director, suggested having a crack. 'Nah, Tone,' I said. 'People don't want to hear my whining Brummie drawl. Don't think I'm suited to it.' Again, that's classic me – underestimating my capabilities, lacking self-belief.

But once I did come around to giving it a whirl, my straight-talking boss, Andy Melvin, offered some simple but very shrewd guidance. 'Alan, tell us what we *can't* see. That's your role.

When you're talking over a replay, don't say, "Oh, he's hit that one just past the far post." We can bloody see that! Tell us *why* he's done that, what he was thinking.'

I've always tried to remember those Melvin *bon mots*. They've served me well in a job so easy to mess up by, among other things, stating the bleedin' obvious. By the same token, start jabbering too much, talking for the sake of it, and the viewer will quickly tire of this annoying voice invading their living space. Consequently, I have always adopted a less-is-more policy, keeping observations short and punchy whenever possible.

As for the nuts and bolts of co-commentary, I tend to alternate between looking at the monitor and pitch from a gantry that might not afford the best view. In one sense, you want to see the big picture by lifting your head but at the same time it's vital you know what the viewer is seeing. This can easily lead to missing something important, such as a player swearing at the referee.

'How the hell did he miss that? This bloke's bloody useless!'

The viewer, quite rightly, doesn't have time for excuses.

Trying to keep those to a minimum, I will talk to my director during a match via a button on the sound desk known as the 'Lazy'. Keep that pressed down and your words won't go to air. Through the 'Lazy', I might ask our director for certain close-ups or perhaps get the VT guys to look at a tackle again just to make sure it wasn't a penalty. Consequently, you are better informed when the replay pops up. All in all, commentating on a live game is very much a team effort. During a frenetic contest, you need all the help you can get.

Thankfully, it isn't quite so frantic commentating on *FIFA*, the enormously popular computer game to which I started contributing in 2011. And what a pleasure it has been helping voice something that has steadily grown into a cultural phenomenon, selling ten million copies at the last count. Talk about street cred. Those far too young to remember me as a player, those who might not even have heard my dulcet tones on Sky, will rush up to ask for a quick selfie. The bolder enthusiasts might ask if I can say a few lines into their phones, lines they have heard many times while playing the game.

This recognition, what's more, extends beyond these shores to countries where the English-speaking version of the game sells very well. I'm told it's a matter of authenticity, hearing English commentary on Premier League games. And because of that popularity, people will recognise your voice before seeing your face. It once happened in Israel where a teenager came round the corner wearing a big grin after hearing me from a distance. Although his English wasn't great, when he said '*FIFA*' I knew what he meant.

And the most common question is how Martin Tyler and I go about recording the commentary. How long does it take? Are we reading off a script? Or do the creators lift all the commentary from Sky's live games?

The answer is that we spend ten to twelve days in the recording studio each year, churning out lines to fit a thousand scenarios, whether it's a thirty-yard free-kick that flew over the bar, a nasty tackle that earned a red card or something more complicated such as the preamble at the start of the second leg of a cup competition when, say, the team in question won the first game without playing terribly well.

'Oh, they've got to step it up, Martin, because they were a bit lucky in that first leg. The manager will be demanding more.'

They get incredibly specific, these recorded lines, in order to bring the game as close to reality as possible. As for the bods in Vancouver at EA Sports HQ, how they match our comments to the action . . . well, that will always remain a complete mystery to me.

It's not as if they tell us exactly what to say. Once given the general scenario, none of our subsequent comments are scripted. It's all totally ad lib to try and replicate the tone of a real commentary. And because our producer normally requires three or four different versions to avoid the same phrase constantly popping up, you quickly have to think of new and interesting ways to describe the same situation. A few hours of that and the brain feels a bit frazzled. It's a stern test of imagination, not to mention vocabulary. At times like this, stuck in that studio trying to come up with different phrases, I think back to my days at school and polytechnic. That prolonged education has served me well in a post-football career revolving around words.

Those words written on the page mostly belonged to the *Telegraph* for whom I proudly worked for twenty years, covering four World Cups and four European Championships. It was an enlightening experience, mixing with people who think about the game in a much different way to my previous circle in the dressing room.

This was made crystal clear in March 2007 when England faced Andorra in a European Championship qualifier played in Barcelona's Olympic stadium. Quite naturally, an England team featuring Steven Gerrard, Rio Ferdinand and Wayne Rooney was expected to beat this bunch of part-timers. But on a tight, bobbly pitch, Andorra set about trying to rough up their famous opponents by clattering into challenges at every turn. It got quite physical, making for a messy contest, and a stop-start first half ended up goalless. But some in the press box weren't having that, feeling England should be comfortably ahead no matter Andorra's tactics. In particular, the *Daily Mirror*'s Martin Lipton thought it a disgrace that Steve McClaren's side hadn't yet managed to score. I tried to offer the alternative view.

'But, Martin, it doesn't matter if Andorra are part-time or not. If they're determined to disrupt our rhythm by fouling all the time, it's going to be difficult out there. They're a big, strong side. It isn't as easy as you think. But once we get the first goal everything changes. The game will open up then.'

But Martin wasn't convinced. And he wasn't alone among his colleagues in thinking our highly paid stars should have done a lot better. Three goals in the second half only partially placated the critics.

It was at times like this that I felt out of place amid a crowd of journalists reluctant to see the situation from the players' standpoint. Mind you, that's not really their job, is it? They write for the general public watching back home, not to mention those travelling fans booing in Barcelona. Reflecting the mood is part of their remit.

For me, it was different. Having been involved in such scraps when a much inferior team tries to level things up through brute force, I understood the problems facing the England lads. And in fairness, that was my job – to give the players' view, to see it from their side. If I didn't do that, what was the point of my being there?

As well as the business of kicking a ball about, people also ask about a well-versed aspect of the modern game. 'Alan, I bet you wish you were playing now, with all this money around. How much do you reckon you'd be pulling in? A hundred grand a week? Two hundred grand?' It's a good-natured question, always asked with a smile, and it does make me wonder how many noughts would have been tagged on the end of my monthly wage slip should I have been born thirty years later. Several more, certainly, than in the 1990s when Arsenal weren't known for their largesse.

On the subject of the salaries of today's players, however, I've always tended to take a philosophical view. For me, a 'good luck to 'em' attitude is the only way to go, or else you become a bitter old pro. And nobody wants to be one of those. It's sad and unseemly, this resentment about money from former players who moan about very average talents getting paid a fortune. Well yes, it is true that plenty of ordinary Joes get lavishly rewarded. But it's hardly their fault, is it? What do you want them to do? Turn down the cash? Of course not. Today's generation is just incredibly lucky to be around at a marvellous time for the bank balance. Nothing more to it than that. No point at all in getting wound up over economics totally out of your control.

To an extent, this moan about money has always been around. Our predecessors from the 1970s, those responsible for Arsenal winning the double in 1971, lamented how little they got paid compared to us. The late, great George Armstrong, for example, used to bring it up during his time as an Arsenal coach. 'Give it a rest, Geordie,' we'd usually reply to this friendly figure everyone loved. 'That's just how it goes. In any case, we're probably not earning as much as you think!'

So yes, comparing eras has always been popular, and it is fascinating to do it now when players come under incredible scrutiny. Money aside, I certainly wouldn't swap my time for the present conditions when a bloated, ravenous media obsesses over every detail for days on end.

As for the social side of media, well, that can be exasperating enough for someone like me. Whatever you say during commentary, it gets wildly misconstrued by angry fans looking at a match through their narrow prism. What they can't understand is that, unlike them, I've got to stay neutral by trying to represent both sides of the argument, a stance, by the way, that sometimes upsets certain sections of Arsenal's fanbase who think I come down too hard on my old club.

They are convinced I should show more allegiance to the team that 'gave me so much', without once considering my duty to the other side. Mind you, I'm far from alone. When Arsenal legends like Ian Wright, Thierry Henry and Lee Dixon get slaughtered for criticising a performance, I know those doing the shouting have lost all perspective. No, as a 'pundit' it's best to take all the flak with a pinch of salt. Take it to heart and you're going to suffer.

That goes for present-day players, too. They really can't afford to be paying attention to the myriad of voices, many of whom talk absolute tosh. But believe it or not, some players are foolish enough to consult the internet on matchdays. In fact, I know of a couple of instances when players have surreptitiously ferreted about in their pocket at half-time to find their phone in order to see what social media is saying about their first-half performance.

That's just crazy. For a start, if you're the type to be fretting about what some random stranger thinks, you're probably not strong-minded enough to survive in this game. Secondly, if the news isn't good, if people are having a go on social media, that's going to affect your second-half performance. The only possible upside to this scenario is if you get a lift from positive reviews. But let's be honest – if you're worried enough to be checking in the first place, the feedback is unlikely to do you any favours.

And the pressure doesn't ease at the final whistle. There's all the post-match analysis when everyone's performance gets clinically examined across TV, radio, newspapers, podcasts, blogs and the rest. A bad game can be brutally dissected, with post mortems stretching into the following week.

In an effort to keep all this 'noise' at arm's length, some footballers may take the decision to cut themselves off from such potentially destructive outside influences, meaning they don't read the newspapers, don't watch TV or even think about seeing what's being said on Twitter. But they're in the minority. For most, it's too tempting to gauge media reaction, especially when you've had a really good game.

The majority of players, just like their contemporaries in everyday life, tend to run various social media accounts. That's just how it is. Nothing unusual in that. There are certain benefits, too. It's a neat way to maintain contact with the public at a time when the gap between footballer and fan has never been wider. A photo on Instagram accompanied by a comment at least gives a glimpse into a player's life, whether it's his professional one or the personal side.

That connection is important, if so much more controlled than previous eras when supporters would bump more frequently into their heroes. For today's big stars, it's a lot more difficult to go out and relax, knowing someone is always likely to be sneakily taking a photo before telling the world your whereabouts. Pictured with a drink in a city bar and you are quickly accused by someone somewhere of being unprofessional. In short, the boundaries of privacy have been drastically reduced, which convinces some, not unreasonably, to live their lives behind gated mansions, away from prying eyes. I don't envy them that. It takes some of the fun out of a profession that should largely be joyous.

Money, of course, will always be cited as more than adequate compensation: 'For ten million a year, I reckon I could cope.' And there is some justification for that kind of sarcasm in a world where the number of food banks quickly multiplies. A football career, after all, has a limited timespan. These lads should eventually go back to leading a normal life free of the money worries burdening many.

But with such a wide chasm between footballers and the average person, resentment tends to grow, causing some to get labelled, fairly or not, as spoiled prima donnas.

In truth, we've got our fair share of those, certainly more than thirty years ago. Financial independence and multi-millionaire status unavoidably affect player attitudes. I hear that all the time talking to managers and coaches, and I heard it when chatting to my old teammate, Steve Bould.

'The difference is enormous, it really is,' he confirms when comparing today's era to the one we shared. 'They're not so committed any more because they don't have to worry about their next contract like we used to. They're earning so much from their present deal that the next one isn't vital. That's what I played for – to win another contract. We never earned enough to live a good life later. We had to work.

'People say we used to play for the club, Smudge. We didn't, we played for ourselves, didn't we, but it just looked like you were more committed to the club back then. But now they've got so much money, the next contract isn't so important. Totally different mentalities now.'

It's essential to remember that reality when commenting on games. You can't judge someone today by previous standards. You've got to bear in mind these are extremely wealthy athletes and the hunger of some will inevitably wane. Should we criticise that? In any profession with the potential to make lots of money – be it an estate agent, accountant, lawyer or investment banker – some will lose their drive, their appetite for hard work, once the millions roll in. That doesn't make them bad people. It makes them human. The hunter-gatherer instinct gradually gets diminished.

One personality, of course, will react very differently to financial security than another. In truth, that's what separates the great from the good. The very best performers don't play for money, they play to get better, to win everything possible. A bulging bank balance therefore has no influence on the commitment of figures like Lionel Messi and Cristiano Ronaldo, driven by achievement rather than affluence.

As for me, I've been driven by the desire to do something proficiently after football, to succeed in a second career that, all being well, lasts a lot longer than the first. And it has. So far, so good.

If there was one thing I was determined to avoid, it was to be forever known purely as an ex-footballer, someone who trundled along after retirement, constantly harking back to the glory days, someone totally defined by his playing career. That, to me, would have been awful.

Thankfully, I don't think that's happened. Quite naturally, I will always be associated with Leicester and Arsenal, with what I achieved during those years. But mention of my name will also elicit comments, flattering or otherwise, about my commentary for Sky and *FIFA*, or perhaps something I wrote.

To me, that goes down as a success. It means I haven't sat on my arse living off the past. I've learned some new skills since hanging up those boots. Admittedly, they still revolve around football but new skills nonetheless requiring constant attention.

Conscientious as a student, diligent as a player, I feel those qualities have helped immeasurably in this line of work; that, and an inclination to talk honestly when asked a straight question.

Hold on a minute. Did I say work? Sorry, a slip of the tongue.

FAMILY MATTERS

Good fortune plays a big part in football. The most talented player in the world won't get very far without the odd slice of luck falling his way. That also goes, of course, for someone's private life, particularly when it comes to choosing a partner.

The divorce rate in football is shockingly high. It gets even worse once the crowd has gone home and the ex-player stumbles into a new life full of frightening pitfalls. They say one-third will be divorced within a year.

So I count myself lucky – extraordinarily lucky – to have chosen a wife who's still around; not only that, who remains my best friend and close confidante more than three decades since arriving on the scene.

But I'm not taking any credit for that. Because how can you possibly know for certain right at the very start if a partnership is made of the right stuff to survive all the ups and downs of everyday life? You can't. It's all a big gamble, one that plenty don't win.

In the football world, one explanation for marriage break-ups is the fact that players tend to spend long periods away from home. But that's not entirely accurate. Of course, a couple of weeks during pre-season are spent away, usually abroad in one or more far-flung countries. That is inevitable, par for the course. Then there are the overnight stays before games, sometimes even the home ones, depending on the manager. And yes, if you're good enough and lucky enough to represent a country that qualifies for a major tournament, three or four weeks away in the summer might put strain on a partner looking after the kids.

But that's it really. Spread out over the year, it's probably not much more than a successful businessperson committed to regular trips, especially if you factor in a footballer's weekday when he might get the afternoon off, meaning he can be home (if he wants) by about 2 p.m. I normally was, which was a godsend to Penny when adjusting to life as a young mother without the support of nearby family.

On the occasions when I have had to disappear, though, she has never given me grief. Pen has always accepted this as part of the job, a sacrifice to be made in this line of work. It helps, I suppose, that her dad loved football, so she grew up in a world that partly revolved around the game, her family's social life dictated by matches, whether it was her dad going to watch Aston Villa, when Penny and brother Greg often went along, or the Alvechurch fixtures that saw vice-chairman Schoey, shiny shoes and all, sipping half a bitter in the clubhouse bar. Her life, in short, has always featured football, hence the acceptance missing in some.

Some wives, for instance, simply won't swallow the unsociable hours, when their husband might be away for the best part of a weekend, just when help is needed with kids. I can understand that. I really can. It must be incredibly hard to cope on your own, especially if you happen to work in the week.

Unfortunately, I've seen a few impasses develop in my time. When a solution can't be found, the dilemma has sadly led to marriage break-ups.

On this, Penny always cites an impromptu chat with Gordon Milne when international call-ups at Leicester started coming my way. 'Remember,' he said, 'the more he's away the more successful he's becoming.' That stuck in Pen's mind in the years to come when she was left holding the babies.

On that subject, I thought it would be interesting to ask my girls for their objective thoughts on having me as a dad; how my career affected their lives, both in a practical and emotional sense. Positively? Negatively? Somewhere in between?

Jessie dived in first. 'Because of your job, you were able to take us to school, pick us up, come to sports events in the week,' she said. 'So many of my friends didn't see their dads so much. And I like that you and Mum are younger than many parents [Penny was only twenty-three when she had Jess]. I guess your career meant you could afford to have us earlier. I think we are closer as a result.

'I'm so lucky to have had the education, opportunities and experiences I have. Again, that's largely down to your career.

'And you made my dreams come true when you got me in the Highbury tunnel to meet Michael Owen. Mega points! Ain't no other dad could have done that! But I also remember playing out in the street when you called me in to say you were retiring. I could feel the worry in you and Mum. I used to think about it a lot lying in bed.'

I didn't know that before. I never considered my enforced retirement would trouble our five-year-old. Granted, Jessie would always cry at the end of the highlights video Arsenal kindly compiled to mark my departure. But I assumed that was more to do with the sorrowful soundtrack accompanying my goals – 'Nobody Does it Better' by Carly Simon.

Emily was only two at the time, so doesn't remember so much about that period. The following years, though, definitely left a mark.

'When I was young and didn't know you were well known. I thought you had friends everywhere because people would always say hi and you'd say hi back.'

Emily is an actor, having graduated from Birmingham University in English Literature and Drama before taking her master's degree in acting at ArtsEd drama school in Chiswick, London. I'm probably partly to blame for her ambition.

'I love it that you followed your dream,' she says. 'You are my main inspiration in pursuing an acting career. I think it's so important to be passionate in life as you only get to live once. You've certainly followed a career you have a passion for and not many get to do what they really love for a living.'

Asking my daughters for their honest thoughts turned into an emotional exercise. Pushed to describe how their dad's career affected their upbringing, they said things they normally wouldn't in the course of conversation. A recurring theme was the closeness of our relationships, which goes back to what I said about a footballer's privileged timetable. Whereas many fathers will be on the 7.30 a.m. train heading for work, only returning twelve hours later once the kids are in bed, I was lucky enough to take more of a part in family life.

Strangely enough, my old routine recently got brought into sharp focus by Paul Merson. Crippled by a gambling addiction, hooked on drink and drugs, my old teammate could never just go home at the end of training. Either the bookies or the pub, usually both, were too strong an attraction for him to resist. As a last resort, he went to see a psychiatrist, hoping some therapy could set him on the straight and narrow. So there he was, sat opposite this counsellor, talking through the problems blighting his life.

'I just want to be like Alan Smith,' Merse confessed with a sigh. 'I want to go into training, do my job and then go straight home to my wife and kids. That's what Smudge does. I want to be like him.'

To be honest, I'm not sure he did really. In the depths of despair, he was just looking for an answer. But it did make me laugh, picturing Merse on the couch hankering after my life-style. It brought home the advantage of keeping things simple in a profession offering so many dangerous diversions.

It's also a profession that can prove cutthroat, with teammates in competition for your place and livelihood. As a result, forg-ing genuine attachments can be quite tricky. No friends in foot-ball – that's what we always joked. Just ships in the night quietly passing through before heading separate ways. To some extent, that is quite true. What feels like a close friendship at one club can easily fizzle out once a transfer or two leave you at opposite ends of the country.

Of course, there are always exceptions to the rule. For some, the bond never breaks, no matter the geography. That was the case with me and Rocky. I should rephrase that: it was the connection between the Smiths and Rocastles that proved incredibly strong,

In the early days, we'd go down to Janet's parents in Brixton for Sunday lunch. Ansell could always be found in the kitchen, lovingly stirring his curried goat stew. Doris, meanwhile, would entertain in the front room, offering us special chocolate mint creams she brought from work at the House of Commons.

When Rocky signed for Leeds United in July 1992, a seven-year journey began, ending in Malaysia with Sabah FA. Throughout that time, we kept in close touch, visiting each other or laughing down the phone. On joining Chelsea in 1994, their lovely house in Ascot saw regular get-togethers featuring Chinese takeaways and cricket in the garden. Melissa, David and Janet's first-born, is Jessie's oldest friend, while their youngest, Monique, became our goddaughter. Wedged in the middle comes Ryan, a young man I would challenge anyone to dislike.

The fact that all three have grown into intelligent, engaging adults with high moral standards reflects tremendous credit on Janet, one of the strongest people I know. To bring up those kids single-handedly following Rocky's death must have taken every ounce of strength and a little more. But she always did it with a smile, on the outside at least, and a very firm hand that kept all three in line.

For Penny and me, Janet's amazing strength first showed itself for real in the early hours of 31 March 2001 when she rang to tell us the devastating news. I will never forget Jan's calming voice that night, as if she was consoling us rather than vice versa. Naturally, we knew Rocky was dreadfully poorly with non-Hodgkin's lymphoma. That was obvious enough when we went down to visit. But I didn't think for one minute our precious friend would die. I'd read that the success rate for curing this type of cancer was encouragingly high.

Later that day, Arsenal were playing Tottenham, a game I was due to cover for the *Telegraph*. Standing there in Highbury's press box just before the minute's silence, I spotted Jerome Anderson, Rocky's agent and friend from the word go. That was it. I completely lost it, burying my head in Jerome's chest, uncontrollably sobbing. This was so unlike me, showing such emotion in a public place. But Rocky's death was too much. It hit me like a hammer.

In some ways, the death of my parents didn't shock so much, mainly because we could all see it coming. My brother David and I, along with Penny and Terri, David's wife, had decided a few months before that it would be wise to put Mom and Dad into a care home. The thing was, Mom was suffering from dementia and it had got to the point when she often didn't recognise the grey-haired old man sitting in her lounge. Imagine how scary that must be. One day, she threw a bucket of water over this 'stranger'.

Dad, in turn, was getting increasingly stressed and bad-tempered, which just wasn't him. Only later did we find out the brain tumour that killed him had been to blame for the change in behaviour. The day he died in September 2009, we went to the care home to break the news to Mom. 'Think you'd better sit down, Mom,' I said. 'We've got something to tell you.'

'Oh, he's not dead, is he?' Mom immediately shot back without a hint of emotion. She started rearranging the ornaments on the windowsill before asking, 'Can we go for a cream cake now?' Over fifty years they'd been married for it all to end like this. Heart-breaking for us, matter-of-fact for Mom, when she would have collapsed in distress had her mind been sound.

Seven months later, Mom was gone too, this time a stomach tumour bringing down the curtain on a happy marriage that provided such a stable childhood for me and Dave. They say everyone is the product of their upbringing and that, I think, is true in this case. A loving, happy home had produced two well-adjusted adults with very few hang-ups. Maybe that can be a handicap in professional sport where a naked desire to succeed can often be rooted in something unpleasant happening in childhood.

You might be desperate, for instance, to disprove a parent who was cruelly intent on constantly denigrating your efforts. In response, the competitor is forever driven on by a burning rage. You hear it so often to explain the champion.

So perhaps I lacked the edge to go that extra mile, too laid-back and content to properly ruffle feathers. If so, that's just the way it goes. You are what you are. I certainly wouldn't swap my temperament for something more suited to pushing the boundaries if it meant suffering a childhood blighted by abuse.

No, Mom and Dad were quietly supportive, which meant they rarely missed the chance to come and see me play. Mind you, it had been pretty straightforward at Leicester, Filbert Street being just an hour's hop across the Midlands. Arsenal was obviously different, tucked away in London, an unknown metropolis. Because of that, they decided to drive down to Highbury after I signed, just to have a look and map out the route. Their best friends, Margaret and Dennis, made the journey too on that hot day in June 1987.

On finally pulling up in Avenell Road, following plenty of stops to consult the map, they pressed their noses against the thick glass of the cast iron door at the main entrance, trying to see if anyone was home. A friendly little Irishman soon opened up. On hearing who it was – the parents of the club's latest signing – Paddy Galligan, Highbury's legendary odd-job man, proceeded to give the quartet a tour of the place, including the dressing rooms where they climbed in the big bath for a quick photo.

Once home, they were full of it, recounting the adventure with great delight. I wasn't so sure. Part of me thought it embarrassing, showing me up like that. Another part thought it reassuring that a big club like Arsenal would treat my parents in such a friendly way.

From then on, they loved coming down and fell into a convenient routine. Rather than drive all the way to Highbury like they did that day, they'd take the M25 from St Albans and park at Cockfosters tube station where the Piccadilly line chauffeured them to Highbury's door. It made for a marvellous day out, especially if I scored in an Arsenal win. Dad would sit in the players' lounge afterwards, sipping his pint as proud as punch.

Mind you, the old lounge we used before the Clock End development, known as the Halfway House, was the scene of a very worrying moment during the winter of 1987 when Dad came along to a night game wearing a thick sheepskin coat. At the end, as always, all the players' relatives and friends piled into a space more like a cubbyhole. It was packed in there. No room to breathe, quite literally for one. But the fact you could hardly move turned into a blessing when Dad overheated and fell onto Penny's brother, Greg, who, being a solid sort, managed to hold him up.

Gary Lewin was called and speedily ushered Dad up the steps to see John Crane, the club's longstanding doctor, who gave him the once over. Nothing serious, he said. Just a little turn.

Maybe this was a warning, for a year later Dad would suffer a heart attack that forced him to retire. That was also the year, 1988, Penny and I got married, an inevitable event from very early on. Luckily, her mother approved, which pleased me no end because, as it happened, I thoroughly approved of her, the best mother-in-law I could ever have hoped for.

Kind, funny, steadfast and glamorous, Linda has always been more like a friend than a relative, rarely failing to make me laugh. She also came in useful when it came to booking the church Penny had set her heart on just down the road. The problem was, it lay outside the parish covering home at the time – Sutton Coldfield Golf Club where Linda's role as stewardess came with a nice flat above the clubhouse.

By chance, however, the club captain's house did fall within the boundary, so he gave us permission to tell the vicar a little white lie by giving his address. Mind you, we didn't half put in the hours over that winter, attending several services, battling through snow and ice, to not just get our banns read but show our faces as 'regular' worshippers. This should do it, we thought. The vicar has to be impressed with our commitment. Yet when it came to meeting said minister to discuss the wedding service, his opening line came as something of a disappointment.

'So, have you been to our church before?'

Oh God (sorry, vicar). What a waste of time. He clearly hadn't noticed us sat at the back.

The day itself didn't begin well. For a start, I came downstairs for my breakfast only to discover Mom had given Mick, my best man, the last of the bacon.

'Mom, I'm getting married today. I was hoping for a full English!'

Never mind. A more important task lay just ahead. For our first dance, Penny and I had picked 'You Bring the Sun Out' by Randy Crawford, a track our chosen DJ didn't have in his collection. Consequently, Mick and I drove to King's Heath shopping centre five miles up the road to buy the album containing that song. That was stressful enough, seeing as the first record shop didn't stock the goods.

But I eventually found it and shot back home with Mick to don our top hat and tails. By this point, time was getting short. We jumped into Mick's car, a white Porsche 944 (flash bastard), to make the tricky journey across town. With traffic unusually busy, my palms started sweating as we broke a few laws to make it in time.

Among those waiting at the church was a fella we'd met the previous summer when searching for a house in Hertfordshire, which wasn't, by the way, as easy as you'd think. For a start, our budget wasn't huge, thanks to an Arsenal salary relatively modest in football terms. Secondly, 1987 was witnessing a mighty housing boom that saw prices shoot up by the week. On top of that, the most desirable houses were getting snapped up literally within hours.

One day, we spotted a real possibility in Flamstead, a picturesque village just north of St Albans, that had come on the market that very morning. Racing up there, we knocked on the door of this quaint cottage only to be told that it had just been sold. *Blimey*, we thought. *They move a bit sharpish down south. At this rate, we'll never find a house.*

By this time, we were getting the help of a local estate agent by the name of Geoff Shreeves, a talkative sort not short on confidence who quickly promised to find the right place. So off we went, hurtling around Hertfordshire's leafy lanes, him in his hairdresser's motor, a white Peugeot 205 CTI soft-top, us in the trusty Capri. Geoff knew his stuff. I only know that because he once told me.

Mind you, we didn't make his task easy. Having originally set our hearts on an old house with beams, inglenook fireplace and AGA, it soon became apparent that the accompanying low ceilings would either give me backache or a bruised head. So having scoured the county for a nice period property, we did a complete U-turn to look for something new.

And it wasn't long before we found the right place in a small development just south of St Albans called Four Trees, named after the tall birches standing at the entrance. Geoff handed over the keys, his work finally done.

It was a lovely first home, that dormer bungalow. It welcomed newborn Jessie, fresh from the hospital. It waved Penny off for her first day at work and it hosted that lively barbecue the night after Anfield. By that time, however, the Great Storm of October 1987 had turned Four Trees into two overnight. Amazingly enough, we didn't hear a thing.

As for Geoff, nothing could blow him down. A resilient character full of initiative, he bounced back from a business fall-out to forge a marvellous career in television, a fixture at Sky virtually from the start. On a personal note, he became a close family friend and godfather to Jessie.

It's very reassuring to have people like that in your life, those who stayed the course to share so much history. It is indeed precious, that kind of relationship, as is the one sealed by the vicar.

Looking at our wedding album now, I can only feel grateful. Tragically, three of my teammates' wives in those photos have since passed away, taken by cancer. A great friend in Rocky went that way too. On top, several other couples have long since divorced.

As mentioned at the start, so much comes down to chance in this crazy life. You just never know what lies around the corner.

Yet 2 July 1988 marked the start of a gamble I could never regret. It gave me a special wife, fiercely loyal. Further down the line, the union produced two beautiful girls of whom we are incredibly proud. Together, I like to think we make a great team, as united as any I've represented in the past. The Core Four: that's us, a family nickname to sum up the bond. This strong alliance, I hope, can cope with anything that lies ahead.

REFLECTIONS

You hear it quite often when retired sportspeople start reminiscing. 'I have no regrets about my career,' they insist. 'Wouldn't change anything for the world.' On hearing that, I'm always a bit sceptical. How on earth can they have no regrets? There must be several episodes, at least, when they'd want to go back and do things differently. That's surely inevitable, simply human nature.

Maybe it's just me, but I'm the sort of person who tends to look back and dearly wish I'd acted differently in certain situations. It's not that I'm unhappy about my career. How could I be? Two league titles, a European Cup Winners' Cup, an FA Cup and League Cup plus two Golden Boots. Oh, and thirteen England caps on top. Never as a young lad did I ever dream that so much success would come my way.

Good fortune, I know, plays a big part – can't kid myself there. It was lucky, for instance, that I joined Arsenal just as George Graham began building something special, thanks to an exceptional raft of youth team products and, yes, some inspired signings. Much better players than me haven't fared as well.

Take Alan Shearer, one of the best strikers England has produced in many a year. Despite countless awards for his ridiculous goalscoring feats, this marvellous centre-forward only has one medal to show for eighteen years in the game – a league title in 1995 with Blackburn Rovers. Shearer would argue, of course, that a return home to his beloved Newcastle United in 1996 was worth so much more than winning trophies with Manchester United, his other choice at the time.

I did the same – turned down United. But what if I had gone to Old Trafford in 1987, where real success didn't arrive for another four or five years? Would I have thrived there like I did at Highbury or have become a victim of United's search for success?

Who knows on that one? It's all academic now. But when it comes to regrets, the decision to choose Arsenal over United, or indeed Chelsea, can never get a mention. Right place, right time – that would sum up the move to London N5. In fact, those eight years at Highbury, plus the five at Filbert Street, define my working life in a wonderful way. Not only did they provide countless memories and some precious mementoes, they built the platform for my subsequent media career, one that has now lasted a lot longer than the playing part. For that, I feel incredibly grateful.

Football has given me everything, not least a good living for my family across three decades and more. Never have I taken that for granted in a world that, when it comes to earning a crust, can often prove cruel. As time goes on, you become increasingly aware of that fact. With two grown-up daughters, I've witnessed first-hand the hurdles people face in the normal workplace. Thankfully, football isn't normal. It has separated me from the crowd, put me in a bubble I hope never bursts.

Even so, I can't help but look back and wonder 'if only' about certain episodes. Sometimes, without realising, I will find myself tutting out loud when thinking back, kicking myself mentally for not taking a different path or making a different choice. Even now, all these years later, those pivotal moments still churn over in the mind.

The biggest by far, the one that still casts a shadow, is the tortuous period between 1992 and 1995 when form and confidence fell off a cliff. If I could only go back to the start of that miserable spell and tackle the problem more effectively and openly.

Talk to Ian Wright, for instance, about the reasons for our partnership failing to ignite. Have a frank discussion with our new signing, tell him how I felt, rather than bottling it up to make matters worse. The elephant in the room badly needed attention.

Not only that, I should have looked at myself instead of blaming other factors supposedly holding me back. I patently failed to do that. I let the situation fester instead of finding a way to turn things around.

As a result, my final three seasons in football (Copenhagen mercifully apart) make for grim reading – three, three and two Premier League goals. How can you not regret something like that? How can you not wish things had been different? I look at the list of Arsenal's all-time top scorers and lament a position that would have been several places higher had I managed just ten goals in each of those final three seasons.

While we're on regrets, I must talk about money, always a favourite subject among footballers. That first contract at Arsenal was nowhere near good enough. I should have dug in my heels, asked for a lot more than the comparatively modest figures being pushed my way.

If only the situation had appeared clearer at the time. I was hot property for goodness' sake, the next big thing on the market, a much-admired young striker courted by several big clubs whose contract at Leicester would soon expire. If those weren't grounds for playing hardball in negotiations, what on earth would be?

The knock-on effect is the difficulty afterwards of redressing the balance in future contract talks. You're always playing catch up, never quite reaching the sums earned by players of the same standing at other clubs. Not that I was alone. Most of my Arsenal teammates were also underpaid. It formed part of dressing-room chatter for many a year.

I realise that talking this way might not go down brilliantly with everyone, especially rabid Arsenal fans who would give anything to pull on that famous red and white shirt. Put in the same position, though, I'm sure their tune would soon change. No matter the environment, everybody wants to be properly rewarded for doing a good job. And we were doing a good job. A top-class one, actually.

All that said, when it comes to harbouring regrets I have got a lot better as time has moved on. I'd put it down to a more philosophical approach, which probably comes with age and a little more wisdom. Reading a couple of books on Stoicism has definitely helped, and I came to understand there is no point in fretting about what you can't change. Those Ancient Greeks had it all sussed, as exemplified by Séneca, a leading Stoic of his day.

'No person has the power to have everything they want,' the great man once opined, 'but it is in their power not to want what they don't have, and to cheerfully put to good use what they do have.'

In other words, be thankful for what you have achieved and acquired rather than moaning about what might have been. There's no mileage in that. It gets you absolutely nowhere.

In any case, I have no real reason to gripe. To put my career in perspective, if someone had offered my eighteen-year-old self thirteen years in pro football full of success, followed by twenty-five years of fulfilling media work, I'd have . . . well, I'd have thought they were kidding before snatching their hand off. Overall, it truly has been a blessed existence.

Yes, of course I would have liked to have played for a few more years, rather than a surgeon calling time at thirty-two. But the more I watch football, the more I come to realise I was very lucky to clock up the number of games I did. Because for the majority of my time, I was free from injury, available to the manager, rarely spending more than a couple of weeks on the treatment table.

At the time, you take this for granted, feeling invincible, never once contemplating the prospect of long-term injury. Yet so much of this is down to pure luck. Some of it, granted, can be due to muscle type – your genes, if you like – and the remainder, perhaps, down to behaviour on the pitch in terms of riding tackles and spotting danger. But good fortune must surely come top of the list.

My heart goes out to those suffering major setbacks, their careers sadly stalled by serious injury. I can only be thankful this didn't happen to me, either at Leicester or Arsenal. If it had, who knows what path my career would have taken. Managers have to think of the team more than individuals. A replacement centre-forward could have easily arrived.

For that reason alone, I have to count my blessings rather than focus on any regrets. I was given a chance to progress in this world and the fates conspired to allow that advancement. So many would give their eyeteeth to sample the same, a fact easy to forget in the middle of it all.

But I'm not in the middle of it now. I can take a step back to appreciate the whole picture and it makes for quite a sight, this love affair with football.

You're a long time retired: it's a well-known saying in the game to emphasise the importance of playing for as long as you possibly can. I understand that sentiment. I really do. At the same time, retirement has treated me well, making the break a little less painful. It certainly helps to have stayed involved in such an enjoyable way. In reality, football has never gone away. I hope it never will.

Acknowledgements

To Ian McFarlane, thank you so much for spotting my potential and persuading Leicester City to stump up the cash. Without your foresight, this wonderful journey may have never begun. After that, I was lucky to have Gordon Milne pointing me in the right direction with his wise words and understanding.

As for the book, thanks to Gary Lineker for trying to remember the old days, to Gary Lewin for adding painful detail about my knee, to Perry Groves for various titbits, to Steve Bould and Paul Davis for their ingrained honesty, and to George Graham for reminding me who was boss.

On the creative side, thanks to Barney Rodgers for coming up with the title, to Alex Fynn for his help and advice, and to Clare and Martin 'Marty' Earl for brainstorming chapter titles on a Spanish beach.

On top of that, I must thank Jonathan Harris for sweet-talking Little, Brown Book Group into offering me a publishing deal. With that secured, the incomparable Andreas Campomar set about knocking me into shape with sound advice and regular reassurance, not to mention a few congenial lunches.

Most of all though, my sensational family deserves special praise for encouraging me to write this book when I kept making excuses. Penny and the girls always recognised the value of recording my life in this way. Now that it's done, I can see their point. Mom and Dad, I wish you were still around to share the moment.

Finally, I want to thank every teammate and coach over the course of my career. We worked hard together, enjoyed the good times, endured the bad, but did it all from a privileged position. For that, we should all give thanks.